BEGINNER'S GUIDE SELLING ON EBAY: 2024 EDITION

How To Start & Grow Your Own Home-Based Reselling Business

By Ann Eckhart

INTRODUCTION

Welcome to the **Beginner's Guide To Selling On eBay: 2024 Edition!** My name is Ann Eckhart, and I have been reselling on eBay since 2005. I have also been educating others about selling on the platform for nearly as long through YouTube videos and books, as well as in thousands of posts on social media sites such as Facebook, Twitter, Instagram, Pinterest, and TikTok. I not only write about making money on eBay, but also on Etsy, Amazon, WhatNot, and YouTube.

However, out of all of the books I've written over the years, this one has remained the most popular. And that is because eBay remains the number two platform for resellers, i.e. people who buy items at thrift stores and garage sales to sell for profit online (Amazon is number one). Millions of people make money selling on eBay; some do it for some extra spending money, while others earn a full-time living on the site.

But for every person who is currently selling on eBay, there is another who hasn't made the leap to making money online. It's not because they aren't interested in selling on eBay, it's because they are afraid. Afraid it is too hard, too technical, and too much work. And that is where this book comes in.

In *Beginner's Guide To Selling On eBay,* I break down every single step necessary for making money reselling everything from antiques and collectibles to clothing and housewares. If you ordered this book, either in eBook or paperback format, you had to use a smartphone or computer. And that right there means you have the first skill necessary for selling online.

However, this book goes beyond just information for beginners. While I will walk you step-by-step through everything you need to know to source, list, and ship items, I will also teach you how to grow your eBay business from a hobby level to a part-time or even full-time business. This book isn't just about how to sell on eBay, but how to sell successfully for maximum profits.

In this book, I will cover:

- **The basics of eBay:** What EBay is, why it's the best platform for reselling, and how to set up your selling account
- **eBay fees and features:** I break down what eBay has to offer you along with how much it costs for you to sell there
- **Reselling equipment and supplies:** Everything you need to photograph, list, and ship items
- **What to sell and where to source:** What sells on eBay and where to find it
- **Taking eBay photos:** How to take and upload photos that will help sell your items fast and for top dollar
- **Creating eBay listings:** I walk you step-by-step through the entire eBay listing process
- **eBay shipping made easy:** A step-by-step tutorial on how to set up your shipping settings and how to print shipping labels
- **Processing orders:** The steps to take when an item sells
- **Marketing and promotion:** How to grow your eBay business through social media and networking
- **Managing an eBay Store:** How to maximize the benefits of having an eBay Store
- **Taking eBay to the next level:** How to go from hobby seller to part-time or even full-time
- **eBay accounting made easy:** How to easily manage

bookkeeping and taxes

- **Customer service:** How to handle difficult customers and other issues that may arise

And I also provide a **BONUS CHAPTER** devoted to reselling clothing, the largest category, on eBay.

I used to break these topics out into shorter eBooks, but now I've complied absolutely everything you need to know into one volume. This book is the ultimate guide to selling on eBay as I cover everything from starting to sell on eBay to how to make it a full-time business. Whether you have yet to create your first listing or have already been selling for a while, this book has something to offer you.

So why would anyone need to read a book about selling on eBay? After all, isn't that information available for free online?

Well, that is true to an extent. Sure, there are active reselling communities on Facebook, Instagram, and YouTube where people post all sorts of information about how to make money selling on eBay. And there are tutorials on eBay's website to walk you through the process of listing and shipping. However, what you likely find online are only the best parts of selling on eBay. The huge hauls, the giant package piles, the impressive gross sales numbers, and the basics of how to photograph, list, and ship.

But those posts only give you a glimpse into the world of eBay resellers. They do not give you the whole picture of the reality of making money on eBay. Not all sellers are always honest about the time and effort required to source items to resell. They do not share how many hours were spent packaging up low-dollar orders. And they do not share the actual net profit after all fees and taxes are taken out. And while online tutorials can be helpful, some people need extra help.

And that's what I aim to provide you with this book. A "friend," if you will, helping you navigate all of the ins and outs of reselling on eBay.

The fun parts of reselling are finding treasures to resell, selling them, and seeing the money deposited into your bank account. However, those are only three parts of the reselling process. There is a lot more that goes into selling successfully on eBay. While huge package piles make for a fun photo opportunity, they aren't telling you the whole story.

This book, however, tells you the TRUTH about selling on eBay, the good, the bad, and sometimes the ugly. I'm honest with you about every aspect of eBay, not to scare you away, but so that you have all the information necessary to make your eBay journey successful and profitable. After all, I'm assuming you want to sell online to MAKE money, not lose it!

Selling on eBay can be a lot of fun, and there is good money to be made on the site. But there are right ways to do things and wrong ways to do things when it comes to selling on eBay. This book will cover everything you need to know to sell on eBay the right way to limit potential issues and maximize your profits.

eBay is a unique marketplace with its own special learning curve to master. However, after reading this book, you can jump into selling on eBay, and start earning money immediately. And if you have already been selling on the site, hopefully, I will have given you some information to help you grow your business.

I know that, for those who have never sold anything on eBay, it can seem overwhelming initially. Even I was scared to sell on eBay initially! However, once you have a few listings under your belt and have shipped out a couple of orders, I promise you will realize how easy it is. And if you are like me, you will wonder why it took you so long to give eBay a try!

CHAPTER ONE: THE BASICS OF EBAY

eBay debuted in 1995 as an online classified ads marketplace, one of the first online shopping websites. It allowed people all over America to list items they had for sale and sell them to customers in every state. The site was very basic; there were no photos, and it resembled a newspaper classified section.

When eBay first launched, it was an online auction site; people put their items up for auction, and customers bid on them. You could not purchase anything for a set "Buy It Now" price. The highest bidder won the item, paid the seller through eBay's payment system, PayPal, and then the seller shipped the winning bidder their merchandise.

Initially, customers could also bypass PayPal and mail checks to sellers; sometimes, they even sent cash. Yes, you read that right: people mailed strangers envelopes filled with cash to pay for their EBay items! And yes, that even happened to me!

After initially being only available in the United States, eBay quickly expanded to sellers and buyers worldwide. Policies and features changed and expanded, including the option for sellers to open their own "stores." Until Amazon took over, eBay was the number on shopping site in the world. While antiques remain what the site is known for, clothing is the largest category on the site, and large brands even have a presence on eBay.

And while auctions were once the standard way to sell, these days, large and small sellers can also sell new and used products through eBay at what is called **Buy It Now** (formerly referred to as **Fixed Price**). When listing an item at *Buy It Now*, the seller sets the price, and there is no auction, no bidding. Today, most items on the site are sold at a *Buy It Now* price, although the auction option still exists.

I sometimes miss the days when you could start every item at a 99-cent auction and watch the bidding go up and up. I remember sitting at my desk and hitting the refresh button on my computer every minute to update the bidding, watching the price rise until the auction ended. Those were fun times!

However, those days are long gone except for scarce, in-demand collectibles. Nowadays, eBay is mainly a buy-it-now shopping site, just like Amazon, Walmart, and other retailers. And while nostalgia for "the old days" remains among those who were on the site in the beginning, eBay now functions much like every other shopping website, giving it an even playing field and making it less confusing for shoppers to navigate.

One thing that was always unique to eBay was **PayPal**, which was eBay's payment processing system. For buyers to shop on eBay, they used to have a PayPal account. PayPal allowed buyers to set up multiple funding sources, everything from their bank accounts and their own PayPal balances to their debit and credit cards, to pay for items on eBay. Sellers also had to have a PayPal account to facilitate their orders and to get paid. PayPal was the payment system that everyone on eBay, regardless of whether they were buying or selling, HAD to use.

However, in 2015, eBay and PayPal split, becoming two individual companies with no ties to one another. And while eBay continued to rely on PayPal as its payment processor for several years, in 2019, eBay introduced its own payment system, **Managed Payments.**

All eBay sellers are now enrolled in eBay's *Managed Payments*. PayPal is no longer an option on the seller's end. While shoppers can still pay for orders using their PayPal accounts (they can link PayPal as their payment method the same way you can link your credit card to pay for purchases), eBay runs all sales through *Managed Payments.*

Now, all listing fees, final value fees, and shipping charges are automatically deducted from each sale, and eBay disperses the remaining balance to sellers on a schedule they choose (daily, weekly, biweekly, or monthly). This is one of my favorite features as sellers previously always had an outstanding bill they needed to pay. Now sellers don't have to worry about racking up fees; the fees are automatically collected at the time of sale.

Note that as a seller you will need to add a bank account to your eBay account for eBay to disperse your payouts. There is no longer an option to request a paper check to be mailed to you. And if you have an eBay Store subscription, you will need to have a credit card on file to charge that fee to.

While PayPal used to be the only option for shopping on eBay, now it is just one of many options available. This opens up the site to new customers who haven't wanted to open a PayPal account. The PayPal requirement turned off some potential customers, but that is no longer an issue.

In short, buyers can now shop on eBay the same way they do on most other websites. And just like PayPal, buyers can pay via *Managed Payments* using various methods, including credit cards, debit cards, bank accounts, and even PayPal. I still use PayPal to pay for my own eBay purchases, although it is connected to one of my credit cards as I no longer have a running PayPal balance from my eBay sales.

For eBay sellers, *Managed Payments* means that eBay, not PayPal, now manages their funds. When someone purchases one of your items on eBay, eBay will process their payment, deduct the fees and shipping costs (after you have printed off the shipping label) associated with the transaction, and then disperse the remaining funds to you.

With PayPal, sellers had to pay for their labels directly on PayPal and then pay their eBay fees every month. Now, however, postage and fees are taken out before your money is released, meaning you don't have to worry about paying for labels or fees. You can choose to have your funds dispersed daily or weekly. The only fee that isn't automatically deducted is if you have an eBay Store subscription. I let my store subscription charge to a credit card that I earn points on.

Don't worry: we will tackle the payment process of eBay distributing your money to you in-depth later in this book.

I have been selling on eBay since 2005 and have shipped items to every corner of the globe. When I started selling on eBay, it was one of the few online shopping sites on the internet, meaning you could sell nearly anything on it. In fact, when I started to sell online, eBay and Amazon were pretty much the only two e-commerce sites available to sell or buy on.

Today, however, eBay competes with Amazon and Walmart for the top marketplace spot. Plus, nearly every retailer, both large and small, has its own website. And sites like Poshmark, Etsy, Mercari, WhatNot, and even Facebook Marketplace are making the online reselling landscape even more crowded.

The competition between online sellers is much fiercer than when I first started selling online, too. Therefore, the types of items that are sold and the methods by which they are sold have also significantly changed. Many sellers now turn to Amazon to sell their new goods, while eBay is more centered on secondhand items.

However, while things may not always sell as fast as they once did on eBay, you can still sell almost anything there, new or used. And, more and more companies are expanding onto eBay to sell their goods the same way they sell them on their own websites and through other retailers. For example, KitchenAid sells products on its website. They also sell through other retailers, such as Target and Kohl's, both in-store and on those stores' websites. And KitchenAid also sells directly to customers on eBay.

Despite the competition, eBay is still the number one site for individuals and small businesses to sell their items to people worldwide. While it is much larger than it was initially, at its core, eBay still functions like the world's largest flea market with items of every type and at every price point available. eBay continues to expand and improve, giving sellers like me confidence that they will be around for years to come. With nearly two hundred million registered eBay users, there are still plenty of opportunities to make money on eBay.

But why sell your items on eBay instead of a garage sale or consignment shop? Hands down, you will get the most money for your items on eBay versus selling them locally. As I mentioned earlier, there are nearly 200 million registered EBay users, meaning there are 200 million more chances to sell your items.

Let's say you have a rare collectible to sell. While only a handful of people will come to your garage sale or enter your local consignment shop, on eBay, your item is available for purchase to the millions of eBay account holders worldwide. You only need to wait for that one special buyer who is looking specifically for your item to find it and willingly pay you top dollar for it. The chances of that same buyer coming to your garage sale are slim to none. Hence when people at garage sales say that something is selling on eBay for a particular amount, I tell them they need to list it on eBay!

The biggest perk of learning to sell on eBay, for me, is that it provides you with a certain level of financial protection. Once you know how to sell on eBay, you can sell your unwanted items for top dollar any time, raising cash quickly if the need arises. While you could earn a couple of hundred dollars fast by selling your stuff at a garage sale, you can rake in a few thousand dollars for those same items after a couple of weeks of them being listed on eBay. I honestly believe they should teach high school seniors how to resell as it's a valuable life skill!

Most people who sell on eBay got their start by selling their extra "stuff" from around their house. And once they were hooked on selling off their own items, they started searching thrift stores and garage sales for more item overstock of gift basket supplies, I went through my house, pulling anything and everything that I wasn't using, and listed it all on eBay.

How To Set Up Your eBay Account: Signing up for an eBay account is the first step towards both buying and selling on eBay. Buyers need to provide payment information to shop on the site, but sellers need to provide more information including a back-up funding source, banking information for payouts, and tax information.

eBay makes the process of signing up to buy or sell very easy. Simply visit **eBay.com** and click on **Register** in the top left corner of the page to get started.

When signing up for an eBay account, you will first need to select a **User Name**, also called a *screen name*. Think carefully about the name you choose; you do not want to give out too much information (such as *singlewomanlivingalone*), but you also do not want to have a crazy name no one understands (what does *dhioatg89yrew* mean, anyway?). Selecting an easy-to-remember user name will help you attract repeat customers and build your brand.

My eBay username is the same name as my eBay store: *Annabella's Gift Shop*. My original gift basket business was called *Annabella's Gift Baskets*; I changed "Baskets" to "Shop" when I began selling single gift items. And even though I have transitioned to selling vintage collectibles, I've kept the name as I've used it since the beginning.

And, no, my name is not Annabella. I just thought it sounded more sophisticated than "Ann"!

Since there are millions of registered eBay users, the first user name you want to use may already be taken, so have a few options ready. If you think you might want to sell on eBay consistently in the future, choose a name that reflects what you plan to sell. But don't narrow your focus too much. You may start out selling sports cards, for example, but eventually expand to other collectibles. "Bob's Sports," "Bob's Collectibles," or "Bob's Sports Collectibles" would be a better choice than "Bob's Sports Cards." Note that if you choose to open an eBay store, you will choose a different name for your shop; although I believe it should match your user name.

Next, American users will need to provide their **Social Security number.** And all users must provide **financial information** to create their eBay account, either a **bank account routing number** or a **credit card**. Some people balk at providing this information, but every single selling platform, whether online or in a brick-and-mortar store, requires these details.

The reason Americans need to provide Social Security numbers is for tax purposes. If you **sell more than $600 a year on eBay,** they will provide you with a **1099 tax form** in January to file with the IRS. And they will report your earnings directly to the IRS. When PayPal issued the tax forms, the threshold for receiving a 1099 form was $20,000; but the new $600 threshold aligns with what most other companies use when issuing 1099 forms. Don't worry: eBay will notify you when you have a tax form available so that you can print out your copy.

If you are registering outside of America, eBay will prompt you with the information you need to enter your country along with what financial documents they will be providing to you and your government.

All sellers need to enter **banking information** to register for **Managed Payments**, which is how eBay distributes earnings. Many sellers open a separate business bank account to attach to their eBay account, although if you are just starting, it's fine to start out using your checking account.

PRO TIP: If you open a business bank account, make sure the name matches your eBay account. When you print shipping labels through USPS on eBay, your user name will show on the label. If you need to file a claim with USPS for lost or damaged packages, they will issue a check made out to your USER NAME, not your legal name. Most banks will not cash checks unless they are made out to the same name on your account.

It is also essential, I believe, to have a **credit card** on file with eBay as a backup funding source. Note that while eBay will deduct your fees and shipping charges from your pending balance, it is still a good idea to have a credit card on file just in case of a charge that your balance or bank account does not cover. I do not want a billing dispute to disrupt my sales, and I do not want eBay to withdraw money from my checking account that may be delegated to something else, so a credit card on file gives me an added layer of protection. And if you open an Ebay Store, the monthly subscription fees will be charged to your card, not taken out of your balance.

As I have already discussed, in 2015, eBay and PayPal split into two separate companies, with eBay implementing their own payment system, **Managed Payments.** All eBay sellers are now enrolled in *Managed Payments.* If you are just now setting up your eBay account, you will be enrolled in *Managed Payments* right from the start. The connection between eBay and PayPal is now officially severed.

When eBay sellers used PayPal, we were billed for our monthly fees, which we had to manually pay from our PayPal balances, credit cards, or checking accounts. The great thing about eBay's *Managed Payments* is that eBay now takes out all listing fees, final value fees, and postage costs once a transaction is completed. That means the money left in your account will all be dispersed to you.

However, as I've noted already if you pay for an eBay Store subscription, that monthly fee WILL be charged to your backup payment account. This fee will show up in your monthly invoice along with any expenses that your balance didn't cover. You can pay for it manually from your checking account or PayPal account, or allow it to be charged to the credit card you have on file.

Once your eBay account is set up and enrolled in *Managed Payments,* it is time to experiment with the eBay site itself. If you've already been shopping on eBay, you are hopefully comfortable with the layout. However, selling on eBay is different from buying. The interface you used to sell has many more sections and options than the shopping interface.

Reselling is a unique skill, and learning a new skill takes some time. To help you learn exactly how to sell on eBay, I believe there are three steps you should take:

Step #1: Buy Some Low-Dollar Items: After you have set up your eBay buying account, purchase some cheap items from several different eBay sellers (there are millions of no-risk 99-cent items on the site) to familiarize yourself with not only eBay's search feature but also the checkout process.

This is not the time to try to get a deal on an expensive electronic; you want to simply go through the eBay buying process so that you will see things the way your potential customers will once you have items listed for sale. By buying a handful of items, you will see how different sellers treat their customers and how they ship their merchandise.

During this buying process, you want to look at how other sellers craft their listings. Are their titles loaded with keywords? Study the photos they provide. Are the pictures clear and well-lit? Read their listing descriptions. Do they provide a lot of details, such as color, condition, and measurements? Note how you receive notification of payment and shipment and keep track of how long it takes your order to arrive. Carefully examine how the item was packaged. Was your order shipped quickly and in clean packaging? Were breakables well protected? Did the seller leave you feedback?

Everything you learn as a buyer will translate to how you function as a seller. Note what you liked and did not like about the orders you received and use that knowledge to create your listings. The biggest lesson you will hopefully learn is how to properly package shipments, which many new sellers fail miserably at. It is the *Golden Rule* of business: Treat your customers as you would want to be treated.

Step #2: Sell Some of Your Personal Items: After you are comfortable *buying* on eBay, it is time to get your feet wet *selling* by listing some items from around your own home. Do not worry about sourcing products until you are comfortable with the selling process.

Again, just as you learned about what other sellers do when you buy from them, selling some of your own items allows you to experience being a seller yourself without the risk of spending money on inventory.

Selling some of the items you already own (books, CDs, video games, clothing, toys, collectibles) will give you experience writing titles and descriptions, taking photos, and preparing shipments. Again, these initial sales are not about making much money; the goal is to gain experience as a seller, both in how the eBay site works and how to ship out items.

You may not even make any money from these sales; heck, you might even lose a few dollars. However, the experience you will gain will be invaluable as you continue your eBay journey.

PRO TIP: Before you list anything for sale on eBay, make sure you have a box to ship it in along with packing materials and tape. The last thing you want to do after an item sells is scramble to find something to ship it in. While it's fine to reuse boxes, make sure they are clean and sturdy.

Experiment with the first items you list. Try 99-cent auctions. Try listing *Buy It Now* both with *Best Offer* and without. Try both calculated, flat rate, and free shipping. Try sending *Offers to Watchers*. eBay offers so many ways to sell; you want to familiarize yourself with all of them so that you will know which ones to use going forward. These days I prefer listing most items at *Buy It Now* pricing and calculated shipping.

By playing around with all the various ways to sell items on eBay, you will find the methods you are most comfortable with. You may decide to offer "free shipping" on small, lightweight objects ("free" is in quotes as shipping is never free; someone, in this case, you, as the seller, will have to pay for it) while using calculated shipping on larger, heavier things.

You may decide that auctions do not work for what you are selling and choose to list items at a fixed price. You may decide that you enjoy the haggling of offering "best offer;" or you may find out that you hate dealing with offers and not add them as an option to your listings. You may try accepting returns but turn them off later down the road.

As you experiment with the various ways to sell, remember that you are not locked into any one listing method. After nearly two decades of selling on eBay, I still frequently change things up. I recently added "Best Offer" to most of my listings, even though I dislike haggling, as these days shoppers like to negotiate. What makes eBay so unique is that each seller gets to decide for themselves how they want to sell their items. The individual control we have as sellers is what sets eBay apart from the other reselling sites. There are no auctions on Amazon, Etsy, or Poshmark; and buyers cannot submit offers on Amazon or Etsy.

Step #3: Source a Small Number of Items to Sell: By now, you have set up your eBay and *Managed Payments* accounts, you have purchased a handful of low-dollar items, and you have sold some things from around your house. Now it is time to get serious and buy some items to resell. In the reselling world, this is referred to as **sourcing** (formerly called "picking").

While it is tempting to head to the nearest garage sale and buy everything they have, do not invest much money in products to resell right away. Start small with some thrift store or yard sale finds. Or try your hand at reselling new items you see on clearance at retail stores. Many resellers frequent the clearance aisles at Walmart searching for items to flip on eBay.

Again, these first few items you buy to resell do not have to be big moneymakers. You are still gaining experience as a seller before you grow into making eBay an actual job. I recommend giving yourself a budget, say $20, the first time you go sourcing. See how far $20 gets you at your local thrift store or neighborhood garage sales. Do not let yourself source anything else until you list what you already bought.

The first few times I went to estate sales to find items to resell were a disaster. I bought things that ended up being worthless. However, since I stuck to a strict budget, I did not berate myself for wasting my money. Instead, I considered these first purchases part of "buying my education." The next time I went sourcing, I did a little better. And then next time, better than that. It takes time to recognize what is worth picking up and what you should just leave behind. We will go over tips and tricks for finding what sells best on eBay later in this book.

Why Take It Slow: Why don't I recommend you jump into selling on eBay with both feet and see what happens? Well, as we've already discussed, eBay is a unique marketplace. You can buy and sell at auction or fixed price. You can accept offers and send offers to interested customers. To sell on eBay, you need to source products, take and edit photos, write up listings, handle customer questions, and ship out packages. You may find that after buying and selling a few things that you do not even like selling on eBay and may decide not to pursue it as a job or even as a hobby.

However, if you find that you enjoy selling on eBay, going through these first steps will give you a good base of knowledge before starting a full-fledged business, whether part-time or full-time. Plus, you will gain some feedback, which is very important in earning potential customers' trust. The more positive feedback you have, the more customers will trust you, and the more benefits you will gain from eBay, such as *Top-Rated Seller* rankings and discounts on fees.

Also, because of the limits eBay now places on new sellers, if you are entirely new to the site, you will be forced to take it slow regardless of how many items you want to list. eBay is constantly changing what it requires of new sellers, and it varies based on several factors, including:

- The age of an account
- Confirmation of identity on an account
- An account's link to an established account
- An account's registered address
- Site of registration
- Selling performance and behaviors
- The volume an account has managed in the past
- The risk associated with the types of items listed on an account

After creating an account, eBay will walk you through their current selling and buying limits and requirements, including exactly how many listings they will give you to start with. Don't be discouraged if you have a low selling limit. If you start off selling strong, you can contact eBay directly to ask them to increase your listing allotment. You will need to prove that you are following eBay's policies and providing the best customer service possible for them to grant you more listings.

Many new eBay sellers dive headfirst into trying to make eBay their full-time business, and many fail miserably. eBay has a steep but manageable learning curve. Take your time to learn eBay's systems and policies so that when you start to list a lot of items to earn real money, you will be successful!

CHAPTER TWO: UNDERSTANDING EBAY'S FEES & FEATURES

eBay as a selling platform and the EBay interface itself have evolved over the years, and they are constantly rolling out new features to help us as sellers. In this chapter, I will be going over all of eBay's seller fees as well as the features you can use to manage your business.

Selling Fees: eBay is sometimes jokingly referred to as *FEEBay* because of the fees associated with selling on the site. Remember, however, that the fees paid for all of the features of the site are numerous. There are three different types of fees you pay when you sell on eBay:

Insertion Fees: As of this writing, eBay is giving all sellers up to 250 zero insertion fees monthly. Those with an *eBay Store* are given more depending on their store subscription level, which we'll discuss later in this book. After you have used up your zero-insertion fee allowance, your insertion fees will be charged per listing based on your selling category. Insertion fees are non-refundable, even if your item doesn't sell. Most items incur a 35-cent insertion fee, although it varies by category.

Final Value Fees: eBay charges you a *Final Value Fee* when your items sell. The fee is calculated as a percentage of the total amount of the sale, including any shipping charges. Final Value Fees are anywhere from 2% up to 15%, depending on the item's category and whether you have an *eBay Store* subscription.

Store Subscription Fees: A great way to save on fees and organize your eBay listings is to open an *eBay Store*. An *eBay Store* is an optional feature you pay extra for, but you do not need to have a store to sell on the site. As of this writing, eBay offers five different store subscription levels. We will go over the store options later in this book.

Listing Variations: As you play around with buying and selling on eBay, you will start to become familiar with the various methods available for listings, including:

Auctions: Auction listings feature items that potential buyers place bids on. Say you find an item you like listed at auction for 99 cents. You put in the minimum bid increment to place a bid, which varies depending on the current bid. Sellers can choose to run auctions for one, three, five, seven, or ten days. Note that seven-day auctions are the most popular, giving potential buyers a week to find the item and place bids.

PRO TIP: eBay now automatically relists unsold auctions, so be sure to keep an eye on your listings if you are running a lot of auctions as those that don't end in a sale will continually be relisted until the items sell or you manually end the listing.

Auctions with Best Offer: Sellers can add a *Best Offer* option to their auctions, which allows customers to submit an offer rather than bid. This can be advantageous if a buyer offers you considerably more than your auction starting price. However, it may also result in shoppers offering you a price that is less than your starting bid. You can accept or decline offers. As soon as someone places a bid, the *Best Offer* option is removed from the listing, meaning customers can only submit bids going forward.

Auctions with Buy It Now: eBay sellers can add a *Buy It Now* feature to their auctions, which not only offers customers the chance to bid on an item but also provides them with the ability to buy the item outright without bidding. For instance, you may see an auction with a starting bid of 99 cents and a *Buy It Now* option of $10. Buyers can either bid on that listing starting at the 99-cent price or buy the item outright for $10. Once the first bid is placed, the *Buy It Now* option disappears.

Buy It Now: eBay began as an online auction site, but today most listings are listed at a fixed price, called *Buy It Now*. *Buy It Now* listings only offer the option of purchasing the item outright; there is no option to bid.

Buy It Now with Best Offer: Many eBay sellers turn the *Best Offer* feature on in their listings, stating a set *Buy It Now* price but with the option for buyers to submit *Best Offers* for consideration. Let's say you see an item listed for $50 with the *Best Offer* option. You submit an offer to the seller for, say, $40. If the seller accepts, you must purchase the item for $40. However, the seller could counteroffer, coming back with a price of $45. You could accept the counteroffer or make another counteroffer of your own. Or the seller could simply reject your offer outright.

Most sellers accept reasonable offers. You can select a minimum threshold amount for eBay to accept on your behalf automatically. Going back to that $ 50 item, let's say the seller turned on the auto-accept feature to accept any offer of $40 or more. So, if you offered them $40, your offer would be automatically accepted; you would not have to wait for the seller to accept your offer manually.

Offers To Watchers: One of my favorite eBay features is *Offers To Watchers,* which gives sellers the ability to send offers to interested buyers. When at least one person "watches" an item you have listed, you can send them a direct offer of either a percentage or a dollar amount off discount. The offer you send is good for up to 48 hours. Note that you will not see the username of the person you are sending the offer to. eBay does not show sellers the watchers' names, just the number of watchers on any item.

Your offer will go to ALL watchers, so if you have ten people watching one of your listings, those 10 will receive your offer. The first person to accept the offer will be the winner, and their payment will automatically go through.

Feedback: Once you have purchased some items on eBay, you will want to follow through with leaving **Feedback**. A unique feature of eBay is its feedback system, where buyers and sellers can leave each other feedback on transactions. Buyers can leave sellers *Positive*, *Neutral,* or *Negative* feedback; sellers can only leave buyers *Positive* feedback.

In addition to the Feedback rating, buyers and sellers can also leave comments. Buyers can also rate their experience using a five-star system on the following factors:

- **Item as Described**
- **Communication**
- **Shipping Time**
- **Shipping & Handling Charges**

Good feedback is key to having a successful selling career on eBay. Getting negative feedback will seriously lower your overall feedback rating. A buyer who "dings" your stars (i.e., leaves you lower than the ideal five stars) hurts your seller rating. And your seller rating directly impacts any potential fee or shipping discounts you may be eligible for.

A solid feedback score and seller rating make potential customers more likely to buy from you and are crucial in maintaining your eBay account. In recent years, eBay started cracking down, suspending accounts, and kicking bad sellers off their site. You want to do everything you can to make sure your buyers are happy and that they do not leave you negative feedback or low star ratings. As long as your listings are accurate and you ship your orders out quickly, you shouldn't have any issues.

As a buyer, you want to leave honest but fair feedback. If you receive the item you ordered when the seller promised, and it is in the condition it was advertised, there is no need to leave the seller anything other than positive feedback with five stars. Sellers typically block buyers who consistently leave negative feedback for most of their purchases (yes, buyers cannot only view your feedback, but you can also see theirs).

PRO TIP: New sellers often become fixated on getting their feedback built up. However, the worst thing you can do is pester your customers to leave feedback. Your job is to list items with accurate descriptions and to ship them out quickly and professionally. Only about a third of eBay users leave feedback, and eBay will remind anyone who has purchased to leave the seller feedback. Let eBay worry about sending out feedback reminders; all you need to worry about is sourcing, listing, and shipping!

Regarding feedback, I take the *Golden Rule* approach in that I leave feedback for others that I would want them to leave me. Because sellers can no longer give negative feedback, if I'm dealing with a problematic buyer, I simply don't leave any feedback. And after all of these years, the truth is that I rarely look at my feedback. After a while, I stopped worrying about it as I was confident in my abilities. In all of my years selling on eBay, I think I've gotten around five negatives. And, to be honest, they were from very difficult customers who were impossible to please. However, since I was selling a large volume of items, those negatives quickly dropped off with the positive feedback from other customers.

Seller Hub: As an eBay seller, you will spend a lot of your time on the *Seller Hub* page of your eBay account. In fact, this is the page that I have bookmarked on my computer as it is the starting point for almost everything I need to access while using eBay.

To access your *Seller Hub*, click on the **Sell** tab at the top right-hand side of any eBay page.

The *Seller Hub* has nine tabs at the top of the page; there are additional options under most of these:

- **Overview**
- **Orders**
- **Listings**
- **Marketing**
- **Store**
- **Performance**
- **Payments**
- **Research**
- **Reports**

Overview: The *Overview* page is the default page for *Seller Hub*. Here you are given a quick look at your current EBay statistics, including:

- **Unread Messages**
- **Orders Awaiting Shipment**
- **Sales for the Past 31 Days**
- **Seller level forecast**
- **Research recommendations**

In late 2023, eBay added the ability for sellers to spend their balances on purchases on the site. This is a program you need to enroll in. If you haven't enrolled, there will be a section with a link prompting you to do so. You can use your funds not only to shop but to cover added selling costs, such as *Store* subscriptions, as well as to buy shipping supplies.

There are then several sections of data that you can really dig into as you scroll further along the page, including:

Tasks: Here, you will see everything eBay needs you to act on, including answering messages or shipping orders. They also offer *Suggested Actions* for things like updating listings and sending offers to watchers. If you have orders to ship, there will be a link to **Print labels and ship.** We'll cover shipping in-depth later in this book.

Other Suggested Actions include **Listings eligible to send offers,** which are listings that have watchers, meaning you can send those watchers offers. They will also prompt you to **Add recommended item specifics** to listings. Note that these are recommendations, not required fields. And finally, there is a link for those with an eBay Store to **Finish setting up your store to help improve conversion.** It's always useful to click on these suggested options to see if there is more you can do to increase sales.

Sales: The next section of the page is **Sales.** This is where eBay shows you your sales from the current day and the *Last seven days, 31 days,* and *90 days.* This snapshot of your sales is a great way to quickly gauge how business is going. Clicking on the > **arrow** will bring up a new page where you can dig deeper into your sales numbers.

Orders: The next section is **Orders,** which is where eBay breaks down your order information and history here, including:

- **Awaiting shipment – print shipping label**
- **All open returns/replacements**
- **Open cancellations**
- **Awaiting payment**
- **Shipped and awaiting your feedback**
- **Orders eligible for combined purchases**

You can click through to any of these options to complete the tasks.

Listings: The next section is **Listings**, which shows you all your listing information, including:

- **Create listing**
- **Drafts**
- **Active listings**
- **With questions**
- **With open offers from buyers**
- **All auctions**
- **With reserve met**
- **Ending today**
- **Scheduled listings**
- **Unsold and not relisted**

Under the title of **Listing reports** you will find the following **Active listings** links:

- **Fixed price**
- **Ad format**
- **Fixed price (GTC)**
- **Ending within the next hour**
- **Duplicate listings not visible to buyers** (If you accidentally create two identical listings, eBay will hide one of them from buyers. If you have multiple quantities of

identical items, you can change the quantity within one listing to account for how many you have.)

Finally, you will see links for your **Ended listings**, including those in the **Last 90 days**, **Sold**, and **Eligible for Second Chance Offer**. If a buyer doesn't pay for an auction win, you can send a **Second Chance Offer** to the next highest bidder.

Traffic: Real-time traffic to your listings for 30 days, including:

- **Listing impressions**
- **Click-through rate**
- **Listing page views**
- **Sales conversion rate**

You can click on any of these line items to gain more data, and you can also click on the > **arrow** to look at data from earlier periods.

Seller Level: Here, you can track your current seller level and the statistics eBay will use to grade your performance in the coming month. All sellers are assigned an individual seller performance level of either:

Below Standard means that your performance has fallen below eBay's minimum standards and as a result, they may place limits on your selling activity, including charging higher final value fees and limiting new listings until performance improves.

Above Standard means you are meeting eBay's expectations.

Top Rated means you're exceeding eBay's performance expectations, as well as having an established sales history and complying with other eBay policies.

eBay calculates your seller level based on one of two metrics:

- If you had more than 400 transactions in the past 3 months, eBay will count all those transactions.
- If you had fewer than 400 transactions in the past 3 months, eBay will count all your transactions from the last 12 months.

eBay evaluates accounts based on factors such as cases closed without seller resolution, transaction defect rate, and late shipment rate. To qualify as a **Top Rated Seller**, you need to meet the following:

- **Cases closed without seller resolution:** No more than 2 (or 0.3% of transactions)
- **Transaction defect rate:** No more than 0.5%, associated with no more than 3 different buyers
- **Late shipment rate:** No more than 5 (or 3% of transactions)
- **Upload tracking:** At least 95% of transactions have tracking uploaded within handling time and validated by carrier
- **Active account:** Your eBay account has been active for at least 90 days
- **Sales:** You have at least 100 transactions and $1,000 in sales with US buyers over the past 12 months
- **Compliance:** You're complying with eBay's selling practices

Top Rated Seller Plus: eBay has one more category that sellers can strive to achieve, which is **Top Rated Seller Plus**. To be awarded the *Plus* badge, sellers must meet the following standards:

- **Offer same or one business day handling**, meaning you need to print a shipping label on the same day as an order comes in or the next day; business days are Monday through Friday.

- **Offer free returns of 30 days or longer,** which means you as the seller pay for the return shipping.

Top Rated Sellers Plus sellers receive a prominent seal next to their listings and also receive a 10% discount on final value fees.

PRO TIP: I believe that you should aim for the *Top Rated Seller* distinction and not worry about receiving *Plus* status. Most small sellers cannot afford to offer free returns. I don't allow returns as I can't absorb the cost. The *Plus* seal is meant for high-volume sellers of new goods who are competing with thousands of other similar listings, not individual sellers who sell single unique items.

Feedback: The next section is **Feedback**, which is where Bay shows you the last 30 days of your feedback, broken down by *Positive, Neutral,* and *Negative.* They also give you links to leave feedback for the items you have bought and sold and automate feedback.

Shortcuts: Here, you will find links to the most popular sections on eBay:

- **Cancel bids**
- **Block bidders**
- **Site preferences**
- **Selling discussion board**
- **Seller Center**
- **Report a buyer**
- **eBay Shipping Supplies**
- **Purchase history**
- **Watch list**

Selling Tools: Like the *Shortcuts* section, this section gives you direct links to several pages that sellers frequently use, including:

- **See my Store**
- **Subscriptions**
- **Merchant Integration Program**
- **Intuit QuickBooks Online**
- **eBay Seller Capital**
- **View My eBay Selling**
- **Manage Store**
- **Markdown Manager**
- **Seller Hub Reports**
- **Automate feedback**
- **Reporting**
- **Seller Dashboard**
- **Sellers you follow**
- **3rd party applications**
- **Promoted listings**
- **Time Away** (formerly called *Vacation* mode)

Selling Announcements: Links to the latest seller news from eBay. This is a section you'll want to keep your eyes on as eBay is always announcing new features and policies.

Promotional Offers: Links to the latest special offers for eBay sellers with an eBay Store, such as any free listing promotions or store subscription offers.

Research: Links to help you gain insight into your pricing, ways to improve your listings, and sourcing opportunities, including **Terapeak**, which I will discuss further later in this book.

PRO TIP: If you are overwhelmed by all these options, please don't worry. To be honest, I rarely look at most of these sections myself. They are great if you want to quickly find a link to a specific section on the site that you don't normally use, such as finding the link to put your store on vacation (now called **Time Away**) or the link to block problematic buyers. And you can *Personalize Your Overview* through a link at the bottom of the page, which lets you add, remove, and reorder the content shown.

Orders: Back at the top of the *Seller Hub* page is the second tab, *Orders*. Clicking on this takes you to the pending orders you need to ship. You can also see if you have orders that are still awaiting payment, orders that have already been shipped, cancellations, returns, and cases. You can also access the *Shipping Labels* you have already printed, which is helpful if a label did not print out correctly. Here eBay makes it easy to print a second copy of the label and/or the packing slip.

Listings: The third tab at the top of *Seller Hub* is for *Listings*, and this, next to *Orders*, is the page I most frequently access. Here I can see all my *Active Listings*. There are several filters available to sort your listings as well as to edit them. eBay shows you the number of active listings and the total dollar value of everything you have listed.

Under the *Listings* tab, on the left-hand side of the page, are the following options:

- **Active**
- **Unsold**
- **Drafts**
- **Scheduled**
- **Ended**
- **Listing templates**
- **Business policies**
- **Item location zip code**
- **Learning resources**

Marketing: The fourth tab under the *Seller Hub* is for *Marketing*. You can manage the following:

Promotions: Offer an order discount or shipping discount, or create a special coupon code you provide to certain people.

Markdown sale: Put select listings or all of them on sale for a select period.

Buyer groups: Create special groups from your previous customers and/or followers to whom you can send personalized offers.

Social: One of eBay's newest features allows you to link your social media accounts to create custom posts. Currently, the options available are for Facebook Pages, Instagram Business Accounts, and Pinterest.

Advertising: By clicking on **Advertising**, you will be taken to a page for eBay's **Promoted Listings**. This is an option program where you can opt to "bid" a percentage to have your listings shown higher in eBay's search algorithm. This is for those who are selling items that have a lot of competition. For example, the clothing category is extremely competitive; therefore, it can be advantageous to enable *Promoted Listings* to have your items shown higher in search.

PRO TIP: The minimum bid allowed is 2%. I enable 2% on all of my listings as it has doubled my sales. While no one wants to pay more money to get their listings seen, you are only charged if someone purchases your item. And eBay automatically deducts the fee from your balance.

Store: The fifth tab in *Seller Hub* is for those with an eBay Store. This area is only accessible to those with an *eBay Store* subscription. Here you can edit your store to customize it. You can also edit your store categories, set up a store newsletter, offer subscriber discounts, and manage your store subscription.

I frequent this section to access my **Store categories**. These are different from the eBay categories; these are categories that I name and arrange in my store. Setting up store categories helps me stay organized as I can quickly narrow down groupings.

Performance: The sixth tab under *Seller Hub* is *Performance*. Here you can dive deeper into your sales data, much of which is also linked under the *Overview* tab, including:

- **Seller level**
- **Sales**
- **Traffic**
- **Service Metrics**

Payments: The seventh tab under *Seller Hub* is *Payments*. This section breaks down your current financials, including your current balance, your next payout, and your current invoice. You can set up when you want your payments dispersed to your bank account, daily or weekly. You can also access various reports and your taxpayer settings. This is my favorite tab as it shows me how much money eBay will be depositing into my account!

Research: The eighth tab under *Seller Hub* is *Research*. All eBay sellers are given free access to **Terapeak**, a database of the past two years' worth of eBay sales across the site. You can research what items have been sold to price your own. While the general eBay search gives you three months of sales data, Terapeak provides two years.

Those with an eBay Store subscription of *Basic* or higher also have access to Terapeak sourcing insights. I use Terapeak every time I create a new listing to research the best price for my item. It also tells me if an item is even worth listing. I generally don't bother listing items that aren't going to sell for at least $10.

Reports: The ninth and final tab in the *Seller Hub* is *Reports*. This is for more advanced sellers who want to upload files, download reports, and schedule reports.

My eBay: Both eBay buyers and sellers have a *My eBay* section, which is everyone's personal eBay page. You will see the *My eBay* link at the top of eBay's homepage. Before eBay introduced *Seller Hub*, *My eBay* was where you went to access all your tasks and data. There are three options here:

- **Activity:** All of your buying activities, including auctions you are bidding on, listings you are watching, and orders you've placed.
- **Messages:** Access all of your messages, both from eBay and customers.
- **Account:** As a seller, most of the information here can also be found under your Seller Hub (remember, this is located under the Sell link at the top of any eBay page).

However, *My eBay* is now just for buyers. Buyers can click on their **Activity** tab to see what items they have recently viewed, their current bids or offers, their purchase history, items on their watch lists, their saved searches, and their saved sellers.

In addition to the *Activity* tab, there are also tabs for **Messages** (where you can see your entire eBay messaging system, not only messages you have received but those you have sent) and **Account** (links to some of the more popular parts of the site). As an eBay seller, you will be using the *Seller Hub* to run your business, likely only accessing the *My eBay* part of the site as it relates to your purchases.

eBay is continually rolling out new features for buyers and sellers, and the choices can seem overwhelming. As I mentioned earlier, I have my *Seller Hub* bookmarked on my computer to access my *Orders* and *Listings* easily. I only check my *Payments* tab a couple of times per week in advance of my weekly payout, and I click on *Research* when I want to look up an item's price history using *Terapeak*.

As a seller, my orders and listings are the most immediate information I need to keep up daily. As you continue your eBay journey, you can slowly begin investigating all the data eBay provides you via your *Seller Hub*. In the beginning, focus on getting your items listed and shipped out. You will have plenty of time in the future to dig into all the statistics available to you in your *Seller Hub*!

CHAPTER THREE: RESELLING EQUIPMENT & SUPPLIES

Just as the eBay platform itself requires learning specific skills, there are also certain tools you will need to have to sell on eBay successfully. I have watched far too many people attempt to sell online without having first acquired the necessary equipment and they struggled to catch up. And as I have already mentioned in this book, I understand that it is tempting to dive head-first into reselling; however, a lot more goes into selling on eBay than just buying items to resell.

Equipment: If you want to sell on eBay, you need a **computer**. And if you are going to ship orders from home, you also need a **printer to print shipping labels**. And you will need a **camera** to take photos. These are the three main pieces of equipment everyone who sells on eBay must have.

Computer: A computer with a fast processor will help you save time when creating your listings and printing your shipping labels. Either Apple or PC products are fine when selling on eBay; it comes down to preference. You will spend a lot of time on your computer creating eBay listings and printing labels, which is a vital investment in your business. Most people these days already have a computer; if you do, you can start with the one you have. However, note that, depending on the specifications, you may need to eventually upgrade so your machine can keep up.

Printer: Unless you plan to handwrite your shipping labels and take them to the Post Office for postage, you will need a printer. When it comes to printing shipping labels, many resellers use thermal printers. DYMO and ROLLO are the most well-known brands. While I have a thermal printer, I use my laserjet printer to print eBay labels. Because I tend to sell fewer items at a higher price point, I rarely have dozens of labels to print at a time, so I print my labels the old-fashioned way onto double-sided label sheets.

If you are just starting to sell on eBay and already have a printer, use it until you see a need to upgrade to a better model. Inkjet printers use a lot of expensive ink, and you must change the cartridges frequently; hence, I use a LaserJet, which takes less ink and lasts longer. Double-sided label sheets print two labels per page, but there's no shame in simply printing your shipping labels onto paper and taping them to boxes. That's honestly how I ran my business for years; it's only recently that I switched to the peel-and-stick labels.

However, if your eBay sales increase to the point where you are shipping dozens of items per day, you may want to look into a thermal printer that prints shipping labels exclusively in rolls (the kind with the peel-off backs that you can stick onto a package). As I mentioned, many online sellers use DYMO or ROLLO printers to print their shipping labels. There are numerous YouTube videos from resellers discussing the thermal printers they use as well as how-to videos on setting them up. Typically clothing sellers who sell a large volume of lower-priced pieces daily use thermal printers; many hard good sellers such as myself who have higher dollar orders use laserjet printers. Which you prefer is a matter of choice.

Camera/Smartphone: In the early days of eBay, there were no photos in the listings. However, that's changed. Now you must put photos into your eBay listings, so a camera is essential. When I started reselling, I used a digital camera to take my eBay photos, using the SIM card to transfer the files to my computer and then upload them to eBay. Now I just use my iPhone to take photos and upload them using the eBay app. Today's smartphones take just as good, sometimes better, pictures as digital cameras, so if you already own a phone, see if you can make it work.

The benefit of having a smartphone is that you can utilize the **eBay App** while away from your computer. I use my iPhone to photograph, create drafts, and answer customer questions. I use my laptop to research, complete listings, and print shipping labels.

PRO TIP: To list items quickly, I **take a batch of photos using my iPhone**. I then open up the **eBay app** on my phone and go to an active listing. I click on the **Sell Similar** option. A pop-up appears asking me if I want to remove the photos in that listing. I answer yes, and then replace those photos with the ones of the product I am listing. I then save the listing as a **Draft** and switch to my computer to finish the listing. Some sellers do the entire process on their phones, but I still prefer completing listings on my laptop.

Computers, printers, cameras, smartphones. They all play a huge part in selling on eBay and can be a considerable expense if you don't already own them. Start with the equipment you have on hand before upgrading. You may find that what you already own works perfectly fine.

Remember that any money you spend on your eBay business equipment can be deducted as an expense come tax time. Be sure to track everything you purchase and keep the receipts to claim maximum deductions. I will discuss how to manage your eBay accounting later in this book.

Internet Access: Fast, reliable internet access is critical to selling on eBay. I pay $50 a month for high-speed internet access. Most phone and cable companies now offer internet services, including modems so that you can have wireless access.

If you don't already have internet access, call around the internet providers in your area and ask about any packages or specials they have for new customers. Be careful about getting locked into a long-term contract, however, and be sure you are aware of any price increases that will take place once the introductory special is over.

Trust me when I say that high-speed internet is worth the price if you plan to sell a significant number of items on eBay; you will easily be able to afford the added cost of quality internet with the additional sales you will be making. And as with all business expenses, you can claim your internet come tax time.

Digital Scale: The number one supply that most people don't have when they start selling online but that you MUST purchase is a digital postal scale. A digital postage scale is necessary to weigh packages to figure out the correct postage. You can buy digital scales for around $20 to $30 on eBay and Amazon, and they are also sold at office supply stores. Look for a "postage" specific scale that measures pounds AND ounces, as you will need to know ounces when shipping items under one pound.

You do not need a fancy digital model, just a tabletop scale that weighs ounces and pounds. I have had the same scale for years; it is a small investment you MUST make if you ship your eBay orders yourself. If you are not willing to purchase a digital scale for your eBay shipping, then be prepared to haul all your packages to the Post Office every day, where you will wait in line and pay for postage as they charge more at the retail counters than they do online. Why do that when you can weigh your packages and print your labels from the comfort of your own home?

Over the years, I have encountered many sellers who sell on eBay without a digital postage scale. They estimate the shipping, overcharging customers in some cases (and getting negative feedback), or undercharging shoppers and losing money. Or they take all of their items to the Post Office BEFORE listing them to get the weight, take the packages back home, list them, and then go BACK to the Post Office to pay for postage after the items sell. That, to me, is a HUGE waste of time and gas money, not to mention that postage is more expensive at the Post Office. Again, you can do all of this from home with a digital postage scale for under $30!

Note that you get a discount on postage when you ship online at USPS.com or on eBay versus paying at the Post Office retail counter. Sometimes the difference can be as much as a few dollars, and when you are shipping multiple packages, those extra costs add up quickly.

Some sellers choose to charge a flat rate for all their orders. These sellers tend to sell the same types of items, such as postcards or clothing. For example, many clothing sellers charge $5.99 to ship clothing that weighs under one pound. This can result in a $1 to $3 overage depending on the weight of the package, which they put towards shipping supplies. In some cases, the cost may exceed $5.99, but the shortfall is absorbed by those that were overcharged.

It is normal to pad the shipping cost to cover fees and shipping supplies, but if you charge a flat rate, be careful not to overcharge your customers too much. Buyers come to eBay for deals, and the shipping charges factor into that. Savvy shoppers will know you are overcharging them on lightweight items. I will go through the complete process to set up shipping and ship eBay packages later in this book.

If you sell a wide variety of items in various sizes and weights, you will want to offer **Calculated Shipping**. *Calculated Shipping* charges the buyer based on the package's weight and the zip code to which it is shipping. Having a digital postal scale enables you to weigh these items before listing them to enter the correct weight. Most sellers who lose money on shipping do so because they do not weigh larger items, causing them to undercharge customers and then pay the difference out of their pocket.

However, if you have a digital scale and offer *Calculated Shipping,* the buyer pays the actual shipping cost based on the package's weight and the zip code it is going to. Using *Calculated Shipping* is a breeze if you have a digital scale on hand. I will talk more about *Calculated Shipping* later in this book

Other sellers offer *free shipping,* padding the item's cost into their estimated shipping charge. While offering free shipping is a smart move for lightweight items (for instance, if you have a piece of jewelry that weighs two ounces and is selling for $50, you can offer free shipping and easily absorb the $4 it will cost to ship), it can backfire on heavier items as buyers know when a seller has inflated the price of an item to cover shipping. You do not want to give the appearance that you are making money from the shipping costs and risk getting negative feedback.

Instead of guessing the postage costs, under-charging or overcharging, or running back and forth to the Post Office, you can save time and money by quickly printing your shipping labels from home....and a digital scale makes that possible. I will cover shipping more in-depth later in this book.

Boxes & Envelopes: You cannot just stick a label directly on a book and send it in the mail. Well, some new sellers do such things, believe it or not. I've even seen new sellers ship packages in cereal boxes!

Shipping packages require *shipping supplies,* and that means shipping boxes and envelopes, such as:

- **Plain cardboard shipping boxes in various sizes**

- **USPS Priority shipping boxes**
- **Poly mailers in several sizes** (if you sell clothing, textiles, or plush toys)
- **Bubble mailers in several sizes** (for shipping items that need a bit more protection than a plain poly envelope offers, such as jewelry)
- **Cardboard envelope mailers** (to protect items such as ephemera from being bent)

The United States Postal Service (USPS) is a great resource for eBay sellers because they offer FREE *Priority Mail* shipping boxes. While *Priority Mail* is an excellent option for shipping many packages, you will need other forms of packaging for *Media Mail and Ground Advantage* (which has replaced First Class Package and Parcel), as well as for international shipments (again, more on these forms of shipping coming up).

Basically, you need two forms of shipping boxes/envelopes: *Priority Mail* boxes and envelopes, and plain boxes and envelopes for the rest.

USPS Standard Priority Boxes: You can get all of these for FREE from the Post Office. Simply go online to https://store.usps.com/store/results/shipping-supplies and click on the **Free Shipping Supplies** option to order; your mail carrier will deliver them to your home.

- **Priority Mail Show Box SHOEBOX:** 14-7/8 x 7-3/8 x 5.24 (not just for shoes, but for anything long and narrow)
- **Priority Mail Box 1097:** 11-5/8 x 2.5x 13-7/16 (rectangle size for clothing, books, and anything flat)
- **Priority Mail Box 1905:** 12.5 x 3-1/8 x 15-5/8 (rectangle size for clothing, books, and anything flat)
- **Priority Mail Box 1092:** 12.25 x 2-7/8 x 13-11/16

(rectangle size for clothing, books, and anything flat)

- **Priority Mail Box 1096L**: 9-7/16 x 6-7/16 x 2-3/16 (rectangle size for clothing, books, and anything flat)
- **Large Priority Mail Box 7**: 12.25 x 12.25 x 1.5 (largest size of the Priority Mail boxes; perfect for shipping several items at once)
- **Priority Mail Box 4**: 7.25 x 7.25 x 6.25 (square size is perfect for shipping mugs, figurines, and small, rounded items)

USPS Flat-Rate Priority Boxes & Envelopes:

- **Priority Mail Padded Flat Rate Envelope**: 9.5 x 12.5 (the go-to choice for shipping heavy clothing, shoes, and anything unbreakable)
- **Priority Mail Small Flat Rate Box**: 8-11/16 x 5-7/16 x 1.75 (sized for small but heavy items)
- **Priority Mail Medium Flat Rate Box 1**:11.25 x 8.75 x 6 (perfect size for mid-size, heavy objects)
- **Priority Mail Medium Flat Rate Box 2**: 12 x 3.5 x 14-1/8 (the flat, rectangle version of the size above)
- **Priority Mail Large Flat Rate Box LARGEFRB**: 12.25 x 12.25 x 6 (this box is smaller than the regular *Large Priority Mail Box*, but it can still come in handy for smaller, heavier items)

USPS Priority Stickers: These are perfect for covering writing on the outside of repurposed boxes.

- **Priority Mail Sticker Label Roll of 1000**
- **Priority Mail Shipping Label of 10**

When you look through all the available choices for *Priority Mail* boxes and envelopes, you will see that USPS offers many other options that I did not list above. As you continue along your eBay journey, you will learn which shipping boxes and envelopes you use the most, and therefore, you need to reorder frequently. While the above selections are the products most resellers use most, here are some other ones you may want to consider adding to your supply as you grow your business:

- **Priority Mail Express Boxes & Envelopes**: I do not offer *Express* or *Overnight* options to my customers (and I have only ever had one person ask me to ship something faster than *Priority*), so I do not bother keeping any of these products stocked. If I needed to send something via *Express*, I would likely just take it to the Post Office packaged in a plain box and have them put the label and *Express* stickers on it. However, these options do exist if you decide to offer them.
- **Tube Boxes:** These long triangular tube boxes work great if you sell posters and/or prints.
- **Envelopes:** There are several options for flat envelopes, but whenever I want to send something that would fit in one of these options, I usually ship it in a manila envelope from my office supplies. The USPS envelopes are geared toward businesses that frequently mail documents, such as law, banking, and medical offices. However, if you sell ephemera, they may be an option.

The Post Office offers free shipping supplies in quantities as low as ten each. I recommend ordering the smallest number possible as you expand your collection. You will soon realize which boxes you use the most, but you will at least have the others on hand if you need them.

Note that sometimes it can take quite a while for boxes to be delivered due to supply issues, so do not wait until you are completely out to order more, especially heading into the busy holiday season. I ensure I order my supply of *Priority Mail* boxes in September in anticipation of the fourth quarter. My own Post Office has to order their supply of shipping boxes the same way, so order early!

While *Priority Mail* is an excellent option for shipping most packages, you will need other forms of packaging for **Media Mail** and **Ground Advantage** as those selections can NOT be mailed in the *Priority Mail* boxes. It is also against USPS policy to alter the *Priority* boxes in any way, so forget thinking you can turn them inside out (they are printed with *Priority Mail* on the inside to thwart this) or put stickers on the outside to conceal the fact that they are indeed *Priority*. Misusing USPS supplies can result in your losing your postal account.

Before you run out and buy new shipping boxes and envelopes, check around your house to see what you have on hand. Plain cardboard boxes, manila envelopes, and bubble mailers can all be used for non-priority mail. If you already have items on hand that you intend to list on eBay, look them over to determine the packaging you need. Perhaps you will only sell books, for which bubble mailers and sturdy boxes are enough. On the other hand, if you only plan to sell large items, you do not need to worry about stocking up on envelopes.

I keep a wide variety of boxes and envelopes in my shipping supply area. While I utilize the free *Priority Mail* boxes and bubble mailers from the Post Office, I invest in plain shipping boxes from Amazon, EBay, Uline, and Value Mailers for *Media* and *Ground Advantage* packages; and I purchase branded shipping supplies directly from eBay. I also have manila bubble mailer envelopes that I buy at Sam's Club and poly mailers that I order on Amazon.

Here is a list of the plain boxes and envelopes on hand:

- **Plain Cardboard Shipping Boxes** (4", 6", 8", 10", and 12" sizes)
- **Oversized Cardboard Shipping Boxes** (14" and 16" sizes for when I have to ship oversized items via Ground Advantage or UPS)
- **Poly Mailers in various sizes** (for shipping clothing, textiles, and stuffed animals)
- **Bubble Mailers in various sizes** (for items that need more cushioning than a plain poly mailer)
- **Cardboard Mailers in various sizes** (for shipping ephemera that I do not want to be bent in the mail)

Note that because I have been selling on eBay for years and am set up as a business, I can buy these supplies and deduct them as business expenses. As you purchase more shipping supplies and office equipment, be sure to track your spending, as you can deduct these costs come tax time. Therefore, I try to limit the places I buy supplies from as I can scan my credit card statements to find my monthly expenses.

Packing Materials: You cannot just throw an item into a box and ship it with no packing materials to buffer it inside the box (well, you CAN, as I have seen many sellers do, but you should not). You need to WRAP up your items to protect them inside the box. You want to ensure that the item is protected from being thrown around, inside planes and trucks and tossed onto customers' porches.

I invest in the following packing materials for my eBay orders:

- **Recycled Packing Paper** (to wrap up items inside of the shipping box)
- **Bubble Wrap** (essential for protecting breakables such as China and ceramics)
- **Packing Peanuts** (perfect for buffering breakables inside of boxes)
- **Shipping Tape** (buy the largest rolls and the strongest type you can)
- **Tissue Paper** (better than packing paper for wrapping delicate breakables)
- **Cardboard Corrugated Rolls** (allows you to create a box-in-a-box around breakables)

Since I have an established eBay business, I invest in **recycled white or gray packing paper** to wrap up the items to arrive neatly packaged inside the shipping box. However, I also use **newspapers** to protect the item further. Do NOT wrap your item in the newspaper directly; you do not want any newspaper ink to bleed onto your products. Also, make sure any newspaper you use is clean.

In addition to packing paper, I also purchase **bubble wrap** to protect fragile items. In my area, I have found Sam's Club to have the best price on bubble wrap; Costco also carries it at the same price.

Bubble wrap is a MUST for protecting ceramics, pottery, and glass. After the item is wrapped securely in bubble wrap, I then use the newspaper to further buffer it inside the box so that the newspaper ink does not bleed directly onto the item itself. If it is a breakable item, I also go a step further and surround the piece with **cardboard wrap** OVER the bubble wrap; this creates a "box in a box" effect that further protects the item.

Packing peanuts are always nice to have on hand to use in shipments, but buying them new is expensive. I save any I get from my online orders, and I let my friends and family know that I will gladly take their unwanted packing peanuts off their hands. Most people are happy to get rid of the packing peanuts as they are a static mess to deal with and cannot be recycled.

When I purchase packing peanuts, I buy them in bulk to save money. I also have a large plastic container on wheels, which was marketed to hold dog food, and I store the peanuts inside. A large, slotted scoop (I use one intended for scooping cat litter!) makes transferring the peanuts from the container into the shipping box quick and easy.

Another shipping supply staple I keep on hand is **tissue paper**. eBay sells its own branded tissue paper, and I also buy any I find at estate sales. Sam's Club and Costco usually sell huge rolls of tissue paper, particularly around Christmas, and after the holidays, if there is any left, you can get it on clearance.

Tissue paper is essential for cushioning small, fragile items such as porcelain figurines and jewelry. Since it is much thinner than newspaper or packing paper, it tucks nicely into small curves to protect delicate pieces during shipment. Tissue paper is also nice for wrapping up designer pieces of clothing. Of course, after I wrap something fragile in tissue paper, I also wrap it in bubble wrap and use other packing materials to protect it further.

PRO TIP: If you are shipping breakables with hollow centers, such as vases, stuff the centers with packaging paper. This helps protect the pieces from shattering from the outside in.

Shipping Tape: You now have boxes, envelopes, packing paper, newspaper, bubble wrap, and maybe some packing peanuts, cardboard rolls, and tissue paper. To seal your packages, you need shipping tape.

Clear shipping tape can be found at drugstores, big-box retailers, office supply stores, warehouse clubs, and even dollar stores. I purchase my shipping tape at Sam's Club. Dollar for dollar, I find it to be the best quality and price. Costco also sells shipping tape in bulk for the same price.

Note that you want to *purchase SHIPPING tape, not packing tape.* Packing tape is for moving boxes and is not as strong, while shipping tape is meant to hold packages together as they travel to their destination by vehicle, boat, and/or air.

I also have both a **handheld tape dispenser** (usually sold right next to the tape at stores) as well as a **heavy tabletop tape dispenser**. If you are just starting out reselling, I recommend buying a kit with a handheld tape dispenser included and some extra tape rolls. You can usually find such kits for $10 to $15 in the tape section of the big box stores. You only need to buy the dispenser once, and tape refills as needed. Throughout the year, the shipping tape at Sam's Club and Costco goes on sale; when it does, I stock up.

eBay also sells branded shipping tape. If you have an eBay Store subscription of *Basic* or higher, you may want to use your quarterly shipping supplies coupon toward some of this tape. Not only is it great for sealing up packages, but it also acts as a sticker when you need to cover up writing that may be on repurposed shipping boxes.

Enclosures: I strongly believe in putting enclosures into my shipments; I personally include a **packing slip** and a **business card-sized "thank you" card, sticker, or magnet** in all my packages.

However, not all eBay sellers agree about the use of enclosures; some do not put anything into their shipments. So, whether to include enclosures is a decision you will have to make for yourself. If you sell similar items, such as certain collectibles or clothing brands, you may find it advantageous to encourage repeat buyers, and enclosures can help you do that.

However, if you just sell a wide variety of random stuff, you may not be as concerned with leaving your customers with any impression of your store. I have personally worked hard to create a "brand" for my eBay Store, and I promote that "brand" via my packing slips and enclosure cards.

If you do decide to include packing slips in your orders, eBay makes it super easy to do, as after you print a shipping label, there is a link you can click on to print a packing slip. The packing slip is just a copy of the original invoice sent to the customer when they purchased the item.

I must admit that when I started selling on eBay, I did not want to include a packing slip as I did not want to spend the money on ink and paper. Fortunately, I was able to chat with some experienced eBay sellers who convinced me that including a packing slip was vital in maintaining a professional image. I am put off when I order something online if there is no packing slip inside. So why should I treat my eBay customers any differently? When running my business, I adhere to the *Golden Rule* and treat my customers how I would want to be treated.

Another benefit of printing a packing slip is that if you are printing out a large batch of orders, you can match the packing slip to the shipping label. For years I would do this and hand the packages off to my late father for packing. He found it helpful to have the packing slips just in case the label got separated as he could easily match up the orders.

In addition to a packing slip, I include enclosure cards in my shipments. Over the years, these have ranged from business cards to large postcards, and now they are stickers and magnets. You can order enclosure cards online from sites such as VistaPrint or at local office supply stores. I now design my stickers and magnets and have them printed online from Sticker Mule.

If you just started selling on eBay, I recommend including a packing slip and perhaps writing "Thank You!" on it to give it a personal touch. If you decide that you want to make eBay a part-time or even a full-time business, you can look into having enclosure cards printed up. The choice, however, is totally up to you.

Shipping Station: Now that you have all your shipping supplies, you need a place to prepare your shipments. It is nice to designate an area just for shipping out your orders if you have space so that you aren't constantly dragging supplies out from a closet or storage room. Although, as often as I have tried to keep all my shipping supplies in one location, they inevitably wind up scattered between several places in my house!

I keep all my shipping boxes and poly bags in my basement, where my eBay inventory is stored. When an item sells, I retrieve it from my inventory, and the box or envelope it will ship out in. I then take the item and shipping container back upstairs to my office to be weighed so I can print out the shipping label and packing slip. I keep all of my packing materials in my office near a table where I package orders.

I have a table in my office where my digital scale always sits at the ready. It is right next to my computer to weigh items as I am listing them and again when I am ready to print the shipping label. The most important thing is to have your digital scale on a flat surface to get an accurate reading. I use the scale both when listing items and when I go to ship them. When I bring an item to my office to be shipped, I package it up and then I weigh it and print the label and packing slip.

I have shelving in the basement and my office for all my boxes, envelopes, and extra packing materials that I can bring up to my office when I run out. Again, since I have an established business, I have a lot of shipping materials; and since I own a home, I have a lot of space to store it all. However, if you are just starting out on eBay, use an out-of-the-way space (perhaps in the basement or the corner of a room) for your shipping supplies. You want to ensure your supplies (and the items you sell) are safe from smoke, pets, or other household odors. Yes, customers WILL complain if they find dog hair inside their packages; and cigarette smoke complaints can lead to negative feedback.

Your shipping area is just as important as your inventory space, so take the time to set it up properly. A well-organized shipping station will save you time and money in the long run, as will making sure you have the right equipment and supplies at the ready before you list your first item for sale on eBay.

CHAPTER FOUR: WHAT SELLS ON EBAY

The most common question I get from people interested in reselling is, "What exactly sells on eBay?" There is no easy answer to this because, for every item that does sell on eBay, there are ten others that don't. There are hundreds of thousands of eBay listings and millions of registered users. Yet the fact is that many sellers barely sell anything because they refuse the educate themselves about what customers are shopping for. Learning what sells and what does not sell takes time and lots of trial and error.

I have been selling on EBay for nearly two decades, and I am still shocked at what sells for me. Similarly, I also pick up things I am sure will sell but do not for whatever reason. As I always tell people, "An item is only worth what someone is willing to pay for it." And there are millions of things for which no one is interested in paying anything for. What sold well last year may not sell this year. To be a successful reseller, you need to be ready to pivot at all times.

As I have already discussed, your home is the best place to find items to start selling on eBay. In fact, when I first got started on eBay in 2005, I sold unused items in my house. I quickly made $3,000 by selling my old clothes (business casual attire I had accumulated from seven years of office work), books, CDs, DVDs, and housewares. These were all items I usually would have donated to Goodwill or sold for pennies on the dollar at a garage sale, but by taking a bit of extra time to list them on eBay, I got a considerable amount of money for them. But more importantly, I learned HOW to list and ship, so that when I was ready to invest in inventory, I was confident in my abilities.

If you are interested in specific lists of items I have personally sold on eBay, be sure to check out my books **101 ITEMS TO SELL ON EBAY** and **101 MORE ITEMS TO SELL ON EBAY**, both of which are available on Amazon. But to get started, look around your house for the following items:

- **CDs** (yes, people still buy CDs)
- **DVDs and Blu-Rays** (full television series do especially well)
- **Books** (out-of-print titles, hardcovers with their dust jackets, and college textbooks)
- **Name-brand clothing and accessories** (I have an entire bonus chapter about reselling clothing at the end of this book)
- **Unused toiletries and cosmetics** (the original seal must be intact)
- **Home décor** from upscale stores such as Pottery Barn, Williams Sonoma, and Crate & Barrel (think small accessories such as desktop clocks and kitchen décor until you are more comfortable selling large, breakable items)
- **Tools** (Snap-On is a brand that is very desirable on eBay)
- **Figurines** (cute animal figures stamped "Japan" on the bottom are always in demand)
- **Ceramics & Pottery** (pieces that are signed and in trendy colors)
- **Dishes** (Fiestaware, Fire King, and Pyrex)
- **Flatware** (people are looking to replace old sets or add to those they've inherited)
- **Anything licensed** such as Disney, Peanuts, or Harry Potter
- **Toys**, both new and vintage (make sure a toy hasn't been recalled before listing it)

- **Office supplies** (unopened printer ink and printer cartridges are two of the most sought-after items on eBay)
- **Craft supplies** (yarn, beads, stickers)
- **Small appliances** (make sure they are clean and in working order)
- **Unused pet supplies** (quality collars, leads, and clothing)
- **Unopened gourmet food** (make sure it isn't expired)
- **Vintage holiday decorations** (Halloween and Christmas are especially popular)
- **Ephemera** (vintage paper collectibles such as postcards)
- **Coins** (make sure you research their value)
- **Genuine leather** (fewer companies still make leather goods, so leather bags and boots are in high demand)
- **Sports cards** (there is still a high demand for trading cards, but be sure you understand how to grade their condition)

These are just a handful of the categories of items that you can sell on eBay. The longer you sell on the site, the more you will discover what things sell (and do not sell) online. Before you know it, you will not be able to browse in a store without wondering if you could sell their items on eBay. Believe me when I tell you that most resellers have a tough time shopping for themselves as they view everything they see as something they could potentially sell online.

So, what DOESN'T sell on eBay? While there are always exceptions to every category, some things I steer clear of are:

- **Precious Moments** (only the Disney licensed figurines and a handful of special editions are worth anything)
- **Collector Plates** (while some complete sets can sell, most are worthless)
- **Cherished Teddies** (as with Precious Moments, there are some desirable pieces; but overall, these are not a good

pick-up for eBay)
- **Counterfeit Goods** (selling fakes is a sure way to lose your eBay account)
- **Liquids** (shipping flammable liquids is prohibited by the USPS)
- **New Vero List Brands** (eBay works with major brands to prohibit the sale of new items on the site. Some of these brands may be sold if they are used, however)
- **Beanie Babies** (most of these plush toys have no value on eBay)

And here is the part of the book I know many of you have been anxiously waiting to get to: **WHERE exactly can you find products to sell on eBay?** Well, grab a pen so that you can write down the directions to the eBay warehouse in Ohio that sells millions of items you can buy to resell online!

Please do not tell me you reached for a pen, because I was joking! When I joined eBay in 2005, this was a popular joke experienced sellers told newbies on the message boards. I just had to include it here!

Unfortunately, there is no conveniently located warehouse or website where you can order products for cheap and make a significant profit on them on eBay. If there were, everyone who sold on eBay would be ordering from them. The penny items you see for sale on eBay are being sold by Chinese manufacturers, not small businesses. And while there are sellers who focus on liquidation and wholesale, most resellers find inventory piece by piece.

Sourcing products to resell is WORK; it is probably the HARDEST part of selling on eBay as it takes time and skill to find profitable items. Sourcing, or "picking" as it used to be called, is also the most addicting part of reselling, as the business attracts people who love to visit thrift shops and garage sales. History is filled with many people who wanted to start reselling but instead found themselves with a shopping addiction and a hoard of unlisted items. Shopaholics and hoarders beware: eBay is NOT the business for you!

Fortunately, for those who are disciplined about sourcing and listings, there are millions of items available to sell and lots of places to look for them. No one will ever tell you where THEY are getting their items, though, and it is tacky to ask. Why would someone tell you where they find items to resell and make you their competition?

Here are the general locations, however, in which you can find items to resell:

SECONDHAND "PICKING": Selling secondhand items, whether they are collectibles, clothing, electronics, or replacement parts is a hot business model on eBay. It has been my method of reselling for most of my eBay career. What most resellers now refer to as "sourcing" is called "picking" by the older generation. I'm sure you've heard of the show "American Pickers." That style of "picking" is still popular among antique dealers.

The great thing about "picking" is that you always have a source of items. Even if you live in an area with brutal winters when no one has garage sales, you can still find items to resell at thrift stores. Sourcing thrifted products is the least risky as the start-up cost is minimal. You can quickly start earning money by spending $20 on a shopping bag full of thrift finds. The trick, of course, is to buy the right items at the right price. And that comes with time and practice.

In theory, you could use the eBay app to research anything you find at garage sales and thrift stores before you purchase it. You can even take a photo on the eBay app and eBay will search the results to see if that item is currently listing. And you can choose the "Sold" setting to see what the item sold for if it sold at all. However, in my case, cell phone service is spotty in many areas where I live. I can't look up things before I buy them. Instead, I try to buy things for as low as possible. Only if I am sure that an item will sell for a large profit will I "pay up" for something.

When you are just starting, I recommend you only pay a dollar or two for items until you gain experience sourcing and selling them. You need time to learn what items are available in your area, what the prices are like, and are those items that will sell on eBay. If you can use the eBay app, do so. But remember to filter the listings by those that have sold. Looking at the active listings only shows you what people are asking for the item, not what that particular product sells for.

Again, it just takes time and practice to learn how to source secondhand items successfully. And there are many places to find secondhand items to resell, including:

Garage/Rummage/Tag/Yard Sales: Garage sales (also called rummage, tag, or yard sales in other parts of the United States, or "boot sales" in the U.K.) are one of the best sources of secondhand goods to resell.

Garage sales are put on by individual homeowners who set items out for sale in their – you guessed it – garages. Garage sales are typically held on weekends and advertised in local newspapers and Facebook groups. Some people don't advertise beyond putting signs out. These sales can be held for one, two, or even three days. And often, several homes in one neighborhood will have sales simultaneously, attracting a bigger crowd of shoppers.

Garage sales are a fantastic source of secondhand clothing at prices often lower than thrift stores. On the flip side, garage sales in neighborhoods where older people live often have vintage treasures to pick up. A good garage sale will have prices at 90% or below retail prices, and items will be clean and laid out nicely for easy shopping. Bad garage sales have retail prices, dirty and broken items, and are unorganized. Part of going to garage sales is taking the good with the bad; after all, the fun is in the hunt.

When I plan to go to garage sales, I start by making a list of all the advertised sales with items I am interested in. For instance, I skip sales where it sounds like all they have for sale are baby clothes. Because I specialize in vintage, I instead look for sales that specifically mention older items. Since many people now post their sales on Facebook with photos of what they have for sale, it is much easier to narrow down the sales I want to attend.

After I have a list of the sales I am interested in, I look up the addresses on Google Maps and make a plan of which sale to drive to first, aiming to easily drive from one to the next and then back home in a loop. Not only does this save time but it also saves on gas. Some weekends I will have sales to go to on Thursday, Friday, and Saturday, while on other weekends, there won't be any sales I'm interested in.

When going to garage sales, make sure to have plenty of cash, especially small bills. I also keep some boxes and newspapers in the trunk of my car to secure breakables as I drive around. Don't be afraid to ask for a lower price on items you are interested in; most people expect some haggling at these types of sales.

Estate Sales: Estate sales, sometimes referred to as "moving sales," have always been my best source of inventory to sell on eBay. While most resellers love garage sales and thrift stores, I have the best luck at estate sales to stock my eBay store with vintage items.

An estate sale usually occurs when the owner of the home has passed away. For their estate to be closed, all outstanding debts paid, and their funds distributed to their heirs, the home needs to be cleared of possessions for it to be put on the market. While some families choose to donate the home contents, others opt to sell off the contents, hence having an "estate sale."

Some families run their estate sale themselves; however, most turn to estate sale companies that have experience in quickly selling a home's contents. My area has several estate sale companies who do this, although each one runs their sales differently in terms of how they price and the services they offer. One company moves the home's contents off-site to a warehouse for sale, while another tells customers they must provide their manpower to carry out items, including furniture. One company prices a bit high to start but then does a fill-a-bag sale in the last hour, while another never lowers prices but instead brings in an auction house to clear any remaining items. Most companies offer everything for half-off on the last day, but it all depends on the family's wishes.

I mentioned that sometimes these types of sales are referred to as moving sales, also called a "living estate sale." These sales are for homeowners who are downsizing or moving into an assisted living or nursing home. They won't be taking most of their possessions to their new resistance, but because they will sell their home, they turn to an estate sale company to clear out their remaining furniture and possessions.

Whether it is because the homeowner is downsizing or has passed away, most estate sales are run the same: What is inside of the home needs to be sold quickly. And this means that the items are priced right where they are inside the house. That means customers walk through the house to shop. Clothes are left hanging in the closets, and price stickers are placed on the pictures on the wall. Any flat surface where items can be laid out for sale is utilized, and the estate sale companies bring in additional tables to handle the rest.

If you decide to shop estate sales for inventory, it's important that you familiarize yourself with each company's policies and procedures, as well as be friendly towards the staff. I make sure to defer to how they want to check me out, asking if I can help or if they'd rather I just let them do it. Since I usually buy quite a lot, I try to be as helpful or unobtrusive as possible.

While you can usually haggle at a garage sale, estate sale prices tend to be firm, especially on the first day. Most companies lower prices to half off the last day, and as I mentioned, some even do a fill-a-bag sale where you can fill a bag for $5 to $10.

It's also important to know what payment methods each company will accept. All accept cash. But in my area, one will accept checks but doesn't accept credit cards. The other companies accept credit cards but not checks. Some ask that you bring your bags and boxes, while others provide all packing materials and even carry your purchases to your car.

Be sure to be respectful of how each estate sale company runs its sales. You may not like some of their policies, but it is their business. Remember that they have their staff and bills to pay as well as giving the profits to the home's owners or heirs. The estate sale company works for the family to facilitate the sale. They are the middleman between the family and the customers. Sometimes the family has specific guidelines about what they want things to sell for. Some would rather have leftover items donated for the tax deduction rather than sell them for less than they believe it is worth. At the end of the day, the family and estate sales company are making the rules; as a customer, you need to respect their terms.

Because of their overhead, prices at estate sales tend to be higher than at garage sales and thrift stores. But while the prices might be higher, estate sales can be a one-stop-shopping destination for resellers. While many resellers visit garage sales and thrift stores weekly, I can usually find more than enough inventory at one good estate sale, meaning I save a lot of time and gas money by only visiting one location.

All that isn't to say that every estate sale is like shopping at a department store. Sometimes the houses need repair, meaning you must be very careful as you walk through. I've had to crawl up narrow stairs into dusty attics and creep into damp basements in search of treasures. I've walked into houses that smelled like mold and were filled with trash. Others were clean and full of items, but everything was from the dollar store and nothing was worth reselling. Just like with a garage sale, every home is different. Sometimes I fill my car; other times, I leave empty-handed.

However, you can't beat a well-run estate sale when it comes to finding vintage collectibles and even antiques at a price that leaves room for profit. Seek out your local estate sale companies on Facebook, and most will post about upcoming sales and pictures of what will be for sale. Strive to create a good relationship with the estate sale owners as they may reward you with special deals.

Thrift Stores: Thrift stores are like a garage sale and estate sale combined into one. You get a wide variety of goods laid out in an organized shopping manner, but the prices are usually consistent. For example, the thrift stores in my area price clothing the same. All shirts are one price, all jackets a different price. They price hard goods individually but typically stick to a pricing system.

Thrift stores rely on donations, and most support a charity. Many now also sell online themselves, making finding items to resell in their stores challenging as many now pull "the good stuff" to sell online for top dollar. I have difficulty finding vintage items in my area's thrift stores, although the clothing is plentiful.

I do not source at my local Goodwill stores as they have an entire department store devoted to selling online, meaning they pull the best items for their online store. They've also raised the price of clothing to the point where because I live in an area where there are no high-end clothing stores, there is no room for profit on eBay.

However, there are other thrift stores in my area that do have vintage items at great prices. While they are a bit of a drive for me, it's often worth it to make an effort to visit them as I always find great items for resale. You, too, may find that your local thrift stores aren't worth sourcing at. But if you expand your search to area towns, you may find hidden treasures.

Every thrift store is run differently, even those that the same company owns. How they price is often left to the store manager; a new manager usually means the pricing changes, sometimes for the worse. But sometimes, for the better. After all, if prices are too high, sales will be slow. Many thrift stores go through periods of pricing up their items only to lower them later when they realize they aren't making sales.

Most resellers who source items at thrift stores visit them often, sometimes daily, hoping they will catch new items on the floor. I know sellers who travel for hours to shop at better thrift stores than those near them. Some will even fly to larger cities and spend days combing through thrift stores looking for items to ship back home to resell.

Most thrift stores accept credit and debit cards, which makes tracking your expenses easy. Inventory is your biggest expense as a reseller, and most garage and estate sales do not offer receipts. Many thrift stores also offer reward programs as well as surprise sale events. Be sure to follow the Facebook pages of the thrift stores near you to keep up to date with their offers.

If you are looking to resell clothing on eBay, your local thrift store is a great place to start. From shoes and purses to dresses and even bras, most thrift stores have every style and size of clothing imaginable. They usually have shopping carts available, which can make the shopping experience easier, especially if you are buying many items.

PRO TIP: Remove the hangers from the clothing before you get to the register. This will make the checkout process go much faster. I create a pile of hangers to hand to the clerk, who puts them aside in a tub, and I then put clothes onto the counter based on price. Jackets, for example, are $7. By putting all of the jackets on the counter together, all the clerk needs to do is count them to enter the price.

As you continue on your reselling journey, you'll learn which thrift stores are worth your time and which you can skip. However, just because you don't find something to resell on your first trip to a store doesn't mean you won't the next time. Thrift stores can be a gold mine for resellers, but it takes time and patience to comb through the various stores to find the treasures.

Goodwill Outlet: Goodwill Outlets, also referred to as "the bins" by resellers, are bulk outlet Goodwill stores. Inside, you will find merchandise (mostly clothing, but some also have hard goods) piled up in blue tubs ("bins") that customers dig through. Pricing is by the pound; at checkout, the weight of your shopping cart is deducted, and you pay as low as 99 cents for every pound of items you purchase.

Just like the pricing is different at various thrift stores, each Goodwill Outlet prices differently. My city's outlet has three pricing levels per pound; you pay less the more you buy. However, other locations charge one rate for clothing, one for glassware, and another for books. As with most stores, pricing can change at any time.

Items at the outlets come from unsold inventory at the regular Goodwill stores but are sometimes unsorted donations. Goodwill receives so many donations that they can't put it all in their regular stores; hence they will send some of it straight to the outlet stores.

Every outlet store has different days and times when they are open. Our rather small outlet is usually open on weekdays for limited hours. Outlet stores in larger cities tend to be open seven days a week. It isn't uncommon for customers to line up outside up to an hour early in hopes that they will score the best deals. However, it's also important to understand that most outlet stores restock their inventory throughout the day, so unless you plan to be there from opening until closing, it will be impossible for you to see everything.

Most outlet stores rotate "the bins" out periodically, creating a sense of urgency for shoppers. With a limited amount of time to dig through each bin, it's nearly impossible that you will be able to get through everything. And "digging" is the name of the game at the outlets.

Items for sale at the Goodwill Outlets are thrown into the blue "bins" exactly as they were delivered to the outlet location. That means sometimes original Goodwill store tags are on them (since the item didn't sell in the retail store), while other times, items are dumped into the bins in whatever container they were donated in. These bins are on wheels, so they can be wheeled out and removed easily. Some stores rotate bins in and out several times a day, while others leave them as is all day.

While some stores try to separate glassware and books from clothes, others just fill up each bin with a wide mix of items. To stay safe and avoid being cut, it's a good idea (and in some stores, it is required) to wear gloves. Also, the bins tend to be very dirty. With a wide variety of donated goods, much of it unsorted, you are bound to find some nasty things mixed in along with soiled items. Wearing a mask can be helpful to avoid breathing in dust and dirt. Not all stores have restrooms, so wet wipes and hand sanitizer are also good to bring with you.

Some outlet locations have a reputation for being very crowded and filled with aggressive shoppers. Going at off times, such as near the end of the day and on weekdays, may help you avoid having to compete for merchandise. Outlet stores have scales that you roll your shopping cart onto. They automatically deduct the weight of the cart; the remaining weight is what you pay for. If your outlet store charges different amounts for clothes versus books, for example, try to separate those items into different piles before you checkout. The clerk will then be able to easily transfer the books to a different cart to weigh them while keeping the clothing in your cart for a separate weight.

The outlet stores are very popular with clothing resellers. Some clothing resellers only source at the outlets and will drive to several different locations in search of inventory. I even know of resellers who fly to other cities to shop at their outlet stores. Washington, Oregon, California, and Colorado have reputations for having excellent outlets, which makes sense as the cost of living in those areas is very high; hence the quality of items donated is much better.

You can find a list of Goodwill Outlet locations at gwoutletstorelocator.com. If you find one near you, see if they have a Facebook page you can follow. If you do, make sure to learn the rules.

Some outlet stores require shoppers to line up against the wall while new bins are brought out; failure to do so can get you kicked out!

Antique Malls: A staple sourcing spot for many vintage eBay sellers are antique malls. While you've likely heard of antique stores where one owner sells items, an antique mall features numerous sellers with individual booth spaces. Antique malls are typically quite large and offer a wide variety of items.

The downside to antique malls is that, just like antique stores, the prices can be quite high. After all, the sellers are experienced in selling antiques and vintage items. Unlike a garage sale where you might stumble upon items that are only a dollar, it's unusual to find rock-bottom prices at antique malls.

However, even if you can't afford to source at antique malls, they can be a great place to learn about vintage items. There is an upscale antique mall in my city where everything is priced the same as if it were listed on eBay. There's no room for me to make a profit off anything they sell, but I still like to wander the aisles to educate myself on different collectibles.

As with most retail stores, some individual dealers may periodically run sales on their items. Sometimes you may even find a booth that has slashed its prices as they are closing. It's these opportunities where you may be able to source for eBay. Frequently visiting the antique malls near you will help you familiarize yourself with the sellers there and see when they are running sales.

Some antique malls are more like flea markets. These "vendor malls" offer a wider range of items versus antique malls, and the prices tend to be better. A simple Google search for antique malls and vendor malls in your area will hopefully show nearby locations you can check out.

SELLING NEW GOODS: While most people think of secondhand goods when selling on eBay, the largest share of items sold are modern, brand-new goods. From clothing and housewares to electronics and toys, eBay is filled with thousands of new-in-box products. And just as there are numerous places to source secondhand items, there are just as many ways to find new items to sell on eBay, including:

Retail Arbitrage: If you love to browse the big box stores and shops at your local shopping mall, finding brand new, not secondhand, items to resell on eBay may be right up your alley. However, it is all about finding the right items for the right price. This type of "picking" is called "retail arbitrage," It works best if you have a smartphone that will allow you to look up items on eBay before you buy them to resell.

As we've already discussed, eBay offers a completed listing search of the most recent 90 days of sales, while Terapeak Research has two years of sales records. Using these completed listing searches lets you see if the game you found for 75% off is selling online and, if so, for how much. Experienced eBay sellers typically look up anything before they buy it, using the eBay app on their phones to research sales before deciding whether to buy an item to resell. If the item has a bar code, you can easily scan it using the eBay app to see what it is currently selling for. You can also take a photo within the eBay app and eBay will search using your picture.

I typically only purchase store clearance items that are 90% off to resell on eBay. Remember that people shop on eBay looking for deals, so it is unlikely you will be able to sell new items for their full retail price. And since many other resellers are also sourcing clearance items to flip, there is a lot of competition. However, sometimes adding in a few items you have scored via retail arbitrage can help bring in traffic to your other listings.

TJMaxx and Ross Dress for Less both have annual clearance sales, slashing prices down to their lowest price. I've scored a lot of name-brand clothing at Ross for as little as 49 cents that I was able to sell on eBay. If you have nice department stores near you, learn when they have clearance sales so you can potentially pick up items at a deep discount to flip for profit. Walmart is also extremely popular among resellers. Not only do most Walmart stores have special clearance aisles, but most also have clearance located throughout their stores. Follow the big yellow CLEARANCE signs and then look for the yellow clearance stickers. Then use the Walmart app to price check unmarked items.

Liquidation: Many people assume that "wholesale" and "liquidation" are the same, but they are entirely different. While wholesale companies deal in brand new items directly from the manufacturer, liquidation companies directly source their products from retail stores where the items did not sell. A retailer buys from a wholesaler, but any inventory that does not sell (including returns or damaged products), is sold by the retailer to liquidation companies. Liquidation companies then sell to resellers, not only those who sell online but also people who sell at flea markets and in their brick-and-mortar stores.

Liquidation sources are closely guarded as competition is fierce among online resellers. And when you are first starting out selling on eBay, it is not something you should invest in until you truly understand how reselling works. No one is going to share their liquidation sources with you, and it's incredibly insulting to ask. After all, a reseller with good liquidation sources has done a lot of work to find their inventory. They aren't going to share their sources with you, the competition.

If you decide to look into liquidation, educating yourself on each liquidation company you consider purchasing from is vital. Find out their terms and precisely what types of products they are selling. Liquidation is usually rated as **Salvage, Customer Returns, Shelf Pulls**, or **Brand New.**

Salvage items, also called *Scratch & Dent,* often come with some damage level, even if it is just to the outside packaging. *Customer Returns* may come to you without the original tags attached or some spots such as makeup on them. *Shelf Pulls* are products that were out for sale on the store shelves but were then pulled for liquidation. While these items are considered new, they may have shelf wear, including torn packaging. Items marketed as *New* may, in fact, be *Shelf Pulls,* so you must understand precisely how the liquidation company you are dealing with is grading their items.

I only buy liquidation lots labeled as brand new and with a manifest, which is a detailed list of every product included in the lot along with the original retail price. Most companies will still warn you that even brand-new lots can contain up to 10% of items that have damage. Just as buying items at wholesale requires a lot of homework, so does purchasing liquidation.

If you sell on eBay, you already know that thrift stores and garage sales are where most resellers find the items they sell. Buying items secondhand for pennies on the dollar will always net you the greatest return on investment. But if you want to try out liquidation, here are some of the biggest companies that cater to resellers:

B&G Trading: B&G Trading specializes in overstock, shelf-pull, and liquidation clothing from Macy's and Nordstrom's. They sell by the case and the pallet, and they even offer smaller starter packs that don't require a large investment. Visit shopbgtrading.com for more information.

Bstock.Com: B-Stock connects you directly with liquidation sources at Costco, Walmart, The Home Depot, Last Chance, Target, Amazon, Ashley Homestore, Kind Snacks, Ace Hardware, Advance Auto Parks, and dozens of other retailers. Most of the sites they connect to sell truckloads of merchandise via auction. Visit bstock.com for more information.

Bulq.com: Bulq.com sells liquidation from Target, Lowe's, and Macy's, but most of their items come from Target. They offer both cases and pallets with conditions of *Brand New, Like New, Salvage, Scratch & Dent,* and *Uninspected Returns.* Shipping on cases is $30; shipping on pallets is $200. They put up new lots daily and continuously mark them down until they sell. Bulq.com is an excellent source for cosmetics, toys, and consumer electronics.

Note that Bulq.com has partnered with eBay to sell their liquidation lots directly on the eBay site. The benefit of this is that when you purchase a lot from Bulq on eBay, the manifest immediately creates drafts of everything in the case. This is extremely helpful in starting the listing process. However, it is essential to note that the photos in their manifests do not migrate to the drafts. Plus, not all the listing details will be correct. You will still need to double-check the listings and provide your own photos.

Continental Wholesale: Located in Iowa, Continental Wholesale offers truckloads, half truckloads, and pallet lots of store liquidation from numerous retailers. Categories include appliances, As See On TV, automotive, baby, car parts, Christmas, clothing, cookware, domestics, Easter electronics, furniture, garden, grocery, health and beauty, holiday, paper goods, patio, pet, rugs, sporting goods, and toys. Visit continentalwholesale.com for more information.

Direct Liquidation: Direct Liquidation offers products from major retailers such as Walmart, Sam's Club, Target, Lowe's, and Amazon in the form of auctions. They sell by the box, pallet, and truckload. Brands you may be able to source include Apple, Samsung, Microsoft, Black & Decker, Mattel, Fisher-Price, and Nintendo. Visit directliquidation.com for more information.

eBay: You are selling on eBay, but did you know you can source on eBay, too? There are hundreds of liquidation lots for sale on eBay at any given time. Search "liquidation" or "reseller box" to see what is currently for sale. As with anything you want to buy on eBay, be sure to check the seller's feedback before purchasing. And don't buy mystery boxes. After all, you don't want to buy another reseller's duds.

Etsy: If you want to buy vintage items or craft supplies in bulk to resell, try Etsy. Sellers are advertising "wholesale" and "reseller lots" of all sorts. As with eBay, make sure you aren't buying another reseller's duds. Avoid mystery boxes and only box lots where the items are laid out. Visit Etsy.com for more information.

Fox Liquidation: Fox Liquidation advertises wholesale clothing from brands such as Ralph Lauren, DKNY, Lacoste, Tommy Hilfiger, and more. Besides clothing, they also sell wholesale napkins and glassware, general merchandise, bedding and sheets, and holiday décor. When browsing their website, you can sort by condition (seasonal shelf pulls, regular shelf pulls, and customer returns) and location (to save on shipping costs). Visit foxliquidation.com for more information.

Goodwill Bluebox: In 2019, Goodwill launched their "Bluebox" website, which sells lots of clothing that did not sell in stores and was headed to one of their outlet locations. New boxes drop on Fridays, although occasionally mid-week boxes launch. Their selection has expanded to include curated boxes on specific brands including Lululemon and L.L. Bean. Also popular are their jewelry boxes, which are filled with jewelry that needs to be sorted.

If you can pick up and transport pallets, they also have pallets of clothing, books, and other items. Note that you need to pick up pallets at the store location in which it is located. You will need a large open-bed truck, box truck, or trailer to pick a pallet up. Visit buybluebox.com for more information.

Liquidation.com: Liquidation.com offers a massive variety of goods to resell, including clothing, jewelry, electronics, computers, housewares, tools, and general merchandise. The twist is that the lots come from different sellers from across the country and are primarily available at auction. If you like hunting for deals, you will love scrolling through Liquidation.com in search of lots to bid on. Visit liquidation.com for more information.

Merchandize Liquidators: Merchandize Liquidators specializes in truckloads and pallets of cosmetics, clothing, housewares, and more. You can visit their Miami Gardens, Florida headquarters or buy from them online. Visit merchandizeliquidators.com for more information.

Poshmark: Poshmark started an app (it is also accessible via computer) where people could buy and sell clothing. It has since expanded to include home, electronics, pets, and beauty categories. They even have a "boutique" section geared towards resellers.

In addition to buying and selling individual items on Poshmark, some sellers sell boxes of items targeted toward resellers. Try typing "liquidation," "wholesale," or "reseller lot" into the search bar to see what is available. Since Poshmark offers flat $7.97 Priority Mail shipping on packages weighing five pounds or less, expect only to find smaller lots for sale. But, again, it is an affordable way to test liquidation or buy in bulk. Visit poshmark.com for more information.

Quicklotz.com: Quicklotz offers boxes, pallets, and truckloads at set prices that ship from three warehouses across the United States. They also sell Mystery Cases that ship for free within the Continental United States. Most of their inventory comes from Nordstrom and Nordstrom Rack, although they recently added Target liquidation. They also sell inventory boxes directly on Instagram. Visit quicklotz.com for more information.

ThredUP: While not a traditional liquidation company, ThredUP, an online consignment store, sells "Rescue" boxes. These mystery box lots contain items that were not accepted for consignment or items that they had listed but did not sell. They offer clothing, handbags, shoes, and jewelry. You can also look through their main website for pieces that are on clearance or have been mislabeled. Savvy resellers look at their "Unbranded" listings to find designer goods that they missed. Visit thredup.com for more information.

ViaTrading: With lots starting at only $100, ViaTrading is an excellent option for testing out liquidation. They sell everything from brand-new cosmetics to salvaged appliances. If you are in the Los Angeles, California, area, you can even visit their warehouse and purchase pallets in person. They also have weekly on-site auctions. Visit viatrading.com for more information.

WhatNot: WhatNot is a new online selling app where you can sell things via live auctions. It started as a site for Funko sellers before expanding to LEGO and sports cards. In the summer of 2022, they opened the site up to thrifted and vintage clothing as well as antiques and vintage.

Whether you sell clothing or collectibles, WhatNot is currently a fantastic place to score great deals on items to resell. Right now, there are more sellers on the site than dedicated buyers, meaning items don't usually sell for as much as they would on EBay as there aren't as many users shopping just for themselves. Follow the sellers who sell in the categories you also sell in and start watching their auctions to see if they sell items that you could sell on EBay. Visit whatnot.com for more information.

Wholesale Ninjas: Wholesale Ninjas sells liquidation by the case, pallet, and truckload. They mainly sell cosmetics, toys, and clothing from Target and CVS. With box lots starting at around $100, Wholesale Ninjas offers an affordable way to test liquidation, and they are my favorite place to source health and beauty. Visit wholesaleninjas.com for more information.

Consignment: Another popular eBay business model is to sell items on consignment for other people. The great thing about consignment is that you do not have to buy any products to resell yourself, so your financial risk is very low. However, selling on consignment is not for a newbie eBay seller. You need to understand how to use eBay effectively before you take on selling other people's items. You also need to be able to deal effectively with people, especially letting them down easily when they show you a pile of junk you know will not sell on eBay.

Most people who sell on consignment take at least a 50% commission fee (although I have seen it as high as 80%), and out of that comes all the eBay fees and related expenses (office supplies, shipping materials). You also must take responsibility for other people's items; having extra insurance to cover those things when they are in your possession is necessary but will cost more money.

However, if you are a people person, already know how to sell on eBay, have a passion for antiques and collectibles, and like the idea of not having to personally source products, then selling on consignment might be for you.

Sourcing items to sell is the most time-consuming part of reselling. Building a successful eBay business means that you need to be adding new inventory to your store constantly. And while buying inventory is usually the most enjoyable part of selling on eBay, it takes time and effort to learn what items sell best and where to get those items for the best price.

The great thing about eBay is that you don't have only to sell one type of item. You can sell clothing, collectibles, and electronics all under one account. If you find it hard to source name-brand clothing in your area, see if vintage collectibles are easier to find.

I've changed my eBay business model several times over the years and have sold in numerous categories. If you aren't successful with selling a particular type of item, try something new. As eBay is always evolving, you as a seller will evolve, too. And knowing how to sell in multiple categories means you can pivot in an instant if needed.

CHAPTER FIVE: TAKING EBAY PHOTOS

Most resellers agree that sourcing is the best part of reselling. After all, treasure hunting for profitable items is just plain fun! However, it is the nitty-gritty work of photographing and listing the items you are selling that will consume most of your time as a reseller. Too many people get into reselling because they like to shop; but if you want to make money, you have to sell. And to sell anything on eBay, you first need to photograph it.

Having good, clear photos of your items is essential in attracting customers and getting top dollar. eBay allows sellers to add up to 24 pictures per listing, and you'll want to take advantage of that allotment to provide as many photos for customers as possible. The first photo in a listing is called the Gallery Photo. This is the photo that will appear next to your listing on the site and is the picture a shopper will see when browsing the site. Make sure it is the best picture you have as it can be the difference between a shopper clicking on your listing or going to someone else's.

But to take photos for your eBay listings, you need a camera. When I first started selling on eBay, I used a digital camera. I saved the photos to the SIM card on the camera, and I then transferred the files to my desktop where I edited them before uploading them to eBay. While it did the job, it was a tedious task.

These days I exclusively use my iPhone for photos. Today's smartphones are just as good, if not better, than many digital cameras, and taking pictures on your phone means you can upload them directly to eBay through their app. I take and edit photos right on my iPhone, and I then upload them to eBay using the eBay app. It's quick and easy.

Whether you use a digital camera or smartphone, the most important thing is that the pictures are clear, not blurry, and well-lit. You want to ensure that your photos reflect the item's actual color and that photos are cropped so that there is not a bunch of white space around them. And you need to ensure the item itself is front and center with nothing else in the photo.

A common mistake I see new sellers make is taking photos of their items on the floor or on a cluttered counter. You do not want any other part of your home showing in the photo, just the item. Would you want to buy something you know has been on someone else's floor or near their dirty sink? Or worse, with personal items or garbage in the background?

And while some resellers invest in expensive photo backdrops and lighting, you can also find space in your home to take good photos. The key is using a white background, which can be a door or wall.

An easy, cheap photo background involves taking two pieces of foam board (I buy mine at Dollar Tree for $1.25 each) and placing them together at a 90-degree angle (one lying on the table and then one propped up against the wall). This gives you a clean, white background both under and behind the photo. I have used this system for nearly a decade.

If you are selling clothing, hang the garment up on the back of a door or against a white wall, or on a mannequin against a solid color wall. While a white backdrop is preferable, a clean, solid wood color will do if you do not have one. Ensure all the wrinkles are ironed out, the buttons are all buttoned, and the piece is lying flat against the door or wall. If you decide you want to become a full-time eBay clothing seller, you can invest in a mannequin; but to start, the door or wall methods are just fine.

PRO TIP: While a white background is preferable for most items, for clear or see-through glass, a black background works better. I have black poster boards that I keep on hand for these situations.

Whatever the item is that you are photographing, you will want to take a lot of pictures of it from all angles. When people shop in a brick-and-mortar store, they touch the items they are interested in and turn them over in their hands. You want to give your eBay customers the same feeling when they are looking at your listings. When I photograph a coffee mug, for instance, I take a picture of each of the four sides and the top looking down into the mug and of the bottom. I also make sure to take close-up shots of the maker's marks or stickers, as well as any flaws, no matter how small.

When looking at multiple completed listings of items that have ended on eBay, the number one difference between those that have sold and those that have not is the photos. Great photos go a long way towards selling items on eBay and can make or break a sale, so take the time to get yours right!

Background Removal Reature: eBay recently launched a background removal feature within listings that is meant to create a solid white space around the item being listed. As of this writing, this feature is hit or miss. Often when I try to use it, it erases half of the item I'm listing! However, eBay is constantly improving features, so give it a try using the following steps:

1. Open a listing in the **eBay app**
2. **Select a photo** to edit it.
3. Select the **Remove background** icon.
4. Crop the photo and select **Continue** to remove the background.
5. If needed, use the **Brush** and **Eraser** icons to manually paint the background back in or remove it.

6. Select **Save** (or **Apply** if using iOS) and then **Done**.

EBay's Picture Policy: Bay has a detailed photo policy that states, *When you create a listing or product, you must include at least one photo that is 500 pixels on the longest side, but we recommend including more to help increase your chances of a successful sale. Photos are one of the most important parts of your listing because they allow potential buyers to see the item's exact condition and help them decide whether to bid or buy. We recommend including more than one picture to help increase your chances of a successful sale.*

eBay also says that the following photos are not allowed:

◈ Photos that don't accurately represent the item

◈ Placeholder images used to convey messages

◈ Stock photos for used, damaged, or defective items

◈ Photos with added borders

◈ Photos with added text, artwork, or marketing material

◈ Watermarks of any type

Note that if eBay decides you violate their photo policy, they can pull your listing. Repeated violations of any of eBay's rules can lead to permanent suspension from their site.

Item Pictures: As I've already mentioned, eBay allows sellers to add up to 24 photos per listing, and you should take full advantage of that and provide as many pictures as possible of the item you are selling. The first photo in each listing is called the Gallery Photo and will be the photo that appears next to your listing in eBay's search.

You can take your photos right within the listing using the eBay app. This is the quickest and easiest way to add your photos and is great when you are just starting. Since I like to edit my photos, I take them using my iPhone, save them to my camera roll, and then add them to the listing within the eBay app. Whether you decide to take your photos within the listing or separately, you want to follow the following tips:

Take photos of the piece from every single angle, including from the top and the bottom. You want to give your customers the feeling they would have if they were in a brick-and-mortar store handling an item. You likely do not purchase something by only glancing at it briefly on the shelf, so you will sell more on eBay if you give your customers pictures of your items from every angle.

For instance, as I noted earlier, if you are selling a coffee mug, take pictures of the front, back, both sides and bottom, along with a shot of the inside (customers want to see if there are any "spoon marks," i.e., scratches or discoloration). For clothes, take full-length shots of the garment's front and back and up-close pictures of hems, cuffs, pockets, and labels. If your item is battery-powered, take a photo of the open battery compartment to show that there is not any erosion. When I list vintage books, I take photos of the front and back cover, the spine, the first couple of title pages, and two to three photos of the text pages.

You want the item you are selling to be front and center in all pictures, so take the time to edit your photos to eliminate as much white space as possible. You can try eBay's background removal feature or use a program such as Canva to eliminate the background and make the item appear with a solid white background. However, this isn't something I personally feel is important. As long as your backdrop is clean and accurately represents the item you are listing, you don't need to worry about white space.

I do not worry about my pictures looking perfect; I focus on ensuring my **photo area is well-lit and against a white background** (such as a wall or piece of posterboard). I worry more about ensuring my pictures are clear with the item in focus than I do about the background. I **make sure to take up-close photos of any condition issues** such as minor wear or damage. I disclose any faults in the listing and direct buyers to look closely at the photos provided, so they know exactly what they are buying. It is rare to find secondhand items that do not have even a tiny bit of wear and tear.

Still, by disclosing all issues and providing photos, you will not only have a better chance of the item selling, but you will also protect yourself from a customer complaining they received something that was not as described. Buyers understand that they are purchasing pre-owned items and do not expect them to be perfect, but they rightly expect that the seller provides them with an accurate condition.

It is important to **take up-close pictures of details** such as the maker's marks on ceramics, clothing labels (both the size label by the collar as well as fabric labels that may be located elsewhere, such as near the inside hem), and any inscriptions, as well as any condition issues. The cameras on most of today's smartphones take pictures that are just as good and sometimes even better than actual digital cameras. In particular, my iPhone is much better at capturing up-close details than the digital camera I used to use ever was.

Adding photos to listings: After taking my pictures on my iPhone and editing them in my camera roll, I open the eBay app, click on one of my active listings, and then click on the *Sell Similar* option. eBay automatically asks if I want to keep or remove the photos from that listing; I select "remove" and then upload the photos I just took directly from my camera roll. I then saved that listing as a *Draft* and switched over to my laptop to complete the listing.

Some eBay sellers complete the entire listing process on their smartphones via the eBay app; in this case, they just skip saving the photos to their camera rolls and are just saving the pictures directly in their listings. Either method is a matter of personal choice. I just personally find it easier to take a big batch of pictures on my phone, edit them on my phone, use the sell similar method in the eBay app to upload them, save the listings as drafts, and then finish listings on my computer. This is mainly because I sell so many different items in various categories with varying shipping weights.

Note that you want the item's main photo, the Gallery Photo, to be the photo that shows your entire item. For instance, if you are selling a coffee mug, you want the mug's front to be the main thumbnail picture. Sometimes when I upload my photos from my phone into an eBay listing, the photos upload out of order. This is yet another reason I like to finish listings on my computer, as it is easier to correct such details.

Ensure all photos are upright, not sideways or upside down, and do not upload blurry photos. I cannot tell you how many bad item photos I see on eBay, and poor-quality pictures can make it next to impossible for an item to sell. It is better to retake photos than upload poor ones.

Lighting: You do not need a fancy photography set-up to take eBay photos, just a space with a lot of light. Good lighting is essential to taking clear pictures that capture color and detail, along with any flaws.

If your home or workspace is dark, you can easily brighten things up with lamps. If you frequently list many items online, you may want to invest in some professional lighting, such as a **ring lamp,** although I never found this necessary.

However, if you mainly list items in a similar category, such as clothing, you may find a professional lighting setup to be beneficial. If you rely on natural light for your photos, a lighting setup will allow you to list even on gloomy days. Ring light systems can be purchased online for as little as $50.

A **lightbox** is a tool that sellers of small items such as jewelry and miniatures like to use. Portable lightboxes can be purchased for around $50 online, although there are all sorts of YouTube tutorials on making your own using cardboard boxes and lights.

I take my eBay photos in a room with lots of windows that provide ample natural lighting. I also turn on all the room's lights and a lamp to add more brightness. I want to make sure to capture the actual color and texture of the items I am selling. Rarely do I use my camera flash, which often distorts the product's actual color, making it appear lighter than it is. My iPhone has some editing features for the light that I occasionally use, especially if an item's color does not show up correctly (this usually happens to me with anything green).

Backdrops: As I mentioned earlier in this chapter, I see many eBay sellers who take pictures of items on their dirty carpet or with their messy kitchen in the background. I have even seen pictures of packaged food products taken on the floor with a pet's tail in the shot!

Taking pictures against a white background will work for most items, whether it is a white wall, a sheet, or a table. My straightforward setup of white poster boards set up on a card table works fine for most of my photos. Note that after a while, poster boards will become dirty and dented. Since these boards only cost $1.25 at Dollar Tree and similar stores, it's affordable to replace them every few months.

For larger items, try to take pictures against a white wall. If you do not have a white wall, draping a white sheet from the ceiling can provide a nice backdrop. I have a blank, white wall in my office with a single nail that I hang clothes from to take photos. You want to ensure that whatever backdrop you use is clean and pattern-free so that nothing takes away from the item itself. For years I sold clothing that I hung on a hook on the back of a door. Try using what you have when you are just starting.

Whatever you use as your backdrop, just ensure that the item you are selling is the only item in the picture. I cannot tell you how many photos I see where other things and even people and pets are in the photos. Make sure to edit your hands/fingers out of pictures. I occasionally need to hold down a book page to get a photo, but I always edit my handout. Unless you are a hand model, no one wants to see your chipped nails and cracked cuticles. Yuck!

Stock Photos: If you sell an item with a bar code in eBay's catalog, a stock photo will often pop up to use as the main picture in your listing. And while many sellers use these photos, I do not like them, preferring to use my pictures. Sometimes I use eBay's provided stock photo, but not as the main picture; I keep it in the listing and have it at the end of my photo lineup.

Stock photos indicate the item is brand new, and even if you have a new, unused item to sell, you likely picked it up secondhand. There may be differences in the item you are selling versus the product's original stock photo, including slight damage. And unless an item is brand new and in eBay's catalog with the photo they provide or you have obtained permission from the manufacturer, wholesale, or liquidation company that the item came from to use their photos, as it is unethical to use stock photos.

In some cases, it is even illegal to use a company's stock photo without their permission. If you are purchasing items via wholesale or liquidation and those companies provide you with stock photos, you will still need permission to use those pictures on eBay. Do not go directly to a company's website and copy their pictures for your eBay listing; not only will that get you into trouble with eBay, but it could also result in legal action from the business whose photos you stole.

Even if the item I am selling matches the approved stock pictures exactly, I still take my own photos as I feel they best represent my specific products. While customers turn to Amazon to buy brand-new items, they often come to eBay looking for gently used products or extreme deals. So, while it is reasonable to expect an Amazon listing with an available quantity of one hundred products to use stock photos, on eBay, most people are just selling one single version of each of the items they have listed. And by providing photos of the exact item you are selling, you assure customers that what they see in the picture is exactly what they are getting.

While you will likely see other sellers using stock photos on eBay, please remember that just because some people are getting away with it does not mean you should, too. Do you really want to risk losing your eBay account because you didn't want to take a few pictures? I know I don't!

CHAPTER SIX: CREATING EBAY LISTINGS

The first eBay listing you create is the most labor-intensive one as you will have to fill out all the various fields, including all the shipping options. However, once you have created your first listing, the second listing and all those that follow will be much easier as you can select the **Sell similar** option from an active listing, which will copy the information from the first listing into the second, meaning you will only have to change specific fields, not start entirely from scratch.

I will discuss how to create a listing using the *Sell similar* option more after I walk you through creating your first listing.

In 2022, eBay completely changed its listing form. While it is simpler for new sellers, for those of us who have been selling on the site for a long time, it's been a bit of an adjustment. However, I will walk you through the entire new listing form step-by-step. While it may seem daunting at first, trust me, it quickly becomes a simple, routine part of selling on eBay. That is because while eBay presents you with an overwhelming list of option fields, you only need to focus on those that are required.

If you are creating your first-ever eBay listing, first **log into your eBay account**, and click on the **Sell** tab at the very top of the page on the right-hand side. Even if you have already been on the site earlier, you usually will have to log in again; don't worry, this is just an added level of eBay security so that they are assured that it is indeed you who is logging into your account. eBay has a lot of protections built into their site, so get used to having to log into your account frequently. Again, it's for your protection.

Clicking on the *Sell* tab will take you to your **Seller Hub.** We talked about this page earlier in this book; remember that this is where all of your selling activities are located. This is the page I have bookmarked as it is the most important page for eBay sellers.

On the right-hand side of the page is a Create listing button in blue. You can choose from *Single listing, Multiple listing,* or *Listings from Bulq inventory.* Click on **Single listing.**

The first field is **Tell us what you're selling.** Here you can enter a UPC, ISBN, ePID, part number, product name, or general description of your item. If you have a new item with a barcode on it, it may pop up in eBay's catalog. If so, you would simply click on the item, and eBay would prefill in the information for you.

However, if you are selling vintage collectibles or secondhand clothing, it's unlikely you'll find your item listed. For example, let's say you type in "Funko Pop", a modern collectible item many people sell online. eBay would show you several options, including if they already have the Funko Pop you are selling in their product catalog. You would then simply select the Funko Pop you are selling, and eBay would pre-fill in most of the information for it.

However, let's say you are selling a men's Ralph Lauren button-front shirt that you picked up secondhand at a garage sale. It's unlikely the shirt you are listing will be in eBay's product catalog. In this case, you would then click **Continue without match.**

A pop-up window will now appear titled **Confirm details.** The condition choices vary slightly depending on the category. For example, clothing categories offer the following choices:

- **New with tags:** *A brand-new, unused, and unworn item (including handmade items) in the original packaging (such* *as the original box or bag) and/or with the original tags attached.*

- **New without tags:** *A brand-new, unused, and unworn item (including handmade items) that is not in original packaging and may be missing original packaging materials (such as the original box or bag). The original tags may not be attached.*
- **New with defects:** *A brand-new, unused, and unworn item. Possible cosmetic imperfections range from natural color variations to scuffs, cuts or nicks, hanging threads, or missing buttons that occasionally occur during the manufacturing or delivery process. The apparel may contain irregular or mismarked size tags. The item may be missing the original retail packaging materials (such as the original box or tag). New factory seconds and/or new irregular items may fall into this category. The original tags may or may not be attached. See the seller's listing for full details and a description of any imperfections.*
- **Pre-owned:** *An item that has been used or worked previously. See the seller's listing for full details and a description of any imperfections.*

Hard goods, such as home décor and collectibles, offer the following options:

◇ **New:** *A brand-new, unused, unopened, undamaged item in its original packaging (where packaging is applicable). Packaging should be the same as what is found in a retail store, unless the item is handmade or was packaged by the manufacturer in non-retail packaging, such as an unprinted box or plastic bag.*

◇ **New other (see details):** *An item in excellent, new condition with no wear. The item may be missing the* *original packaging or protective wrapping or may be in the original packaging but not sealed. The item includes original accessories. The item may be a factory second.*

◈ **Seller refurbished:** *An item that has been restored to working order by the eBay seller or a third party not approved by the manufacturer. This means the item has been inspected, cleaned, and repaired to full working order and is in excellent condition. This item may or may not be in its original packaging.*

◈ **Used:** *An item that has been used previously. The item may have some signs of cosmetic wear but is fully operational and functions as intended. This item may be a floor model or store return that has been used.*

◈ **For parts of not working:** *An item that does not function as intended and is not fully operational. This includes items that are defective in ways that render them difficult to use, items that require service or repair, or items missing essential components.*

Using the Ralph Lauren shirt, let's say you bought it at a garage sale, and it did not have the original hang tags attached. In this case, you would select *Pre-owned* and then click **Continue to listing.**

A page titled **Complete your listing** will next appear. The first section you will need to complete is **Photos & Video.** If you are using the eBay app to create your listing, you can take photos right from your phone or upload them from your camera roll. If you use a desktop computer and have the photos saved on your system, you can upload them from your system. For this step, I have typically already taken my photos on my iPhone so that I can upload them into the listing from my camera roll.

PRO TIP: If you are uploading photos from your phone, you can have two options. The first is to upload your photos to a draft you have already started. The second is the start a draft on your phone. For example, if you draft a listing on your desktop, you can save it and then switch to the eBay app and upload your photos from your phone. You would then be able to publish your listing from your phone. However, if you start the listing from your phone so you can upload the photos first, you can then save a draft from your phone, switching to your computer to finalize the listing. Which method you use is up to you. I prefer to take photos of several items at once. I then open the eBay app and create new listings using the Sell similar option from an active listing. I upload photos into new listings, save those as drafts, and then switch to my computer to finish them.

eBay also now offers the option to add a video to your listings. Currently, you can't upload a video directly into the listing; rather, you must use a third-party program or enter HTML code. The easiest way is to film a short YouTube video and add that HTML to the listing. Since this takes more time, it's best to save videos for expensive items, especially those with music or moving parts.

For this example, we'll stick to just adding photos. Remember that you can add up to 24 pictures to each listing, so take advantage of that number by taking photos from every angle, up-close photos of intricate details, photos of labels, and photos of any flaws.

After you've uploaded your photos, the next field to complete is the **TITLE.**

A great keyword-loaded title is key to selling your item, as it will help buyers find your listing. You want to use all the 80-character spaces allowed, even if it does not read like a proper sentence or headline. "Red Men's Shirt" is a lousy title as it will be drowned out in the search against all the other red shirts listed. However, "XL Red Blue

Plaid Mens Ralph Lauren Button Front Shirt Long Sleeve Thick Cotton" not only tells the customer exactly what the item is but it is loaded with keywords that buyers are likely to enter into the search bar to make finding the listing in the search much easier.

There is a **Subtitle** option available directly under the *Title*, but this feature costs extra. There is no need to pay $2 to add a subtitle; this is just an added feature for which eBay charges you extra fees. In all my years of selling on eBay, I have never once paid for this option. A keyword-loaded title is all you need for buyers to find your listing.

The next field is **ITEM CATEGORY.** eBay will automatically choose a category for you based on your listing's title. In the example of the Ralph Lauren shirt, eBay chose: *Clothing, Shoes & Accessories > Men > Men's Clothing > Shirts > Casual Button-Down Shirts.* This is correct for that item listing, so if eBay chooses the correct category for your item, you can move on to the next field.

However, if, for some reason, the category eBay chooses is not correct for the item you are listing, you can easily change it by clicking on **Edit** (it has a pencil graphic next to it). This will open a box for you to search for other categories. Click on the **First category** option and a new page will open. Here you will see the *Category* eBay originally offered you, but you will also see a few **Suggested categories**. Usually, you can find the category you prefer here. But if not, you can look at all of the categories under the **All categories** field and search to find the one you want.

You can also add a **Second category.** However, just like I don't advise paying for a *Subtitle*, I don't advise selecting a second category as you will pay additional fees. One title and one category are enough.

The other field under **ITEM CATEGORY** is **Store category.** Store categories differ from eBay categories; only those with EBay store subscriptions can create store categories. Unlike the eBay categories, you can choose two store categories for no extra fees.

If you have an eBay store, you can create categories to help shoppers narrow down the items in your store. My store has a "Clothing" category. So, in the example of the Ralph Lauren shirt, I would select CLOTHING under **First category.** If I wanted to add the item to a second store category, I could do so under **Second category.** Again, there are no fees to add your items to your store categories; and having items in two categories may mean more customers see them.

PRO TIP: You can only create store categories from the **Manage My Store** section. You cannot create new store categories within a listing. If you are listing an item you don't have a store category yet set up, let it go into the *Other* category. You can then go to your store, create a new category, and move the listing there. Since I batch list items, I don't stop to create categories when I'm listing. I wait until I've finished listing to then create new categories as I can do this in bulk. We'll discuss managing an *eBay Store*, including setting up store categories, later in this book

The next field is **ITEM SPECIFICS.** Depending on the category you are listing in, the selections in this area will vary.

There are two sections under *Item Specifics:* **Required** and **Additional (optional).** *Required* fields must be filled out. eBay will not let you complete the listing until you select the required fields.

Some categories don't have any *Required* fields, but most do. Fortunately, they are usually very straightforward. For clothing, the required fields will be things like the brand, size, and color of the item you are listing. You cannot list an item for sale until all required fields are filled out.

After you complete the *Required* section, you'll move on to the *Additional (optional)* section. The options under *Additional* are completely optional, but the more fields you can fill out, the better chance your item will have to be found by customers in search. However, these fields can be very overwhelming, especially if you are new to listing on eBay.

In the example of the Ralph Lauren shirt, there are 27 optional fields available. Some are logical, such as the material and country of manufacture, both of which are printed on the shirt's tag. But others are confusing and seem to have no relevance to the item. For instance, there is a field titled *Character.* The selections under *Character* have licensed toy brands such as Barbie and Hello Kitty. Neither of these has anything to do with a men's Ralph Lauren shirt. So why are they listed as an option?

eBay introduced this new listing form in 2022, and it's been a work in progress. Many sellers have complained about the numerous and odd choices in the *Item Specifics* section. So, if you see choices that don't connect to the item you are listing, know that you aren't alone. eBay continues to work on the listing form and is making improvements to it, and they are well aware that sellers aren't happy with some of the features.

The bottom line is that when it comes to the *Additional* options, choose the ones that are easy to fill out and just ignore the rest. And if you want to skip over all of them, that's okay, too.

After you finish the *Item Specifics* section, you will move on to the **VARIATIONS** section. This field is for those who are listing multiple variations of the same item. For example, let's say you have six brand new shirts from the same brand and in the same color. However, you have two mediums, two larges, and two extra larges. This section would allow you to create one listing for the sweaters and offer variations for the sizes. This section is typically for sellers who are selling liquidation new goods that they have multiples of.

The next section of the listing form is **CONDITION.** We covered the condition options earlier in this chapter, but to recap, they differ slightly between categories. However, you are usually looking at listing something as new or used (also called *pre-owned* in some categories). Remember that you chose the condition of your item when you first started the listing process; however, you can change it here. Perhaps you thought your item was *New with Tags,* but when you went to list it, you saw that there was a flaw and needed to change it to *New with Defects.*

Representing your item's correct condition is very important as buyers can file a claim with eBay and force you to issue them a full refund if you say an item is new but is used or if it is in worse condition than you state. Legally, once you take an item out of a store, it is classified as secondhand, so even if it still has the original hang tags and has never been worn, it is technically used. However, new in the box or new with tag items are almost always listed as "new" by eBay sellers.

Depending on the category, there may be more choices than just new or used. For instance, remember that there are four in the clothing category: *New with Tags, New without Tags, New with Defects,* and *Pre-Owned.* If that Ralph Lauren shirt we've been using as an example has been washed but never worn, you need to list it as pre-owned.

There is also a **Condition description** field for you to write in any specific information you want the customer to know about. Be sure to disclose even the tiniest of issues. Flawed items can still sell, and most shoppers understand that used items aren't brand new; but you want to make sure you detail all missing parts, stains, rips, or cracks an item may have.

One of the best pieces of advice I ever got for selling on eBay was to under-promise and over-deliver. I often understate the condition of my items. If an item is in like-new condition, I say it is in "very good condition." If it is in good condition, I will say it is "fair." Not only is condition highly debatable among buyers, but when a customer gets something in better shape than they thought it would be, they are always pleased. My feedback reflects this as several of my customers write, "Better condition than expected!"

The following section to fill out is **DESCRIPTION**, which is where you really get to "sell" your item. Put in as much information as you can think of; the more details you give, the more likely you are to sell your item, plus it will drastically cut down on questions from potential buyers.

For instance, when listing a vintage book, I type in everything that is on the cover page, including the publishing house. I also measure the book. You would not believe how many questions I get when I do not put in the measurements for vintage books! Measurements are one of the most requested details customers want, so take the time to provide them in your descriptions.

Even obvious information, such as brand and color, should be repeated in the *Description* field. While all these details may seem like a waste of time for you, remember that you are competing with thousands of other listings, especially if you are selling a popular item such as a current toy or video game. Let your buyers know the REAL condition of the item, and if it comes from a smoke-free home, mention that, too.

PRO TIP: While eBay offers **Templates** you can create for your listings, I've never bothered with these. I prefer to simply include the relevant details and skip the fancy layout. eBay favors simple text with a 14-point black font. Remember that people access eBay from various sources and different computer models, meaning graphics can change depending on the platform. Simple text ensures everyone can read your listing.

Note that even if you have added information under the *Additional* section under *Item Specifics*, such as measurements, it is helpful to add these details to your description. Is that repetitive? Yes. Does it require a bit more time? Yes. However, it will help reduce questions from potential buyers who don't look at the *Item Specifics* section. The more information you can provide throughout the entire listing, the less likely you will be bothered by questions from shoppers.

The next section of the listing form is **PRICING.**

The first decision you need to make is whether to list the item at **Auction** or **Buy It Now.** Note that *Buy It Now* used to be called *Fixed Price.*

If you choose *Auction*, you will be presented with several fields to fill complete, including:

Auction duration: Choose from one, three, five, seven, or 10-day auctions. Note that one and three-day auctions have an additional listing fee of $1. Most sellers choose seven-day auctions as that gives shoppers a full week to discover the listing.

Starting bid: While most eBay auctions used to start at 99 cents, in today's market, you don't want to start your auction at less than the minimum you'll be happy with it selling for. When eBay first started, you would only list items at auction, and most things were typically bid up. However, as more sellers came on to the site and competition increased, *Buy It Now* sales became more popular. If you are hoping an item will sell for $15 but would be happy with $10, start your auction at $9.99.

Buy It Now: You can offer a set amount that allows shoppers to buy the item outright without bidding. eBay requires your *Buy It Now* price to be at a minimum of 30% more than your starting bid.

Reserve price: You can enter the lowest amount you are willing to take for your item. However, there is an additional fee for selecting this option. Instead, I recommend starting your auction price at your minimum price and saving on the extra fee.

Offers: You can choose to *Allow offers* or *Don't allow offers*.

Allow offers: See all offers, or if you want, set up rules for when you'll review or accept offers. You can set a minimum offer amount and also an auto-accept amount. While low-ball offers are annoying, the general rule of thumb is to allow all offers to come through for you to see, as just the activity of people making offers shows eBay that your listing is creating engagement, which can help push it up in the search.

OR

Don't allow offers: When it comes to running auctions, I don't allow offers. I do add the offer feature to fixed-price listings. However, it's up to you what you decide. You can always play around with the feature. You may decide you like getting offers on auctions, or you may be like me and save, allowing offers for fixed-price listings only.

Scheduled start time: If you are running an auction, it can be advantageous to schedule when it will start and therefore end. However, if you are listing at a fixed price, it makes no difference to schedule your listing. Rather, you can leave it at the default to *Start immediately*.

Buy It Now: If you choose to list your item at a *Buy It Now* price, the fields will change slightly from those for auctions. When you select *Buy It Now* for your listing, you will first enter your **Price**. Depending on what you are listing, eBay may show you what the average sale price is for that particular product. But remember that it is just an average and a suggestion. I often find I can price my items higher than what eBay recommends.

You will then enter the **Quantity** of the item you are selling. If you are only selling a single shirt, the quantity would be one. If you are selling multiple, identical copies of the same item – for instance, you have three copies of a video game – then you would type in the number of items you have. Note that multiple items must all be IDENTICAL, not only in that they are all exactly the same item but that the conditions are all the same, too. If you have two of the same shirt, one brand new with the tags and one that has been washed and worn, you will need to create two separate listings and list their respective conditions accordingly.

Next, you can choose whether or not you want to **Allow offers**. You can enter a **Minimum offer** that eBay will automatically implement on your behalf. As an example, if you have a *Minimum offer* of $20 and someone offers you $3, eBay will automatically decline that offer. You can also enter an **Auto-accept** amount. Let's say you enter an *Auto-accept* amount of $10 for your $20 listing. eBay will automatically accept any offers of $10 or more on your behalf. If you don't offer a minimum or auto-accept, you will need to manage all offers manually.

Add volume pricing: If you are selling items you have multiple quantities of, you can offer a discount when buyers purchase more than one item at a time. eBay offers three options here: *Buy 2 and save, Buy 3 and save,* and *Buy 4 and save.* Each option has a drop-down menu where you can select a percentage discount.

Scheduled start time: Just as you can for auctions, you can also schedule fixed-price items. However, while it can be advantageous to schedule auctions to select an ending time when more people will be online, in my opinion, it makes no difference to schedule your *Buy It Now* listings. Rather, you can leave it at the default to *Start immediately.*

Sellers used to be able to choose the duration for how long they wanted *Buy It Now* items to be listed. However, eBay no longer offers that option. All *Buy It Now* listings renew automatically every month until the item sells or you, the seller, manually end it.

The next section of the listing form is the one that trips up a lot of new eBay sellers, which is **SHIPPING**. This is the section where you set up the shipping for the item you are selling. I will cover shipping in-depth in the next chapter, but I'll briefly review it here as it appears within the listing form.

The first field you encounter is **Shipping policy**. Here are the step-by-step instructions for this section:

> 1. Select an existing policy from the *dropdown menu* or select the *three-dot menu* to create a new shipping policy or edit an existing one. If this is your very first eBay listing, eBay will likely prompt you to **Create a shipping profile.**

> 2. If you click on the three-dot menu and select *Create shipping profile*, a popup window will appear.

3. Your first choice is to choose a **Policy name.** These days I ship most items via *Ground Advantage* and *Priority Mail.* So my policy is called "Ground/Priority". I also check the **Set as default shipping policy** box so that I don't have to continually update this section.

4. You can write yourself a note under **Policy description.** This field is not visible to customers.

5. The next section will be specific to the country you are selling from. In my case, this is U.S. Shipping. The first drop-down menu requires you to select from the following:

◈ **Flat: Same cost to all buyers**

◈ **Calculated: Cost varies by location** (eBay will calculate the postage based on the weight of the package and the distance from your zip code to the person who buys your item)

◈ **Freight: Large items over 150 lbs**

◈ **No shipping: Local pickup only**

6. If you choose *Calculated* or *Flat*, select your preferred **Services.** We covered the various forms of postage earlier in this book, but most sellers are shipping via *USPS Media Mail, USPS Ground Advantage,* and/or *USPS Priority Mail.* I offer *Ground Advantage* as the first option and *Priority Mail* as the second.

7. You can select *Free shipping* on your first shipping option.

8. If you're offering a flat rate, enter the shipping cost.

9. If you are listing multiple quantities in the same listing, you can offer a discounted charge for every item of two or more under *Each additional.*

10. Set a **Handling time.** This is how long it will take you to process and ship the order once payment is received.

11. You can add a handling cost (calculated shipping only) to cover shipping supplies.

12. Choose whether you want to offer **International shipping.**

13. Select **Save and close.**

A note about **Handling time**: The **default setting is 2 business days.** However, you can change it anywhere from the *Same business day* up to *40 business days* (this is used when sellers change their handling time due to vacations). I have always chosen *2 business days,* which are Monday through Friday in the United States. Weekends and Federal holidays do not count as business days. I usually ship the following business day, but selecting *2 business days,* not only gives me a little leeway in case an issue arises, but if I do ship faster, the customer is happy.

The next two fields are **Package weight** and **Package dimensions.** This is where having a digital postage scale is essential as you need to enter the package, not the item, weight. I weigh all items in a box, mentally noting that the box will weigh more once packing materials are added. I then round up to the next pound.

PRO TIP: If a box with an item inside weighs one pound 14 ounces, I know that it will eventually weigh over two pounds once packing materials are added. But rather than entering 2 pounds and guessing on the ounces, I simply round up to the next pound, which is three pounds. You only need to know the weight ranges, not the exact weights. Over one pound but under two pounds is rounded up to two pounds. Over two pounds but under three pounds is rounded up to three pounds.

The next field is **Package dimensions.** As long as your shipping box is under 36 cubic inches (12x12x12 inches), there is no need to enter the size of the box. After all, you likely won't know the exact box you will using until the item sells. However, if you know the package will be over 36 cubic inches (I sometimes have to ship boxes as big as 16x16x16 inches), enter those dimensions as it will change the postage rate considerably.

I will be going over shipping more in-depth in the next chapter, as well as giving you some inside tips and tricks to use when setting up your shipping profile. But for now, just note that unless the item you are selling will require a box larger than 12x12x12 inches you don't need to enter the *Dimensions* or select *Irregular package.* The main thing is that you've entered the weight. Most eBay packages do not require you to enter the shipping box dimensions, nor do they qualify as an irregular package.

The next section is **International Shipping.** ebay automatically enrolls all sellers in their **International Shipping Program.** This program makes it easy to sell to customers outside of your country as eBay handles the process for you. With the *International Shipping Program*, international orders will ship to eBay's domestic shipping hub. There, eBay will prepare all customs and tax forms before sending the package off to your customer. Your sale is complete once the package arrives at eBay's hub, not at your customer's home. eBay issues a refund at no cost to you if the buyer opens a return, and eBay also assumes all responsibility for damages and loss, including removing negative or neutral feedback.

In my opinion, eBay's *International Shipping Program* is the best service they offer. The ability to sell to customers all over the world without having to deal with customs forms, language barriers, and lost or damaged packages is a huge benefit to sellers. When I first started selling on eBay, I had to fill out lengthy customs forms for international shipments, and I had to then take those packages to the Post Office for review and special stamps. Now I can just print a shipping label from home, one that doubles as a customs form. And I can hand the package to my mail carrier the same way I do domestic packages.

The next field of the listing form is one of two sections titled **PREFERENCES.** Here you can adjust **Your settings.** A pop-up form will appear when you click on the little pencil icon. Under **Item Location** will be your country, zip code, city, and state, all of which determine *Calculated Shipping* charges between your location and that of your buyer.

Under **Returns,** you can choose whether or not you will accept **returns.** Clicking on the little three dots will allow you to see, edit, or create a return policy. For your first listing, choose the **Create a return policy option.** If you turn the **Accept returns** option off, then all sales are final unless there is a problem with the order.

If you turn the **Accept returns** options on, you can create rules for domestic orders, including how many days returns are allowed, whether you the seller, or your buyer pay for the return shipping, and the refund method. Sales through the *eBay International Shipping*

Program are eligible for returns that eBay handles on the seller's behalf.

Whether or not you decide to accept returns is up to you. I do not accept them because, as a small business, I can't afford to absorb the cost. If I make a mistake with someone's order, I will usually just issue them a full refund and allow them to keep the item. If I suspect the person is trying to scam me by saying an item wasn't as described, I will tell them I will accept the return just to call their bluff. Often they will balk at this. Usually, this indicates the buyer wants to keep the item but is fishing for a partial refund.

The next section in the main listing form is **PROMOTED LISTINGS.** eBay now offers the option to essentially pay for advertising to help you reach more buyers. Fortunately, you only pay for these ads when someone purchases after clicking on your ad. This feature is optional, although most seasoned sellers do opt into the program. I personally always have a 2% listing ad rate on all of my listings as I have seen an increase in sales. Around half of my sales come from Promoted Listings, so, for me, it's worth it to pay the fee, which is automatically deducted from my account after the buyer pays.

Finally, the last section of the listing form is the second field titled PREFERENCES. Clicking on the eBay Payments icon will bring up a pop-up window where you can create different policies for requiring immediate payment and if you will accept checks, money orders, or cash on pickup.

Finally, all the fields in the listing form have now been filled out, and it's time to list your item for sale LIVE on EBay! You can **Save for later** or **Preview your listing**. But if you are ready, you can click on **List it,** and it will be for sale.

However, don't fret if you realize after clicking on *List it* that there is an error in the listing. You can easily edit the listing after it goes live. And if something happens to the item and you can no longer sell it, you can end the listing at any time.

Your Second Listing: Once you have gotten one EBay listing under your belt, the second one will be super easy to complete as the first listing created a template for all your future listings. When you are ready to create a new listing, you simply open a listing that is either active or has ended, then click on **Sell similar.** You can find this option if you open a listing; or, if are looking at your listings list, you simply click on the drop-down menu next to **Edit.** *Sell similar* is the first option.

What *Sell similar* does is copy the information from the original listing into a new listing. Then you only need to change the title, photos, item specifics, and shipping weight for your new item. If you list the item in the same category as the first, you will not even have to change that section, which is why listing goes much faster if you list like items back-to-back, as you will have fewer specifics to alter. Plus, you do not have to recreate every one of your settings with every single new listing.

Let's say the first eBay listing you created was for a book. You have created that listing, which is live on eBay's website. Now you want to list a jacket. You simply click on the listing for the book and then click on *Sell similar* at the top left-hand corner of the listing. A new page will open that will look exactly like the book listing, but you can now edit it.

You'll want to change all of the fields that don't match the book's listing, including *PHOTOS & VIDEOS, TITLE, ITEM CATEGORY, ITEM SPECIFICS, CONDITION, DESCRIPTION, PRICING,* and *SHIPPING.* However, the other sections that relate to your policies, such as your handling time, payment details, and return policies can all stay as they are since they are universal to all of your listings.

Back to the book example: Perhaps you had the book listed at *Auction* with the buyer paying for calculated *Media Mail* shipping. However, for the coat, you want to list it at *Buy It Now* with *Free for buyer shipping*. Note that you must change the selling format and the shipping options within the new listing. However, you still do not have to worry about changing your return policy or excluded shipping locations as those carried over from the book listing.

Under *SHIPPING*, since you are doing *Calculated shipping* and have set up those specifics in your first listing, you only need to change the item's weight and how you will ship it. Since clothing cannot ship via *Media Mail,* you will have to choose *Ground Advantage* or *Priority*. I give my customers a choice: the lower-cost *Ground* which I sometimes offer for "free" (meaning I will have to pay the postage out of the selling price), and the more expensive *Priority*. The customer feels they are getting a deal with the "free" *Ground* shipping option I am offering in this instance, but they can also pay to upgrade to *Priority* if they want the coat faster.

PRO TIP: As I will talk about in the next chapter of this book, often *Ground* and *Priority* postage cost nearly the same amount for packages weighing under four pounds. When a buyer selects *free Ground shipping*, I can often upgrade them to *Priority* as it costs me the same amount. The buyer is happy as I've given them "free" upgraded shipping, meaning they will get their item faster. However, the cost was the same on my end, and I could use a free *Priority Mail* shipping box. It's a win-win for both my customer and me!

As you did with the first listing, you simply hit the **List it** button after changing all the relative fields and adding in the new photos.

You can then open that listing, click on *Sell similar* again, and start on your next listing.

The "sell similar" trick is fast and easy; in fact, I cannot remember the last time I created a new listing from scratch. The listing process gets easier and faster with every new item you list. While it can be overwhelming at first, trust me that you will be listing items like a pro in no time. And when you are ready to take things to the next level, here are some of my advanced listing tips:

Research: Before I list anything on eBay, I first research it to see the current average selling price for the item is; or if it is even selling at all. The way I do this is by doing a completed listing search. I simply type in a general description of my item in the search bar (for instance, "Pink Pyrex Bowl"), and I then narrow down the search fields, which appear on the screen's left side. Included in those search fields is one for **Completed Listings.** Selecting *Completed Listings* will show me what, if anything, an item has recently sold for.

If a completed listing search brings up several hundred listings, I will further narrow it down by selecting the **Sold** listings. Instead of showing me every item listed in the past few months, regardless of whether it sold or not, selecting *Sold* will only show me the listings that resulted in a sale. I can then sort the results using several options, including most recently ended, distance, or price. I prefer to sort using the highest price so that I can see which items sold for the most money. Note the price will also include shipping, regardless of whether the buyer or seller paid for it.

If you want to see results from further back, simply click on the **Research** tab in your **Seller Hub**, which will take you to **Terapeak**. All eBay sellers have access to *Terapeak* research, which shows you sales from the past two years.

Terapeak takes researching sold eBay listings up a notch by providing you with two years' worth of data. While the *Completed Listing* search on eBay only gives you three months of sales records, with *Terapeak,* you can see what an item has been selling for during the previous twenty-four months. This is incredibly useful when you are researching off-season items. After all, it's hard to gather data on Christmas items in July. With Terapeak, you can see holiday sales from the past two years, which will help you price items for the busy fourth-quarter shopping season.

When you are researching sold listings, whether via *Terapeak* or through eBay's completed listings search, you will often find that your item has sold for a wide range of prices. This is when you need to examine the results to see why some sold for a high price while others only sold for a few dollars, if at all. Sometimes, the seller had a low asking price, either starting an item at auction for only 99 cents or listing it at *Buy It Now* for just a few dollars. Perhaps the pictures in the listing were terrible, or maybe the item itself was in awful condition. Compare the highest sold price listing with the lowest one to determine what factored into the difference. And then price your item accordingly.

If my item is in the same condition as the listing that sold for the highest price, I base my price on that listing. I also note *when* the item was sold to account for seasonality. Back to the example of Christmas items: If I am listing a Christmas collectible, I want to base my price on what it sold for during the previous holiday season, not what it may have sold for during the summer months. I am willing to let some items sit in my store for longer, specifically vintage collectibles and seasonal goods, until the right buyer comes along. The exception to this is clothing, as I prefer to move clothes much faster, specifically if it is a trendy piece that may go out of style if it is listed too long.

Note that it is imperative to base the selling price of the item you are listing on the comparable sales results and conditions. While a brand-new book may bring in top dollar, a used one may only bring in a few bucks. Ensure that you base your item's price on those in a similar condition to yours when looking at the completed listing results. Remember that "brand new" refers to items with absolutely no flaws. The original tags attached were basically in the condition it was in as they rolled off the manufacturing line. However, most of the items you will sell on eBay are likely to be secondhand, and condition plays a huge factor in how much pre-owned items will sell for.

I also use the *Terapeak* and eBay search results to tell me if an item usually only sells with "free" shipping. As I say in every eBay book I have written, shipping is never actually "free" as someone, either the seller or the buyer must pay for the postage.

However, some categories, such as clothing, are so crowded and competitive that building the cost of postage into the asking price to list the item with "free" shipping is often necessary to get the sale. Health and beauty items are also products that typically sell best when listed with "free" shipping. And if you sell similar items, such as jeans in the same size or a line of specific collectibles, offering "free" shipping may help convince a buyer to purchase multiple items from you as they will not be wondering about the shipping charges.

While I typically research pricing on my computer, I sometimes look up items on my smartphone using eBay's mobile app when I am out and about. That way, I can quickly determine if an item is worth picking up or if I should pass on it. The downside to using eBay Mobile for me is that I often run into problems finding an internet connection (especially when I am at an estate sale in the country). I have even had difficulty getting an internet connection inside Goodwill stores.

So, while it would be nice to look up every item before I buy it, I often rely on instinct and wait until I return to my office to do any research. If the item you are researching has a bar code, you can use the eBay app to scan it to check its current price. Note that if the eBay app is not working for you for whatever reason if you are listing an item produced within the past few years, you can also use the Amazon Seller app for scanning purposes.

Remember that an item is only worth what someone will pay for it. Therefore, looking at the *active* eBay listings will not be much help as those results only show what sellers are currently ASKING for the item. The *completed listings* will show you what customers have actually paid for the item. This is often the biggest mistake new eBay sellers make; they only look at the active listings, not the sold results. I also hear this a lot from people selling their items at garage sales. "It's selling for $1000 on eBay!" they will claim, but they have usually only looked at the active listings, not the sold results.

Some categories, specifically clothing, require you to list the size of the item you are selling. While most clothing sizes are straightforward, I sometimes need to research how various clothing brands size their garments. For instance, Chicos, a women's clothing company, has its own unique sizing chart ranging from 000 (extra small) to 4.5 (extra-large). I also often have to research whether a piece of clothing is vintage (say, a pair of Levi's jeans) and how to spot counterfeit items (such as telling an authentic Coach purse from a fake).

I also pick up vintage items from overseas that are not labeled in English; fortunately, Google can quickly translate most languages to English. I have found several German Bibles and hymnals over the years that I needed help translating, and I have also gotten pottery marked in a foreign language. I simply type in the book title or maker mark into the Google search bar, followed by "translate to English" to get a translation.

If you are dealing with vintage and collectible items like me, you may need to do further research on a piece to provide as much information about it as possible. For instance, I sell a lot of vintage flatware sets. These sell best when I can identify the pattern, so I visit sites such as *replacements.com* to find the name, manufacturer, and date of the sets I am selling.

Using Google Images will bring up all kinds of resources for most objects you are selling. You simply snap a picture of your item and Google will scan the internet to see if there are photos that match. Most of these results lead you to sites such as eBay and Etsy, where you can further narrow down your research. And these days, nearly every collectible item has at least one dedicated website, often run by actual collectors, that you can use to research everything from pottery to clothing.

Don't rely on eBay alone to do your research; use the World Wide Web to learn as much as possible about the items you are selling. Yes, all this research takes time; but remember that the more information you can provide in your listings, the more likely your item will sell fast and for top dollar!

Auction vs. Buy It Now: What makes eBay such a unique selling platform is the different ways you can sell items. You can run *Auctions* from one to ten days, and you can also, for an added fee, include a *Buy It Now* price to your auction listing. Or you can list items solely at a *Buy It Now* price (formerly called *Fixed Price*). While eBay used to allow you to list items for a set period, now all

Buy It Now items are automatically relisted every month until the item sells or you, the seller, manually end it.

Then there is the **Best Offer** option, which you can add to both *Auction* and *Buy It Now* listings. *Best Offer* allows potential buyers to send you a direct offer on your item. You can either accept, decline, or negotiate with a Counteroffer. You can also set up **Automatic Accept,** and **Automatic Decline** options to instantly agree to or decline offers that meet or do not meet the thresholds you have set.

There are so many choices, I know! But the bottom line is that all eBay listings, despite the length and added options, will either be *Auctions* or *Buy It Now.* Many eBay sellers start out selling their items using one format and get stuck using the same option for all their listings. However, some items sell better at *Auction,* while others do best at *Buy It Now* price. But how do you know whether you should start an item at *Auction* or just list it at *Buy It Now*? The answer depends on the item itself.

If you have done your research, using either eBay's *Completed Listing* search or *Terapeak,* and found that the item you are selling commands a steady price of, say, $50 on eBay, then go ahead and list yours for $50 at *Buy It Now.* If you find your item sells for a wide range of prices, you may want to price yours in the middle.

As I discussed earlier in this book, condition is a huge factor in pricing your items. If the items you see selling for top dollar are in like-new condition, but the item you are listing is in poor condition, you need to price accordingly.

However, if you see that the item typically brings in many bidders at *Auction,* you may want to try listing yours at *Auction,* too. While you can run an eBay *Auction* from one to ten days, I prefer listing them for seven days. Seven days gives potential customers an entire week to find your item listing and decide if they want to bid.

Note that if you have a particularly "hot" item that you have started at *Auction*, you will likely receive messages asking you to sell the item outright. This is a tell-tale sign that you should keep the item at *Auction* just as you listed it, as it indicates just how desirable it is. And it is also a good reminder that you were wise not to have added a *Buy It Now* option, as the bidding will likely go higher than the price you would have set.

If I think an item should realistically sell for $19.99, I will not list it at *Auction* for $9.99 with a $19.99 *Buy It Now* price as the item would likely end up only selling for $9.99, anyway. And if an item has the potential of selling for $50, I will not start it at an *Auction* of $9.99 with a *Buy It Now* of $19.99 as I am severely limiting my profit potential. In both cases, adding in the *Buy It Now* option would result in my items likely selling for less money.

While eBay started as an auction site, the landscape has changed significantly over the years. It is now tough to get the price you want for an item when you start it as an *Auction* as customers are becoming used to and now typically prefer to buy things at a set price rather than bidding on something and then having to wait up to a week to see whether they win. More than ever before, eBay is in direct competition with Amazon and Walmart, so you need to adjust your selling strategies to meet the changing times continually.

While I typically stick to listing my eBay items at *Buy It Now*, I will occasionally use *Auctions* to clear out stale inventory, especially clothing. *Auctions* are an excellent way to bring in traffic to my eBay Store, and even if someone does not bid on anything I have up at *Auction*, they may end up checking out my other listings and buying one of my *Buy It Now* items.

Best Offer: When you list an item for sale on eBay, you can allow buyers to send you offers via the *Best Offer* feature. There is no additional fee associated with adding the *Best Offer* option to your listings. You can add *Best Offer* to all or only some of your listings, and you can also remove it at any time if you change your mind. It is easy to add *Best Offer* to your listings; you can do so individually within the listing itself by checking the box under the price to enable customers to submit offers to you.

If you want to add *Best Offer* to multiple listings, the **Bulk Edit** feature makes adding and removing options such as *Best Offer* easy; just go to your **Seller Hub** and click on **Listings**. Select **Active** from the drop-down menu and click on the boxes next to the listings you want to edit. Then click on **Edit** and select **Edit Selected** from the drop-down menu. You will then be taken to a page where you can bulk-add, edit, or remove features, including price, payment, and shipping.

When dealing with *Best Offer,* remember that you can choose to accept or decline offers automatically, or you can choose to review each offer personally. For instance, if you have an item priced at $50, you can choose to accept any offer of $40 or more automatically; and you can choose to decline any offers under $24.99 automatically.

However, as I said, you can leave the settings open to review every offer. Some sellers prefer to review all offers manually and never set up an auto-decline price as they believe that it is best to attempt to negotiate with anyone who sends an offer. And there is evidence that just getting offers helps your listings show up higher in the search results as the eBay algorithm favors activity. However, what you decide to do is up to you.

When you get an offer on an item, you have 48 hours to review it and respond. You can accept the offer, and the buyer will automatically be committed to completing the purchase and the payment should process automatically. The same is not true yet for auctions, however, although eBay is promising that immediate payment for auction wins is coming any day.

Back to receiving a *Best Offer:* Note that you can also outright refuse any offers, closing the communication between you and the buyer. If that buyer wants to send you another offer, they will have to start the *Best Offer* process again. Some buyers like to send ridiculously low offers, such as offering $1 for a $50 item. These people have no genuine interest in buying the item, so I do not engage with them; I simply decline their offer. If they continue to message me or submit more low offers, I will block them.

However, if you get a reasonable offer, you can choose to send the customer a counteroffer; most sellers send counteroffers for reasonable offers from buyers who they suspect really want the item. Let's go back to that $50 item. You have it listed at *Fixed Price* with the *Best Offer* option. A potential customer sends you an offer of $30. You can then send a counteroffer of, say, $40. If the buyer accepts, they are committed to the purchase and payment should process instantly. However, the customer may want to continue negotiating by submitting a counteroffer to you of $35; again, you can accept this or counteroffer yourself, either for your original $40 offer or, for one, a couple of dollars less, say $38.

Sometimes, however, counteroffers are not accepted or completely ignored. While this can be frustrating, it is just a part of the unique eBay selling platform. Don't get discouraged by customers who send lowball offers or refuse your counteroffers; move on, and eventually, the right buyer will come along. Again, many sellers believe that just the fact that someone has engaged with your listing by sending an offer helps the item show up higher in eBay's search algorithm as the action tells the eBay system that people are interested in the item and that it has the potential to sell. And at the end of the day, eBay is a business; they want your items to sell just as much as you do so that they can charge you *Final Value Fees* on top of your *Insertion Fees* and *Store Subscription Fees*.

Note that you want to carefully review all offers to ensure the offer does not include a change to the shipping price. I have had buyers send me an offer that also stipulated I would give them free shipping. For instance, they would offer me $10 plus free shipping for an item I had listed for $20, with the buyer paying the postage cost. Had I accepted those terms, I would have essentially had to PAY to ship them the item. So, be very careful to understand the terms you agree to when you accept a *Best Offer*.

Regarding adding the *Best Offer* option to my listings, I only do this after an item has been listed for a month or so. If I list something for $50 and after 30 days it hasn't sold, I might end the listing and then relist it (using the **Sell similar** option to show up as a brand-new listing on eBay's site) in the *Best Offer* option. I typically do not do this the first time around as I want to try for the maximum selling price, and when you have the *Best Offer* option active, most customers are likely to try and negotiate.

I set my *Best Offer* listings to automatically decline any offer that is less than 50% of my asking price. If I were willing to take half for an item, I would just list it for that. As for which offers I will accept, I look carefully at the item itself, what I originally paid for it, how long I have had it listed, and what I think it should go for. I will generally accept offers of 25% or less off my asking price; if the offer is between 26-51% off my asking price, I will usually send a counteroffer to try to get closer to the 25% off mark. However, some sellers happily engage with any customer who sends offers. What you decide to do is up to you and how much time (and patience!) you have for fielding offers.

I only negotiate sale prices using the official eBay *Best Offer* feature; I do NOT accept offers or make deals using the eBay messaging system or with people who email me directly. It is very common for buyers to message sellers directly with their offer terms, including requests for free shipping; I generally ignore these messages or reply by telling them that I only negotiate on items that have the *Best Offer* option on them.

Do not let potential customers bully you into selling your items for less. Buyers who send direct messages asking for a discount usually do so because they know that the item is indeed worth what you have listed it for, and they are trying to snatch it away before another buyer comes along. Or if you have the item up for *Auction*, they know that it will have multiple bidders and are trying to get you to sell it to them outright, so they do not have to compete in a bidding war.

Offers To Watchers: A recent feature of eBay's site is sellers' ability to send offers to interested customers. When someone "watches" an eBay item, eBay allows the seller to send an offer. You can choose a percentage or a set amount of the item's price, and the customer has 48 hours to accept. You can also enable the customer to submit a counteroffer. Sellers do not see the user's name of the person they send the offer to.

For me, *Offers To Watchers* has proven to be the most effective way to generate a sale. It has worked better for me than either allowing buyers to submit offers or running sales in my store. I typically send offers out once or twice a week. eBay makes sending offers incredibly easy. When you access your *Active Listings* in your *Seller Hub*, you will see a highlighted **Send offers – eligible** button highlighted above your listings. Clicking on this will take you to a new page to see all the items that currently have watchers.

You can choose to send offers through each individual listing, or you can send offers on all the items by bulk selecting all the listings, clicking on the **Send Offer** button, and choosing your terms. You can choose to offer a percentage off, or a dollar amount off. Although eBay provides an automated "Here's your chance to get this item at a great price!" option, you can add a personalized message. And you can also allow counteroffers from those to whom you send offers.

Buyers have 48 hours to either decline or accept offers, although they can and often ignore them as not all watchers are buyers, but are sellers watching items to see how to price theirs. Or it may just be someone who is curious to see what an item eventually sells for. So, don't be discouraged if you send out several offers and get no response. I still get enough of a response from customers who are interested in purchasing the items that it is worth it to me to send out offers regularly.

Pricing: While I do a completed listing search for every item I list on eBay to determine a price, I tend to stick to a few key price points: $9.99, $24.99, $49.99, and $99.99. I chose these amounts for two reasons: One, these were the price points eBay used to charge different fees for back when I first started selling on their site, and while they no longer do this, it was this way for years, and I've yet to break the habit.

Two, customers have been trained to look for prices ending in 99 cents. After all, aren't you more willing to buy something priced at $24.99 instead of $26.45? When a customer chooses between spending UNDER $25 or OVER $25, even if the difference is only pennies and the shipping is more expensive or slower, they are more likely to spend the price point under the threshold.

Sticking to these price points has worked well for me over the years. Of course, if I have researched and found that an item is selling for a different amount, I will undoubtedly price it accordingly. And I will also accept offers or run sales for lesser amounts. These numbers are my base prices, not always my final prices.

Many sellers will price items at $9.97 or $24.98, hoping their items will appear before $9.99 or $24.99 in eBay searches. However, it is essential to remember that EBay shows items based on the *total* price, including shipping. So, if your shipping is higher than the competition, your listing will still appear after other listings despite any difference in the item's price. And factors such as photos and keyword-loaded titles also factor heavily into where eBay places your item in the search.

For auctions, I generally will not start the bidding lower than $9.99 unless I know for sure that I have a very desirable item OR if I just want to move stale inventory. If you start your auction at 99 cents, do so only if you are using the auction to draw traffic to your other listings, you are trying to move old items, or you are confident that a bidding war will ensue. Otherwise, don't be upset when your item only sells for 99 cents.

eBay is flooded with 99-cent items, so be careful not to devalue your items by getting them lumped into the 99-cent listings that permeate the site. Even upping your starting bid to $1.99 or $2.99 will help cover your fees if your item only sells for the opening bid. And you can always add a dollar or two to your shipping fee to act as a buffer. I have seen many successful sellers run 99-cent auctions with a $9.99 shipping charge to ensure that all fees are covered and that they make a small profit off the overage the buyer paid in postage.

The bottom line is that you want to price your items at the amount you will be happy with. If you want at least $20 for something, do not start the auction at $5; start it at $19.99. Many new sellers lose money by pricing their items too low, both at *Auction* and *Fixed Price.* These sellers do not make as much money, and the item itself gets devalued across the board. Again, do your research to determine what your item goes for on average and price yours accordingly. You may realize that it is almost always best for you to list them at *Fixed Price* for the types of items you sell, so you make precisely what the item is worth.

Immediate Payment: One way to protect yourself from customers clicking to buy your items but not paying is to require *Immediate Payment.* This can only be done on *Buy It Now* items, not *Auctions.* And it may not be practical for you if you are a seller that frequently sells multiple items in the same transaction as it prevents you from combining a customer's order. For instance, if you specialize in golf accessories, you may sell several items in one transaction to the same customer; and sending them an invoice with combined shipping is essential as the eBay combined shipping system will likely overcharge them. However, if you are like me and sell primarily unique, individual items, requiring *Immediate Payment* can save you the hassle of dealing with non-paying buyers.

TO RECAP: One of the biggest benefits of selling on eBay is that they offer so many different ways for sellers to list their items. However, these numerous options can be overwhelming for new sellers. My advice is to stick to the basics when you are just starting. As you get more comfortable with reselling, you can start to experiment with different options to find the features that work best for you and your business!

CHAPTER SEVEN: EBAY SHIPPING MADE EASY

Now for the most confusing part of selling on eBay for new sellers: **Shipping!**

While I touched on shipping in several previous parts of this book, in this chapter, I will dig into the details and walk you step-by-step through all your options, including how to print your shipping labels. This chapter has some overlap from earlier in this book, but readers have asked for a dedicated section where everything is located, so here it is!

There are dozens of carriers and ways you can ship packages. While UPS and FedEx are viable shipping options, when you sell on eBay, you will want to stick with shipping your packages through the United States Postal Service (USPS), especially when you are just starting out. The USPS provides the best value and service for small sellers, and eBay has partnered with them to make shipping easy and cost-effective. Shipping your packages through eBay costs significantly less than taking them to your local Post Office and paying at the counter. Since the USPS is eBay's preferred shipping partner, if you sell on eBay, you will be using them a lot.

While there are numerous ways you can ship a package through the USPS, most EBay sellers ship via one of four methods, all of which are for shipments within the United States (including San Juan, Puerto Rico, and military bases):

- **First Class Mail**
- **Media Mail**
- **Ground Advantage**
- **Priority Mail**

First Class Mail: *First Class Mail* is for flat letter envelopes that can be shipped using stamps. The minimum size is 5x3.5x.007-inches and the maximum size is 11.5x6x.25-inches. Only certain categories on eBay will allow you to print *First Class Mail* labels: trading cards, coins and paper money, postcards, and stamps. If you are selling other pieces of ephemera that you can ship via *First Class Mail*, you will have to use stamps.

Media Mail: *Media Mail* is for, surprise, MEDIA! It is preferable to ship books via *Media Mail* because they are heavy, and you get a discounted rate. However, the low price also means that *Media Mail* is extremely slow, sometimes taking up to one month (although the Post Office claims delivery is two to eight business days).

The following items qualify to be shipped via *Media Mail*:

- **Books of at least eight printed pages**
- **16-millimeter or narrower-width films and catalogs of films 24 pages or more**
- **Printed music**
- **Educational testing materials and printed educational materials**
- **Sound recordings**
- **Playscripts and manuscripts**
- **Loose-leaf pages and their binders of educational medical information**
- **Computer-readable media**

Media Mail can NOT be used for advertising, video games, computer drives, or digital drives. The maximum weight for a *Media Mail* package is 70 pounds.

Some sellers try to cheat the system by shipping heavy, non-media items via *Media Mail*. This is a violation of the USPS policy and can result in you losing your postal account. Post offices are notorious for opening boxes marked as *Media Mail* to ensure they only contain approved media items, so be careful to follow the rules.

Media Mail items can only be shipped in plain boxes or envelopes, NOT in the *Priority Mail* boxes. When you print a label via eBay (more on how to do this coming up), it will clearly state on the label which service you paid for. So, if you print a *Media Mail* label, it will say "MEDIA MAIL" at the top. eBay has also cracked down on *Media Mail* misuse by only allowing sellers to select it in approved categories.

Ground Advantage: In 2023, the USPS eliminated *First Class Package* (for packages weighing between 4 and 15 ounces) and *Parcel Select* (a cheaper yet slower option versus *Priority* for packages weighing a pound or more), combining the two services into the newly branded *Ground Advantage*. Ground Advantage is now for all packages weighing four ounces or more.

USPS promotes *Ground Advantage* as "an affordable and reliable way to send packages inside the United States" with a delivery time frame of 2-5 business days. *Ground Advantage* ships to all 50 states, U.S. military bases, territories, possessions, and Freely Associate States. This is the shipping method for sending hazardous materials that can't ship via air.

Ground Advantage shipments must be in plain boxes or envelopes; just as with *Media Mail,* you can NOT ship *Ground Advantage* shipments in *Priority Mail* boxes. The maximum weight for *Ground Advantage* packages is 70 pounds.

Ground Advantage postage cost depends on the weight of the package and where it is going. That is why you always want to use eBay's *Calculated Shipping* as the customer pays for the exact shipping for their zip code.

While *Ground Advantage* is an excellent option for packages weighing under one pound or one to four pounds, you want to make sure to check the cost between *Ground* and *Priority* when you are creating your shipping label through eBay (again, I will be going over how to do this coming up). Depending on how far away the package is going, *Priority Mail* may be the cheaper option.

For example, I am in Iowa, centrally located on both coasts in the middle of the country. For packages weighing between one and four pounds, it is often cheaper for me to ship via *Priority* over *Ground*. Plus, I get to use a free *Priority Mail* shipping box, and I get a discount on postage by shipping directly through eBay.

For packages under 1 pound or over 4 pounds, it is now less for me to ship via *Ground Advantage*. While *Priority Mail* takes up to three days to arrive, *Ground* takes up to five. This is a big improvement over the old *Parcel* option, which sometimes took up to two weeks. And for packages under 1 pound, Ground has proven to be the same cost as the old First Class Package rate. Faster shipping at a lower cost is a great feature of *Ground* over *Parcel.* The only disadvantage is that you cannot use free *Priority Mail* boxes, but rather have to find plain boxes for shipping.

What is great about shipping through eBay is you can look at all the package and price options before paying for and printing a label. That way, you can find the best rate AND fastest shipping time for each order. My goal is always to get customers their orders as quickly as possible, and the new *Ground Advantage* helps me achieve that while also keeping costs in line.

Priority Mail: *Priority Mail* is for packages weighing over 4 ounces that need to get to their location quickly, typically 2-3 business days. Note that "business days" means weekdays and does not include Saturdays, Sundays, or federal holidays. If you ship an item out on a Friday, realize that it may not be processed and scanned at your area Post Office until Monday. From there, it will have an additional two to three days before it reaches the customer.

As I explained above when discussing *Ground Advantage,* sometimes *Priority Mail* can be the cheaper option. For me, this is often true for packages weighing less than four pounds that go as far as the East or West coasts. I also get a shipping discount because I ship directly through eBay, and I get the *Priority Mail* boxes for free. In fact, since I mainly sell small items, most of my shipments go via *Priority Mail* as nine times out of ten, it ends up being the cheapest option for packages between one and four pounds. I do, however, ship packages weighing between 4 and 15 ounces via *Ground Advantage* as the savings are usually a few dollars over Priority.

Both *Ground Advantage* and *Priority Mail* include FREE tracking when you purchase the label online, insurance up to $100, Saturday delivery, and FREE **Carrier Pickup.** I utilize *Carrier Pickup* to have my mail carrier pick up my packages and scan them in immediately. Since I work from home, *Carrier Pickup* is a blessing as I do not have to make multiple trips to the Post Office every week!

Of course, the best thing about *Priority Mail* is the FREE boxes! As we discussed earlier in this book, there are many sizes of *Priority Mail* boxes, including *Regular* and *Flat Rate.* If you are just starting on eBay, I recommend ordering 10-count packages of all the available boxes and envelopes (JUST the regular *Priority* and *Flat Rate* options, not the *Express* and *Overnight* versions) so that you will have an adequate supply on hand. The boxes are FREE, and your postal carrier will deliver them right to your door for FREE, too!

While the Post Office promotes their *Flat Rate* boxes and envelopes as having the best postage costs, regular *Priority Mail* is usually cheaper for packages less than four pounds. Why? When it comes to *Priority Mail,* it is not just the weight but also the distance a package has to travel.

As I mentioned previously, I live in Iowa. I can send a two-pound package to Minnesota for a little over $9. However, that same package costs over $13 to ship to California. If that package goes to New York, the postage is around $12. To Hawaii or Alaska, the cost jumps to $16. Again, it is not just the weight but the distance the package must travel.

The type of *Priority Mail* box (*Regular* or *Flat Rate*) does not affect the speed of delivery. *Priority* is *Priority*. The difference in the shipping cost depends on the type and size of the box.

Regular Priority Mail: A regular *Priority Mail* box is priced by weight and the zip code to which it is being shipped. You can also ship *Priority Mail* packages in regular boxes and envelopes, not only in the branded *Priority* boxes. The label that prints off from eBay is branded as *Priority*. Still, we also keep *Priority Mail* stickers (again, FREE from the Post Office) on hand to ensure the package is easily spotted as *Priority* as the postal carriers do their initial package sorting. The stickers are also nice for covering up writing on boxes that we are repurposing.

The maximum weight for a *Priority Mail* package is 70 pounds. If you are using your own box, note that the maximum combined length and girth are 108 inches, which means the combined measurement of the longest side and the distance around the package's thickest part cannot be more than 108 inches. An easier method I use is to aim for boxes that are no bigger than 12x12x12 inches as boxes over this size are oversized and cost more. I keep a small supply of 14x14x14-inch and 16x16x16-inch boxes on hand, but I ship those sizes via *Ground Advantage* or *UPS Ground*. With increasing postage rates and limits on box sizes these days, I try to stick to items that fit in 12x12x12-inch boxes or smaller, just to make my life easier!

As I mentioned, the Post Office provides FREE *Priority Mail* stickers to put on plain boxes and envelopes. I keep a roll of stickers on hand for when we ship *Priority* packages in plain boxes. But don't feel that you must use the stickers; the shipping labels are designated as *Priority*. The *Priority* stickers are just another shipping supply item we like to keep on hand.

Flat Rate Priority Mail: *Flat Rate* envelopes and boxes have a set price. You can pack them up to 70 pounds and pay one flat rate no matter where the package is going. However, there are various sizes of *Flat Rate* boxes and envelopes, each with its own price. Note that the prices are cheaper online than at the Post Office counter. For example, a *Priority Padded Flat Rate Envelope* costs $8.80 when you print the label through eBay. At the Post Office, it will cost you $10.40 to ship the same package.

However, while the Post Office heavily promotes *Flat Rate* boxes as the best option, *Flat Rate* is often more expensive than shipping via regular *Priority*. For instance, say you have a ceramic dish that weighs three pounds once it is in a shipping box. Putting it in a *Medium Flat Rate Box* will cost over $14 to ship anywhere in the country. Now, if you are in Florida and your buyer is in California, that works out to be a great deal. However, if your buyer lives in your state or in a surrounding one, you could save as much as $7 in postage by choosing regular *Priority Mail.*

Again, by using eBay's shipping tool, you will be able to see and compare all the available options to find the best deal on postage for each order. However, note that if a customer pays for *Priority*, you need to ship the item *Priority*. *Priority* is an *Expedited Service* and is the fastest option compared to *Media* or *Ground Advantage*. So, if your buyer pays for *Priority* but you downgrade them to *Ground,* they are rightfully going to be angry and will file a claim against you on eBay.

Regional Priority Mail: In 2023, USPS eliminated the *Regional Priority Mail* boxes. If you have any of these boxes on hand, you can still use them for shipping regular *Priority Mail* packages.

More About Priority Mail: When packages are sorted for shipment at the Post Office, the most expensive postage options go first as they are guaranteed space on the trucks and planes. *Overnight* and *Express* are obviously the most expensive since customers pay for one-to-two-day delivery. *Media Mail* and *Bulk Mail* (bulk mail is usually "junk" mail that is sent out in mass) are the cheapest and, therefore, the last packages to be put out for delivery. It is all about available space; the more room on the truck or plane, the more packages they will ship out.

The Post Office promotes *Priority Mail* as being delivered in two to three business days. Again, that is BUSINESS days, i.e., WEEKDAYS. While some large postal facilities process mail on the weekends, the vast majority do not. Mail and packages are not processed on federal holidays, either. eBay stands behind sellers in shipping times when it comes to mailing out orders on weekends and holidays; keep these rules in mind if you have a customer demanding that the order they placed on Friday arrive by Monday!

After *Priority*, *First Class Mail* is next as it can also be shipped via air. *Ground Advantage*, which is typically shipped via truck or train, is next. Last are *Media Mail* and *Bulk Mail*. It is always in your best interest as a seller to use the fastest option available, depending on the price. The faster the customer receives their order, the happier they will be!

International Shipping: International shipping used to be such a massive headache that most sellers avoided it altogether. While you certainly do not need to ship to Canada, South America, or overseas, doing so will significantly increase your business. Fortunately, eBay offers its **International Shipping Program** (formerly called *Global Shipping*). While the program is technically optional, eBay will most likely put you in it whether you opt-in or not. I specifically opted OUT of the program twice, only to be put back in it. However, now that I am enrolled, it has been smooth sailing, and I kick myself for waiting so long to opt in.

When a seller offers *International Shipping,* their international packages are sent to a sorting facility here in the United States. So, when I get an international order, the label that prints out and the postage paid is to a Kentucky facility. After the package arrives at the facility, eBay takes full responsibility for it, including filling out customs forms and putting on the postage to send to the buyer's country. Once a package reaches the eBay facility, it is entirely in eBay's hands, meaning if it is lost or if it arrives damaged, eBay, not the seller, is responsible.

Because international shipping is now so easy using eBay's *International Shipping* program, there is no reason not to opt into it. Opening your sales to international customers will significantly increase your sales, and now printing a label is as easy as printing one for the United States.

However, some sellers still prefer to ship internationally on their own. While I certainly do not recommend that new eBay sellers who are struggling with shipping within the United States try tackling international shipping, too, here are some essential points for those of you who at least want to know a bit more about how to ship your eBay orders internationally if you are not using eBay's *International Shipping Program:*

- International orders ship via *First Class Mail International* (letters), *First Class Package International* (packages up to four pounds), *Priority Mail International* (6-10 days for packages weighing four pounds or more up to 70 pounds), *Priority Mail International Flat Rate* (same as regular *Priority Mail International*), *Priority Mail Express International* (3-5 business days), and *Global Express Guaranteed* (1-3 business days).

- While shipping a letter via *First Class Mail* to Canada may only cost a few dollars, most international shipments cost much more. Therefore, if you offer international shipping, you will want to ensure that the buyer pays the postage cost to have the item delivered to their country.

- When you set up your domestic shipping, the same package weight and dimensions carry over to the international options. eBay's shipping calculator will determine the postage cost based on the buyer's location. Let's say you are listing a coffee mug in the 1-2-pound range; you will likely offer *Ground* and *Priority* for US customers and *First Class Package International* and *Priority Mail International* for international customers. eBay's *Shipping Calculator* will then do the rest.

- When you pay and print your shipping labels through eBay, the shipping label and the customs form will be printed out together. You simply sign the customs form and attach both the label and the customs form to your package.

- If you do not print your labels but instead take your packages to the Post Office for postage, note that you will need to fill out the customs forms there. The form requirements change frequently, so you will need a postal clerk to give you the correct forms and explain how to fill them out. This is just another reason you should print your shipping labels out yourself at home!

- Due to customs regulations in other countries, some buyers will ask you to mark their orders as a "Gift" to avoid paying customs fees. Note that this is illegal to do and could result in being suspended from using USPS services; be sure to tell any buyer who asks you to do this that you cannot and will not. Always mark international orders as "Merchandise." If the buyer persists, you can put in a cancellation order through eBay under the terms that the customer is asking you to violate a shipping policy.

If you ship international orders on your own, be aware that international packages' tracking varies greatly and is quite unreliable. More than the hassle of dealing with customs forms is the frustration of not always tracking international shipments. And without tracking, it is very easy for a customer to claim they never received their order, which means you will have to issue them a full refund. If you are shipping items yourself, you will ultimately be responsible for any lost or damaged packages. However, when you use eBay's *International Shipping Program*, eBay is accountable for any shipping issues.

While Canada, the United Kingdom, and Australia all offer easy-to-track, generally reliable shipments, there are some areas of the world you may want to consider avoiding if you are shipping outside of eBay's *International Shipping Program*. Before I shipped through eBay's *International Shipping Program*, I blocked several countries and regions, including Central and South America, Africa, the Middle East, and Italy.

While the other European countries offer fairly reliable shipping, Italy is notorious for holding packages up in customs and losing them. Mexico and other South American countries also offer poor tracking, and shipping anywhere in Africa or the Middle East is risky as many online scams originate from those countries. Most international customers who buy from American eBay sellers are in Canada, England, and Australia; for many years, those were the only areas I would sell to.

Once a shipment arrives in the buyer's country, it must first go through customs. As I have mentioned, some countries do this very quickly, while others (Italy) are notoriously slow. International shipping can take as little as a week to arrive in Canada or up to a month or more for countries overseas. When I shipped internationally on my own, I always dealt with messages from overseas buyers wanting to know where their packages were. But by using eBay's *International Shipping*, I never hear from international customers as EBay handles any questions about their packages.

So, those are the basics of shipping internationally on your own. While it can offer cost savings to the customer as they do not pay both you AND eBay for postage, the time and confusion for new sellers can be too much. Doesn't using eBay's *International Shipping Program* sound much better? It is so easy, and eBay protects you from lost or damaged packages. I will never go back to shipping internationally on my own!

How To Set Up Shipping In Your Listings: So now that you understand the basic four categories of USPS shipping options, it is time to choose the ones you want to offer for your listings. One of the biggest mistakes new eBay sellers make is to guess shipping costs, resulting in either overcharging customers or undercharging them and losing money on shipping. However, **Calculated Shipping** will protect you and your customers from incorrect postage costs.

I firmly believe in using *Calculated Shipping* on eBay for packages. If you have a digital scale, there is no reason not to use it. *Calculated Shipping* means the buyer pays the exact shipping cost for the item's weight and the zip code it is being shipped to.

While more seasoned eBay sellers like to experiment with "free" shipping (i.e., building the shipping cost into the price of an item), I recommend you stick to *Calculated Shipping* when you are just starting out and have the buyer pay shipping. This will protect you from LOSING money by trying to guess shipping costs. It also ensures a fair shipping rate for the customer, which means you will not get angry customers who figure they were overcharged for shipping. You can experiment with "free" shipping once you are more comfortable selling and shipping.

Oh, and the reason I always put "free" in quotes is that shipping is never free. Someone has to pay for it, either you or your customer.

So, you have a digital postage scale and are ready to create a listing using *Calculated Shipping*. It is so easy to do. We already covered creating an eBay listing in the previous chapter. But we'll go over the steps of setting up shipping in a listing more in-depth now.

First, **put the item you are listing into a box similar to the one it will ship out in**. Note that the box does not have to be the exact one you will end up shipping the item in; you just want a box close to the size and weight of the one you will be using. Boxes can easily add up to one pound of weight to a shipment, with larger boxes adding up to two pounds, so you definitely need to know the general type of box you will use.

For example, if you are selling a coffee mug, place it in a 7x7x6-inch *Priority Mail* box or a similar-sized plain cardboard box. Set the box on the digital scale and note the weight. Perhaps it comes out to 1 pound and 4 ounces.

Within eBay's listing form, under **SHIPPING**, you will first see the field for your **Shipping policy**. Here you can set up your shipping options. I have **Calculated Ground Advantage/Priority** selected for all of my listings except those that qualify for *Media Mail*. Remember that *Ground Advantage* is the economy option while *Priority* is the expedited option. I like to give customers the option of which to pay for.

The next field is **Package weight.** There are two sections, one for **pounds** and one for **ounces**. Using the coffee mug example that weighs 1 pound 4 ounces, you are likely thinking that you should enter 1 pound 4 ounces into the fields, right?

WRONG!

When you are dealing with postage weights, you do not need to know the exact weight, only the ranges. Under 1 pound, 1 to 2 pounds, 2 to 3 pounds, etc. And when you know the range, you simply round up. If the package weighs under 1 pound, you can enter 15 ounces. If the package, like our coffee mug example, weighs 1 pound 4 ounces, you round up to 2 pounds. If you have a package that weighs between 2 and 3 pounds, you round up to 3 pounds.

Understanding that you only need to round up to the highest weight between the two ranges will make your shipping process go much more smoothly!

PRO TIP: For packages weighing under 1 pound, there is a slight difference in the ounce ranges, which are 4 ounces to 7 ounces, 8 ounces to 11 ounces, and 12 ounces to 15 ounces. You can do the same here as with pounds by rounding up to the highest range. For example, if you have a package that weighs 13 ounces, you can enter 13 ounces or round it up to 15 ounces. I realize this is a bit confusing when you are just starting, so it's perfectly fine to list all packages that weigh under 1 pound at 15 ounces. The difference in cost is minor. Even I usually just use the 15-ounce weight to make things easy!

eBay used to have you enter weight ranges in this section. For instance, you could select 1 to 2 pounds, 2 to 3 pounds, 3 to 4 pounds, etc. However, in late 2022, eBay changed the listing form. Now you must enter a package weight in pounds and ounces, but again, you just need to round up. If the item you are selling will ship within the 1-to-2-pound range, you simply enter 2 lbs 0 oz under **Package weight**. By entering in 2 pounds, it will cover the postage for items that weigh in the 1-to-2-pound range when shipped.

Because you are rounding up to the nearest pound, you do not need to worry about exact ounces. In fact, because the box will actually weigh MORE when it ships out due to packing materials, an initial weight with exact ounces would no longer be correct.

See how easy it is when you only need to know the weight RANGE and ROUND UP? Under 1 pound rounded up to 15 ounces. 1 to 2 pounds rounded up to 1 pound. 2 to 3 pounds rounded up to 3 pounds. Easy

PRO TIP: Packing materials can add more weight than you may realize to packages. When I am getting an initial weight on an item, I use a box with some packing materials stuffed in it such as bubble wrap, packing peanuts, and/or packing paper. Adding these materials can easily push the weight of a box into the next pound range, so always make sure you are thinking ahead to what a package will weigh once the item is completely wrapped up.

The next section under **SHIPPING** is **Package dimensions** with three fields to add the size of the shipping box in inches. While you technically don't need to enter exact box measurements unless the package is oversized or irregular, eBay wants you to enter something in these fields.

My trick is to just enter 12x12x12 inches into these fields as that is the maximum size for regular *Priority Mail.* Most of my packages are smaller than 12x12x12 inches, but it doesn't matter. The system just wants to make sure your package isn't oversized. If, when you go to finally print your shipping label, you can certainly enter the exact box measurements if you want to. But unless the box is oversized or irregular, it honestly doesn't make a difference in the cost of postage.

Oversized packages are defined as large packages whose length plus girth is over 84 inches, and less than or equal to 165 inches. You can only send packages with length plus girth between 130 inches and 165 inches through UPS, not USPS.

If your package can't be sorted with mail processing equipment because of its size or shape, it is classified as **Irregular.** Examples include the following:

◇ Boxes larger than 34 inches long or 17 inches wide or 17 inches high

◇ A square envelope

◇ An envelope on which the address is written parallel to the shorter edge

◇ A glass container with more than 24 ounces of liquid

◇ A metal container with 1 or more gallons of liquid

◇ A plastic container with 1 or more gallons of liquid

◇ An insecurely wrapped parcel

◇ A metal banded parcel

◇ A wooden or metal box

◇ A tube or roll

◇ A book, printed matter, or business forms weighing more than 25 pounds

◇ A high-density parcel weighing more than 15 pounds and exerting more than 60 pounds of pressure per square foot on its smallest side

◇ A film case weighing more than 5 pounds or with strap-type closures, except any film case the USPS authorizes to be entered as a machinable parcel and to be identified by the words "Machinable in United States Postal Service Equipment" permanently attached as a nontransferable decal in the lower right corner of the case

Printing Shipping Labels: So, what do you do when you've made a sale and need to print a shipping label? You proceed to the next chapter, where I will walk you through the entire process!

CHAPTER EIGHT: PROCESSING ORDERS

Finally, the most exciting part of selling on eBay has arrived: You have SOLD something! Now it is time to print your label and package up the order.

If you want eBay to notify you via email or even text when you have made a sale, simply **log into your account and look for the "Hi, (your name)" text in the upper left-hand corner of the page**.

From the **drop-down menu**, click on **Account Settings.** You will be taken to your **My eBay page,** where you can access your account settings and preferences, including:

- **Personal Info**
- **Payment Information**
- **Account Preferences**
- **Selling**
- **Donation Preferences**

Under **Account Preferences**, click on **Communication Preferences.** Scroll down to the **Seller** section and click **Edit** next to **Selling Activity.** Here you can select when you would like eBay to send you notifications. Note that you can edit this section at any time. I have the following notifications set:

- Item Sold
- Shipping reminder after handling time has passes
- Item shipped
- Item received
- Refund issued

Note that not selecting options doesn't mean they won't show up for you in your Seller Hub. It just means your email inbox won't be filled with notifications. And in all honesty, the most important notification is **Item Sold** as you want to ship orders as quickly as possible.

If you are using the **eBay App**, you can also set up notifications to be delivered to your cell phone whenever you make a sale. Simply **open the eBay app**. Tap the **My eBay icon** at the bottom of the screen. Click on **Settings** at the bottom of the screen. You will be taken to a new screen with several options for both buying and selling.

PRO TIP: Take time to set up your eBay app account the same way you did on your desktop. The eBay app is available on both Apple and Android devices. These days you can run your entire eBay business on your phone, although I still prefer to do most tasks on my desktop computer. And there's nothing better than hearing the CHA-CHING sound when something sells! However be careful about how high the volume is set on your phone as you don't want to startle those around you when you are in a public place, haha!

Back to processing your first order: If you have an order or message waiting for you, there will be a notification on the **Bell** icon at the top of the page that you can click on. Or you can go straight to your **Seller Hub** (remember, click on the **Sell** link at the top of any eBay page to go directly there), and click on the **Orders** tab at the top of the page. If you have an order awaiting shipment, eBay will default to the Manage orders awaiting shipment page. But note that there are other options on the left-hand side of the page, including:

- **All orders**
- **Awaiting payment** (you can send invoices from here to anyone who hasn't paid)
- **Awaiting shipment** (a list of orders that have been paid for

and need to be shipped)
- **Paid and shipped** (a record of recent orders that you have already shipped)
- **Cancellations** (orders that either you or a buyer has requested to cancel)
- **Returns** (even if you don't offer returns, this link will still be there)
- **Requests and disputes** (orders that have open claims with eBay)
- **Shipping** labels (if you need to reprint a shipping label because it didn't print correctly the first time or you misplaced it, you can easily print a new one here)

Clicking on the **Awaiting shipment** link will bring up a new window setting titled **Manage orders awaiting shipment** with a list of orders that need to be shipped. You will notice that within each section for every item, there is a tiny down arrow that opens a drop-down menu. Here you will find numerous options:

- **Print shipping label**
- **Cancel order**
- **View payment details**
- **Add/edit note**
- **Relist**
- **Sell similar**
- **Contact buyer**
- **Report buyer**
- **Send refund**
- **View order details**
- **Archive**

If the buyer has yet to pay for the item they won at auction, you will also see a **Send an Invoice** option. Note that some buyers will wait for you to send them an invoice after winning an auction, even though the shipping options are already set up for them. Fortunately, a quick click sends an invoice, so be prepared to do that occasionally. And you will also need to send an invoice to anyone who buys two or more items from you to combine shipping for them. But for customers who have purchased a single item at *Buy It Now*, their payment should go through automatically, so there will be no need to send an invoice.

I have my *But It Now* listings set so that buyers must pay immediately. However, buyers obviously cannot pay immediately when they are bidding on items through an *Auction*, so you will likely have to send invoices to auction winners.

If you have chosen to sell internationally using eBay's *International Shipping Program,* eBay will handle the invoicing for you. So, if someone in the United Kingdom buys an item from you, you will not be able to invoice them. eBay will do it on their end as they will be figuring out the shipping. This is because the customer will pay you the cost to send the item to eBay's *International Shipping* center, and then they will also pay eBay to ship that item internationally.

eBay requires sellers to give buyers at least four days to pay for their purchases. After that, a seller can cancel the order and an unpaid cancellation will be recorded on the buyer's account. eBay will also refund all of a seller's fees and, if you wish, relist the item for you.

If I do not have immediate payment required on an item and someone buys it but does not pay within an hour or so, I send them an invoice. Then the next day, I send a "friendly" reminder that their payment is due by the following business day. If they still do not pay after four days, I cancel the sale. While it is frustrating to have someone not pay for an item, in the end, there is nothing you can do except eventually cancel the sale, relist the item, and add the buyer to your **Blocked Bidders List,** which is located under the **Overview** tab in your **Seller Hub**. Scroll to the bottom of the page and, under **Shortcuts**, you will find the **Block bidders** link. Note, however, that most eBay customers do pay for their orders promptly.

Once a customer pays for their item, it is time to print out the shipping label. The default selection in the drop-down menu next to the item will be to **Print Shipping Label.** All you need to do is click on that link, and you will be taken to eBay's **Ship your order** page. Please note that sometimes you may have to log in a second time here due to eBay's tight security settings.

The eBay label printing screen has **Ship your order** at the top, with the **Order details** underneath. Listed here will be the **Ship to** address for the buyer and the **Ship from/Return to** (your) address. You only need to choose **Print format** once; eBay will remember it for the next time you go to ship an order. I have my settings at *PDF 8" x 11"* as I print on two-to-a-sheet mailing labels. However, eBay offers several label printing options to choose from. The 4" x 6" option is for those using thermal printers. You can also preview what the shipping label will look like.

You will also see the item that sold, which is clickable and will take you to a copy of the listing. And you will see the buyer's eBay screen name, the shipping service they selected (or that you chose for them when you set up the listing), the order value, the delivery charge, and the expected delivery date.

In the middle of the screen is the section called **Package.** This is where new eBay sellers typically get tripped up, so take a breath as we go through it. After you have shipped out a few packages, I promise this will become a routine step for you in no time!

Since you set up your shipping preferences when you created your listing, the selections here will match those from the listing. Let's say you are shipping that Ralph Lauren shirt we used as an example earlier in this book. It weighs under a pound, so you listed the Weight as 15 ounces and put 12x12x12 inches under Dimensions. Those choices are automatically entered for you here.

Now, you don't need a 12x12x12-inch box to ship out a shirt. But remember how we discussed box sizes earlier in this book? The *Dimensions* are in case a package is oversized, which for USPS is anything OVER 12x12x12 inches. As long as your package isn't oversized, you don't have to enter the exact *Dimensions* here, although eBay will ask you if your package size is correct. This is why I have 12x12x12-inches entered in all of my listings as I don't have to alter these numbers.

However, if you have the measurements for the box or envelope you are using, you can certainly change the *Dimensions*. I usually ship clothing in poly mailers that measure 12x9x2 inches. Because it's quick and easy to do, I would likely enter those dimensions in for the shirt.

The next section is **Service**. Here is where you will first select the carrier you are buying postage from. The system will default to the option you chose when you first listed the item, which was likely USPS. Note that FedEx and UPS are also options here, which are for oversized, heavy packages.

Next is a **Ship on** drop-down menu for you to select the date when your package will be mailed. I ship packages out the following business day after I have printed a label, but I usually just leave this field as-is, which is for the day I'm printing out the label. If you aren't shipping out the next business day, you will want to select the date you will be handing the package off to the Post Office.

The next section is **Service.** Here you will see ALL of the shipping options available through the carrier you are using. In this case, we are shipping through USPS, so every shipping service they offer will be listed here, including ones that your item may not even be eligible for, such as *Media Mail.* The shipping service your customer chooses will be chosen for you at the very top.

Remember that I usually offer *Ground Advantage* as the first option and *Priority Mail* as the second. Let's say that my customer chose *Priority Mail* for their order. In this case, *Priority Mail* would be selected at the top.

PRO TIP: Be sure to look at the prices for all of the qualifying services. For example, while *Ground Advantage* may have shown as the cheapest option to your customer when you are logged in to your account and looking at all of the shipping options for that order, you may find that *Priority Mail* costs the same or even a little bit less. This is because eBay sellers get a discount on USPS postage when they buy their labels through the system. Because of this discount, you could upgrade the package from *Ground* to *Priority.* Not only will your customer get their package faster, but you will also be able to use a free *Priority Mail* shipping box. If you change the postage option, make sure you are choosing an upgrade, not an option that will be slower than what the customer paid for.

There are some **Additional Options** available to you, including:

- **Require Signature at delivery** (because you, the seller, will have to pay for this service, and use it only for items of high value)
- **Add additional liability coverage** (this is added insurance that you, the seller, will have to pay for; only buy this if your item is valued at over $100 as the USPS automatically insures all packages up to $100)

- **Display postage value on the label** (I make sure this is NOT checked so that the buyer does not see that they may have paid a bit more for shipping than it cost)
- **Add custom text on the label** (this is if you want to add an inventory number)

I leave all these options unchecked. In fact, I rarely even notice them!

Underneath these options is **Shipping label format. Printable label** is the default selection here. The other option is **QR code**, which is a code that is saved to your phone for you to scan where you ship. This option requires you to take your package to a USPS location; you cannot use *Carrier Pickup.* This is not an option most eBay sellers use.

The final section of the shipping form is **Pay with.** There are two options here:

- **Your funds:** eBay will deduct the amount of the shipping label from the funds that are in your account from your sales. If there isn't enough money in your fund to cover the label, eBay will charge your backup funding account, which is the credit card, debit card, or bank account you have on file.
- **Your saved PayPal account:** Even though eBay no longer owns PayPal, PayPal is still a very popular option for online shoppers. eBay sellers and buyers used to be required to use PayPal, so many sellers still have their accounts linked. If, for some reason, you keep funds in a PayPal account, you can pay for your labels from that account. Most sellers, however, pay for shipping labels out of their funds. If your buyer paid for shipping, the amount they paid will be in your funds, and eBay will simply use that amount to

purchase your shipping label. However, if you offer "free" shipping, the amount will come out of the sale price of the item, so you will see a significant reduction in your balance.

And finally, you will see the total postage cost above a big blue button titled **Purchase and print label.** By clicking on that, your eBay shipping label will be purchased and a new window will open with your label for printing. You then attach the label to your package and either take it to the Post Office or request Carrier Pick-up.

And that's it: You've shipped your first eBay order!

Once your shipping label prints, the postage and the fees associated with the sale will be taken from your eBay pending balance account. The cost for the label is paid directly to the USPS within eBay's system. So once the label is printed, all your eBay fees and postage costs related to that order have been paid; you do not owe any more money to eBay or USPS regarding that order.

After you print your shipping label, you also have the option of printing a packing slip. Simply click on **Print packing slip** if you would like to print one. I always include a packing slip in my orders, but not all sellers do. Again, the decision is yours to make.

Reprinting a Label: If for any reason you need to reprint the label you already generated (perhaps it jammed in the printer or you accidentally misplaced it), simply click on **Shipping labels** on the left-hand side of your **Orders** page. This will bring up all of your orders. Simply find the order for the label you need to reprint and click on **Actions.** From the drop-down menu, you can **Print Another Label** and also **Print Packing Slip.**

Canceling An Order: Sometimes mistakes or accidents happen, and you cannot fulfill an order after the buyer has paid. Perhaps you misplaced the item and cannot find it. Or maybe the item broke when you were packing it up. In either case, you can cancel the order.

To cancel an order, find the order under **Manage all orders.**

From the drop-down menu next to the item, click on **Cancel order.** A new window will pop up where you will need to choose one of the following:

- **Out of stock or damaged**
- **Buyer asked to cancel**
- **Issue with buyer's shipping address**

If you choose that the item is out of stock or damaged, the cancellation will count as a strike against you for your **Top Seller Rating.** However, if a buyer asks to cancel the order, eBay will send them a confirmation. If the buyer confirms they want to cancel the order, there will be no consequences for you. The same is true if there is an issue with the buyer's address.

Regardless of the reason for canceling the order, eBay will issue a total refund to the buyer. If the buyer asks to cancel or there is an issue with their address, eBay will also refund you all fees associated with the sale.

PACKING YOUR ORDERS: Once your label has been printed, both you and the buyer will receive a notice from eBay that the package is in pre-transit along with the tracking number. Once the package is scanned in by the Post Office, tracking will be updated and you may be able to follow the package as it makes its way to your customer. I say you "may be able" because tracking doesn't always update on time.

But before USPS can begin tracking your package, you have to finish packing it up. Since you weighed the item in the box or envelope you planned to ship it in before you ever listed it, you will now want to go ahead and start packaging the item for shipment.

PRO TIP: Many resellers wait to print their shipping labels until AFTER they have packaged up their items. This is because, as we've discussed, packing materials such as bubble wrap, packing peanuts, packing paper, and the shipping boxes themselves add to the overall weight of orders. The larger the box, the heavier it is and the more it will weigh. And while you can get an idea of the weight of a package by weighing your item in a box before you list it, you won't know the actual weight until it is sealed. This is why I talk about bumping packages that are close to the next pound into the next range. If you weigh an item in a box and it weighs 1 pound 14 ounces, you will want to list it at the 3 pound range as once packing materials are added, the package will weigh over 2 pounds. And with *Ground Advantage* and *Priority Mail*, you round UP package weights.

Even when selling used items and using secondhand packing materials, it is still essential to take time to package up your items in a clean and professional manner. I keep all sorts of packaging materials on hand, everything from recycled packing paper to bubble wrap. As you are just starting out, try and use items from shipments you have gotten. If you do not have anything around, ask friends and family for any boxes, bubble wrap, and packing peanuts, they may have.

If you are just going to sell on eBay occasionally, you might be able to get most of your shipping supplies for free by reusing what you have or asking for people to give you their leftovers. However, it is important that whatever you use is CLEAN and from SMOKE-FREE HOMES! If you are a smoker, be sure to keep your inventory AND your packing supplies in an area away from the smoke. If your buyer detects even the slightest scent of cigarettes, they WILL complain!

Using a combination of packing paper, bubble wrap, and/or packing peanuts, carefully wrap the item you are shipping and ensure it is surrounded by a buffer of packaging material in the box. I use newspapers to create a barrier around the item and the box sides, but I always ensure the item itself is wrapped in paper or bubble wrap away from the newsprint to prevent any print from rubbing off on the item.

Once your item is securely packaged, use shipping tape to seal it. Make sure you press down on the tape to adhere it to the box and make sure any open seams are covered with tape. If the box has any bar codes on it, be sure to cover those with stickers or blackout with markers so that they don't interfere with the USPS scanning system. If you are repurposing a box, black out any personal information from any old labels, and use stickers or a marker to cover text and graphics. While you don't have to complete block writing and logos out, it's a good idea to cover them up as much as possible. If you are shipping the package via *Priority Mail*, you can use free *Priority Mail* stickers from the Post Office. And you can purchase eBay branded stickers right on their site.

PRO TIP: Once your package is sealed, pick it up and shake it. If you hear or feel anything inside moving around, open the box back up and add more packing materials. Packages are tossed around throughout the entire shipping process and even seemingly sturdy items can break from the motion. When you can't feel or hear the item inside of your shipping box moving, you will know it's packaged well.

If you are printing your shipping labels onto actual peel-and-stick labels, you will just need to remove the backing and stick the label to the package. However, if you are printing your labels onto paper, you must use clear packing tape to adhere the label to the outside of the box. It usually takes me three small pieces to cover the label and make sure it is stuck tightly. The only part of the label that I do NOT cover with tape is the bar code. You want to leave the bar code free of the tape so that the Post Office's scanning equipment can easily read it.

Once your label is affixed to your package, it is ready to be shipped out! If you are at home and can arrange for pickup, you will want to take advantage of the FREE *USPS Carrier Pickup* service where your postal carrier will pick up all your packages for free. Note that you need to request this service online the night before you want your packages picked up.

If you cannot be home for *Carrier Pickup* and need to take your packages to the Post Office, note that you will likely have to stand in line and hand them to a clerk. If you end up scaling your business to the level that you are shipping out multiple packages daily, be sure to develop a good relationship with the clerks, as they may allow you to leave your packages on the counter without standing in line. If you do hand them directly to a clerk, they can scan them and give you a receipt. I usually skip this since I have the tracking information from eBay loaded onto my account.

And that is it! Your order is packaged and ready to be shipped off to the buyer. Again, once you have printed the shipping label, eBay will notify the buyer that their order has shipped, providing both them and you with the tracking number. Both you and the buyer can then track the progress of the shipment. Note that the tracking numbers for each order are easily accessible next to the item itself in your *Seller Hub* list of orders that have shipped. Most buyers know how to access the tracking number, although new eBay users may not. So, it is not uncommon for buyers to ask you directly for the number.

Now that you have sold and shipped your first order, you are ready for the next one!

CHAPTER NINE: ADVERTISING YOUR EBAY BUSINESS

As I've noted previously when I first started selling online, eBay and Amazon were the only two e-commerce retailers. Customers who shopped online only had those two sites to choose from, so there was no need for sellers such as myself to seek out buyers as I was one of a small number of online stores.

However, nowadays, it is often not enough to simply list an item on eBay for it to sell; you now must do some promotion and marketing to drive sales, both on the eBay site directly as well as on social media platforms, to compete with the thousands of other eBay sellers and the other e-commerce sites out there.

Fortunately, most of these promotional tools are free and easy to use, especially when it comes to utilizing social media sites to promote your eBay listings. By adding some or all of the following marketing methods, you will see your eBay traffic and sales increase. In some cases, you may need to spend a little bit of money (such as if you decide to set up a website and/or have enclosures printed up); but even then, the costs are still relatively low compared to the huge differences these efforts can make for your sales.

Blog/Website: If eBay is your full-time business, it may be worth it for you to set up a blog or even a full-fledged website to further connect with customers. If you are going to have a site, however, be sure to commit to maintaining it. Nothing is worse than going to someone's blog and seeing that they have not updated it in months.

However, if you are only selling on eBay on a part-time level or less, then you do not need to burden yourself with the work of maintaining a site. Ask yourself the following questions:

- Do you plan to write lengthy articles discussing the items you sell?
- Are you looking to use your site not just as a sales channel but also as a teaching tool?
- Would you like to sell products directly from your website outside of eBay, or are you selling your items on other online sites (Amazon, Etsy) and/or at brick-and-mortar retail locations (your own shop or at an antique mall)?
- Would you like to explore affiliate advertising and/or sell advertising to earn extra money for your site?

If you answered "yes" to any of the above questions, then you may want to consider starting a site. However, you will need to decide whether to go with a free blogging platform or a paid website. If you decide to go the paid route, you can invest in a sophisticated system or choose a simple, low-cost one. Yes, there are lots of decisions to make!

Both **Blogger** and **WordPress** offer free blogging platforms. Note that **Google** owns *Blogger*; therefore, you can apply for a **Google AdSense** account and place ads on your blog. So not only will you be helping drive traffic to your eBay listings to increase sales, but you will also be able to earn advertising revenue.

However, if you decide to go with a paid website, do your research, as there are many out there to choose from. If your main business is selling on eBay, you want your *eBay Store* to be your brand, with your blog/website acting as an additional tool to drive traffic to your listings. There are a lot of low-cost website options out there. For instance, you can not only register for the website URLs on **GoDaddy.com,** but they also offer website inexpensive hosting and simple websites.

If you sell on other websites besides eBay, a blog/website is a great place to provide the links to those places (Amazon, Etsy, flea markets, and/or antique malls). In addition to posting about new inventory and sales, you can include photos and talk about what is happening behind the scenes with your business. Having a site gives people a more personal look at who you are. Also, it confirms that you are running a legitimate business, both of which can go a long way toward building up trust and reassuring people that they can buy from you with confidence.

Note that in addition to posting updates on your blog, you will need to maintain it. If you allow visitors to leave comments on your posts, you will want to make sure to respond to them. You also want to make sure all links are active and up-to-date so that people do not click through and get an error.

Suppose you are selling a significant number of items on eBay and plan to continue with it as your primary business. In that case, you really should register for a domain name, i.e., a personal website address that matches your *eBay Store* name. For years, I have maintained a URL of my *eBay Store* name that sends people directly to my *eBay Store*. Having a URL gives you an easy web address to share with customers that is shorter and easier to remember. You can purchase domain names on a website like *GoDaddy.com*.

You will also have to decide *where* you want the URL to direct users. Do you want people to go to your blog FIRST, or do you want them to always go to your eBay Store? Remember, you should use a blog/website to *complement* your eBay Store, not as a replacement. If you decide to go with a free blog on a site like *Blogger,* you may want to choose a URL that sends people directly to your *eBay Store* (i.e., www.MyStore.com) and keep the URL you get from *Blogger* for your website as-is. Or choose another URL, such as MyEBayStoreBlog.com, just for your site.

My advice is to have a personalized URL address that points to your *eBay Store,* as getting eBay sales should always be your priority. Your website should work to direct traffic to your eBay listings, not to intercept them. I only recommend you consider a site after you have been selling for a good length of time and see the need for it. Otherwise, a free *Facebook Business Page,* which we will discuss further in this chapter, can serve you just as well as a paid website.

Mailing List: When I sold new gift items, I tended to get a lot of repeat customers. I developed my own email mailing list using the PayPal email address that I had access to once someone paid me. I simply copied and pasted email addresses into a Word document and then put them into the *Blind Carbon Copy* section of my email program when I wanted to send out a message.

However, with eBay's *Managed Payments,* sellers no longer have access to customer emails. If you sell a lot of similar items, you can always create your own mailing list by using a service such as **Constant Contact** or **Mail Chimp** and letting customers know that they can sign up for the list in an enclosure card included in their order. Note that it is against eBay's policy for you to use their messaging system to direct people off their site, so if you want to cultivate a mailing list, be sure to do so off the eBay system.

Again, I would only consider a mailing list if you sell similar types of items and have a massive quantity of them. For example, if you specialize in Hummel figurines or only sell vintage hats, then cultivating a list of customers may be worth your time. If, like most resellers, you have a wide variety of different items for sale on eBay, I would skip the mailing list and instead focus on creating listings that will show up high in internet search rankings (keyword-loaded titles, good photos, and accurate descriptions).

Facebook: If you plan to sell a lot of items on eBay, it is worth your time to set up a **Facebook Business Page** to promote your listings. Some sellers choose to make their personal Facebook page their business page, but I discourage that. Suppose you are already actively participating on Facebook by using your personal page to communicate with your friends and family. In that case, I recommend setting up a separate business page. A personal page is one where people add you as a "friend," while a business page is one people must "like."

I prefer the business page format for promoting eBay listings because it keeps your personal life and business separate. There is a limit to how many "friends" you can accept on a personal page, but you can grow an unlimited number of business "followers" on a business page. However, to start a business page, you must first have a personal page.

To set up a *Facebook Business Page*, simply visit **facebook.com/about/pages.** You will need to log into your personal Facebook account first, and then the system will walk you through the steps needed to create your business page. It is FREE and easy to set up.

The first decision you will need to make is to name your page. I have several Facebook business pages for my various businesses, including one for my eBay Store. If you are starting your Facebook page specifically for your eBay business, then you will want to make the names match. My *eBay Store* and the accompanying *Facebook Business Page* are both called *AnnabellasGiftShop.*

In fact, as you go forward with creating more social media accounts related to your eBay business, you will want to make sure they all have the same name. Make sure your store name is a good fit before starting a Facebook page with the same name and then carrying that name over to various other sites. For instance, if you have been using the eBay user name "i_luv_cats," you may want to change it to something more professional. Well, unless you only sell cat products. Then that would be an acceptable name!

To change your eBay user name, simply go to **My eBay** and then **Account**. Click **Personal Information** on the left side of the page. Then click **Edit** to the right of the information you want to change.

To change the name of your eBay Store, simply go to **My eBay, Account** and then **Subscriptions**. On the **Manage My Store: Summary** page, scroll to the **Set Up, Sell and Track** section and click the **Design Your Store** link. In the **Display Settings** section, click the **Change** link and make your edits.

Once you have gotten your eBay user name and *eBay Store* names straight, you can proceed with naming your Facebook page the same.

There are all kinds of things you can personalize on your Facebook page. You want to add a profile picture and a banner. I have my logo as my profile picture, and I had a custom banner made on **Fiverr.com**, although you can also design your own graphics using sites such as **Canva** and apps such as **WordSwag**. Whatever photos or graphics you choose, remember that this is your BUSINESS page, so keep it professional.

You will also want to fill out the extensive **About** section to provide people with information about your page and business. Facebook will prompt you to do this when you are setting up your page, but you can also find an *About* tab at the top of your page to make changes at any time.

Remember, since this is your BUSINESS page and separate from your personal page, you want to be careful with how much information you provide. While you may share your cell phone number on your personal page so that friends and family can call or text you, unless you have a brick-and-mortar location that you want people to call, you will want to leave that section blank on your business page.

You will first need to choose the **Category** for your page; as an eBay seller, there are several you can choose from, such as *Companies & Organizations*, *Local Businesses*, or *Websites & Blogs*. Any of the three would be sufficient for your eBay page; it is up to you which you prefer. And don't worry about being locked into your selections; you can easily change them anytime.

Once you have your page set up, it is time to start building your audience by getting people to "Like" your page. You can invite friends and family to your personal page to "Like" your new business page. To bring customers (past, present, or potential) to your Facebook page, include your Facebook page handle, i.e. your username, on any package enclosures.

So, you have set up a Facebook page for your business and have started getting people to "Like" it. Now what? Providing helpful content on your page will be vital to keeping it up to date and attracting new followers.

eBay makes sharing your active listings to Facebook and other social media websites easy as there are **SHARE** buttons both on the desktop and mobile versions of the site. Simply locate the *SHARE* link in your listing and choose the site you wish to share it to. If you have an *eBay Store*, you can share your storefront on several social media sites simply by clicking on the *SHARE* icon at the top of your store. If you don't see the word *SHARE*, look for an **UP arrow**.

In addition to sharing listings, it is also a good idea to engage your Facebook followers by posting status updates about what is going on with your business, such as if you are getting in new inventory or if you are running a sale. You want to keep your business page postings POSITIVE; stay away from religious, political, or other controversial topics. Remember, your goal with eBay is to make money, and you cannot do that by offending people. Save the personal commentary for your personal Facebook page.

Posting pictures of your office, new inventory, or even a shot of orders ready to ship out are all fun ways to keep your audience interested. And sharing unique content is vital to ensure people actually see your posts. The reselling community is very active on social media, so Facebook will also connect you with other sellers, which is a great way to have "co-workers" in a business that can sometimes be rather isolating.

As I mentioned earlier, you may decide that a Facebook page can act like your blog or website rather than setting up a separate site. Most eBay sellers do not have a blog or website; instead, they use their Facebook page as their business homepage. So, unless you have the time to maintain a separate website, consider just using Facebook and other social networking to promote your eBay business.

Facebook is just the first in a long list of social media sites you can create in conjunction with your eBay business. Master your Facebook page first before moving on to the next social media account: Twitter!

Twitter: If you do not already have a Twitter account, you can create one for FREE at Twitter.com. If you do have an account that you are active on, consider creating a new one just for your eBay business. As with Facebook, you want to keep your personal and business lives separate on Twitter. Ensure your Twitter handle is the same as your eBay user name, *eBay Store* name, and *Facebook Business Page* name.

Twitter allows users to share posts of 280 characters or less. And just like Facebook, Twitter is a fast, easy, and free way to promote your listings as well as connect with other resellers.

As with Facebook, eBay makes sharing your active listings to Twitter easy using the **SHARE** buttons both on the desktop and mobile versions of the site. If you don't see the word *SHARE*, look for an **UP arrow** at the top of the page.

Adding hashtags is another easy way to ensure potential customers see your Tweet. A hashtag is a pound (#) sign followed by a keyword, and it is what experienced Twitter users enter in the search field to seek out relevant Tweets. For example, let's say your eBay listing title is "Red Mens Polo RALPH LAUREN Dress Shirt LARGE Pony Logo Stretch." Copying the link to Twitter will automatically add the title. And after the link, add hashtags such as #RalphLauren #Polo #MensClothing.

Just as you share your Facebook page with customers, you will also want to share your Twitter handle with them in the hopes they will follow you on Twitter, too. And to find even more followers, you want to engage with other Twitter users actively.

Some Twitter users follow everyone who follows them, which can certainly help build up your followers. You can also "network" with other users on Twitter by replying to, retweeting, or favoring tweets.

What you want to gain from Twitter is people clicking through to your eBay listing links and either purchasing that item or finding something else to buy from you. You will also likely see that some people "favor" your Tweets by clicking on the little star icon under each message. It is always nice when someone retweets one of your Tweets, too, so that it gets shared with their followers.

Note that just as people can message you on Facebook (unless you change the privacy settings to block them), you can also send and receive messages on Twitter. And finally, you can create "Lists" on Twitter to group people you follow together (such as "customers," "resellers," "thrift stores," etc.).

Pinterest: Pinterest started as a way for people, mainly women, to "pin" craft ideas and recipes on virtual boards. However, Pinterest is quickly becoming a tool for businesses to get the word out about their products and develop brand loyalty. Pinterest offers eBay sellers another fast and free way to promote their listings in the hopes that people will click through and purchase products.

As with Facebook and Twitter, eBay makes sharing your active listings to Pinterest easy using the **SHARE** buttons both on the desktop and mobile versions of the site. If you don't see the word *SHARE*, look for an **UP arrow** at the top of the page.

I have a "For Sale on eBay" board on Pinterest to which I "pin" my listings. Not only can my Pinterest followers see my new listings, but they can share the pin with THEIR Pinterest followers by pinning it to their boards.

You will find many other eBay sellers on Pinterest, many of whom have created eBay group boards to which you may be invited to post. Networking with fellow eBay sellers on Pinterest is another excellent way to promote your listings while getting to know other eBayers such as yourself. Re-pinning THEIR pins is a nice gesture and a great way to network.

One concern some eBay sellers have is that once items sell, the "pin" is no longer relevant. Should you delete old pins of items that have sold? While you certainly can take the time to do this, you don't have to. In fact, it may be beneficial for you to leave the pin active. Why? Let's say someone sees a pin of a collectible you have for sale. When they click through, they find that the item has sold. However, they are now connected with you on eBay and may click on the link to visit your eBay Store or to see your current listings. While they may be annoyed that the item they wanted is no longer available, they also might find something else to buy from you.

Just as you should be doing with your Facebook and Twitter links, be sure to share your Pinterest page with customers by including the link on your blog/website (if you have one) and in the General Information section of your Facebook page. You can also provide the URL to your Pinterest account in any package enclosures. Be sure to periodically share your Pinterest link on both Facebook and Twitter to attract new followers.

You may be noticing by now that a big part of social networking is to have all your sites working together. Include all your social media links on your blog/website, if you have one, and in package enclosures. Post your Twitter and Pinterest links to Facebook; share your Facebook and Pinterest links on Twitter. The more you can get your eBay links out there, the more brand awareness you will create.

Instagram: Like Facebook, Twitter, and Pinterest, Instagram is easy and FREE to use. While eBay does not yet provide a "share" button for Instagram, it is still a valuable tool for promoting your listings. You can currently only add photos and videos to your Instagram page through their app, so note that you will need to have a phone or tablet to use the site.

In addition to helping to drive traffic to your eBay Store, Instagram is also great for connecting with customers on a personal level by sharing photos that may not always relate directly to your business.

However, as with anything you share on your business accounts, be sure to keep Instagram pictures non-controversial and lighthearted (i.e., avoid politics and religion!). Take photos of your office or of all the packages you are shipping out. Include pictures of your pets and even what you are having for lunch. Make it your goal to post at least one photo to Instagram every day.

As with Twitter, hashtags are a big part of getting your content on Instagram found. I like to include at least five with every photo I share. The goal of these hashtags is that people will search for them and find me.

When I post a photo related to eBay, I use hashtags such as:

- #eBay
- #eBayer
- #reseller
- #reselling
- #picker
- #thrifting
- #workfromhome
- #selfemployed

Other helpful hashtags on Instagram can be used to connect you with fellow resellers, including:

- #resellercommunity
- #resellingcommunity
- #eBayseller
- #eBayreseller
- #eBaycommunity

Instagram allows you to include one website link in your profile; so, if you are using Instagram to bring in eBay customers, you will want to make that the link to your eBay Store. And while you can include the link when you share a photo, it will not be active. Therefore, a tip is to put something like, "25% off sale going on right now in our eBay Store; direct link in profile @yourinstagramaccount." The "@" link will take users to your profile page, where the active link to your eBay Store will be. Then the user simply clicks on your eBay Store URL, taking them straight to your eBay listings.

If you have other websites you'd like to post links to, you can use a plug-in from a site like **Linktr.ee**. Linktr.ee allows you to include multiple links under one main link. If you visit my *Linktr.ee at linktr.ee/anneckhart*, you'll see what mine looks like. This format allows me to list all of my links under the umbrella of just one link.

Some resellers also use Instagram to sell items directly, skipping eBay altogether. These sellers will put up a picture of an item and offer it up for sale right on Instagram. All someone must do is message the poster (Instagram has a "mailbox" system that allows users to message one another) to give them their email so the seller can send them a PayPal invoice.

Another way some people sell on Instagram is to post items for sale in their stories. And some are now starting to go live on the app and have live sales.

Just like with Facebook, Twitter, and Pinterest, you will want to network with other eBay sellers and even your customers by following them back on Instagram and "liking" their posts. Include the link to your Instagram page on package enclosures and Facebook page. And share your Instagram link periodically on Facebook and Twitter to gain more followers.

TikTok: TikTok is the newest entry into the social media world and is promoted as a video-sharing social network. The TikTok app allows users to create short-form mobile videos. The platform has a vast catalog of sound and song clips, special effects, and filters. Other users can "react" to TikToks, allowing them to record their reactions in side-by-side frames to other creators' content. TikTok is growing by the day as more users, particularly celebrities, join the app.

As with any fast-growing platform, businesses are jumping on the TikTok bandwagon, too; and as an eBay seller, you can also leverage it to drive traffic to your listings. Creating a TikTok account and putting the link to your eBay Store (or creating a Linktr.ee page with all of your links) in your profile can potentially attract customers by showing off newly listed items.

Reselling content on TikTok varies from sellers posting their garage sale and thrift store adventures, sharing hauls, touting sales, and offering tips. If you use TikTok as a way to promote your eBay business, but sure to keep things lighthearted but professional. It's okay to have fun and be silly but stay away from potentially offensive or divisive topics such as religion, politics, or current events.

YouTube: A blog/website. Facebook. Twitter. Pinterest. Instagram. TikTok. Are you feeling overwhelmed? Take a deep breath and relax; no one expects you to master these social networking sites and techniques in one day. Take one at a time before moving on to the next one. Once you have mastered the second site, continue to the third, and so on.

We have already covered the biggest sites eBay sellers are using to drive sales and make more money, but there are still others you can use, including YouTube. Not only can you use YouTube to drive traffic to your eBay listings, but you can also make money on your videos through Google's AdSense program.

But what kind of videos can you make that will help you increase your eBay sales? One way to use YouTube to help sell your eBay items is to take videos of products you have listed and include those videos in your eBay listings. And you can also share the video via your other social media accounts, hoping that viewers will click through to the actual listing.

Note that making videos can be time-consuming, so shooting a video for every single item you have listed would likely not be worth it, especially for lower-priced items. However, for items you sell that have moving parts, play music, or are higher priced, adding a video to the listing may help sell it.

Under every YouTube video is a description box where you can include information and links. I include the links to my Amazon store (where all of my books are sold), my eBay store, my two Etsy shops, and all of my social media sites. These links enable viewers to easily click on the links to visit my various sites.

Many eBay sellers grow their sales via YouTube by filming haul videos of the new inventory they will be listing. I do haul videos on my YouTube channel showing all the items I picked up at estate sales and thrift stores that I will be selling on eBay. Not only does this help educate others about how they can make money on eBay, but it also lets customers know what items will be showing up in my eBay Store soon.

Probably the most popular videos made by resellers are "shop with me" vlogs where they film themselves sourcing inventory at garage sales and thrift stores. Some resellers wear GoPro cameras to film, while others, like myself, simply film on their smartphones.

However, more than driving sales, making videos about your eBay business is about connecting with other sellers. Selling on EBay can be a bit lonely when you do not know anyone else who does it. And chances are your friends and family do not understand what you do (or they just want you to sell their stuff for them). By sharing your EBay business through YouTube videos and by searching out others, you will quickly find yourself networking will fellow resellers. And once you connect on YouTube, you can also connect on Facebook, Instagram, and other social networks.

You may think eBay sellers compete with one another, but I have found the opposite to be true. People who sell on eBay love meeting others who do, too. They enjoy watching YouTube videos about selling on eBay, and they support each other on social networking.

And if you, like me, source secondhand items to resell on eBay (from thrift stores, garage sales, and estate sales), YouTube is a fantastic resource to learn what items to look for to make money. When I transitioned from selling new gift items to secondhand goods, YouTube videos helped teach me what items to look for when I was out "picking."

You do not need a fancy camera or high-price editing software to make YouTube videos. As I mentioned, I film my videos on an iPhone! After you upload a video, you can monetize it so that it brings in AdSense revenue. And once your video goes live, you can share it to social media via the convenient "share" icons YouTube provides under each video.

I make all kinds of eBay-related videos, including the hauls I mentioned earlier. I have also filmed many how-to videos teaching people everything from how to list items to what shipping materials I use.

A newer YouTube trend is for resellers to have live sales on their channels. Some people who sell on eBay now go live on YouTube periodically to sell their items directly to customers. Not only does this add another sales stream to their business, but it can also get more people to check out their eBay stores to see what else they are selling.

LinkedIn: LinkedIn is a social networking site specifically for the business community. Rather than sharing family photos as you do on Facebook, you want to keep LinkedIn strictly professional by only sharing your business content, such as blog posts and Tweets, both of which can be automatically linked to your account, related to your eBay business.

Creating a LinkedIn account is free and easy, and you can connect your account with your other social networking sites. As with Facebook, LinkedIn allows you to connect with fellow users. You can search for friends and past co-workers. Think of LinkedIn as an online resume where you highlight your past accomplishments and share your current business activities.

Does my LinkedIn activity bring me any eBay customers? Not really. However, since it is free to create an account, it is something you should take the time to do to add to your social media presence. There are eBay seller groups on LinkedIn that you may want to check out, too. And if you are open to selling on consignment, LinkedIn could be a way to find clients. However, out of all of the social media platforms, LinkedIn is the last one I would worry about.

Putting It All Together: When you sell on eBay, your primary concern should be sourcing new inventory, creating new listings answering customer questions, and shipping out orders. A keyword-loaded title, clear photos, and an accurate description complete with measurements are crucial to creating an eBay listing that will result in a sale. Think of social media as the final step in that listing creation process.

As I have mentioned several times before, eBay makes it easy to share your listings on Facebook, Twitter, and Pinterest via the *SHARE* buttons located in every active listing. After I finish creating a listing, I click on the active listing and go to the upper right-hand side of the page where the *SHARE* buttons are. If you don't see a link titled *SHARE*, look for an upward arrow that will bring up the links. I click through each link and post my listings to the respective sites. Note that connecting your eBay account to your social media networks is a one-time step; once you have set up the connections, they will remain permanently linked. It only takes about 15 seconds for me to share a listing on Facebook, Twitter, and Pinterest; a little longer if I add hashtags.

One tip is that if you list a large batch of items, share each individually on Twitter and Pinterest but hold off on Facebook. Why? Facebook manipulates its search algorithm to show more popular posts first, those with engagement. Flooding your Facebook page with listing after listing will cause Facebook to suppress your posts.

Instead, wait until you have finished listing for the day and then post a single photo of the items you listed or individual photos of each on Facebook with a link to your eBay Store. I like to use an app for creating photo collages to make one photo showing several items. Facebook tends to show photos with added text and hashtags versus simply direct links, so it is much more likely followers will see the one photo you post and click the link to your listings.

Remember that you can share your listings directly from eBay to Instagram. If you are using Instagram, you will need to manually post photos there. I recommend that you try posting a photo at least a few times a week, if not daily. You can upload shots of your office, new inventory, or even what you are having for lunch. Include three to five hashtags so that users can find you. And be sure you are following other users and "liking" their content. I like to spend a few minutes scrolling through my Instagram feed to connect with other users at the end of the day. The reselling community is very active on Instagram, so it's easy to grow a following there simply by connecting with other eBay sellers.

Having a blog/website and/or YouTube channel will add a considerable amount of more work for you, so only use them if you feel they are benefitting your sales or you are getting something from them personally (as in networking with other sellers). If you do utilize those options, be sure to share the content you create over to all your other social networking sites.

When I upload a new YouTube video, I share it on Facebook, Twitter, and Pinterest using the social media sharing buttons under the video. I also manually share the link to the video on Instagram by sharing the thumbnail photo with a link to the video.

While I put in a lot of effort to market my eBay business online, I also have promotional tools I use offline. As I mentioned earlier, I include a packing slip in all my eBay orders (you can print these directly from eBay after your shipping label has been printed); and I also include a sticker or magnet that contains my Linktr.ee URL in hopes that customers will not only return to my *eBay Store* but may also check out my other businesses and social media pages.

eBay's Own Marketing Tools: While the various social media sites help advertise your eBay business, you can also utilize several features directly through eBay to drive sales.

In the **Seller Hub**, click on the **Marketing** tab at the top of the page and look on the left-hand side of the page under **Summary**. Here you will be able to access:

MERCHANDISING:

- **Promotions**
- **Markdown sale**
- **Buyer groups**
- **Social**

ADVERTISING:

- **Dashboard**

Learning Resources

Promotions: Under *Merchandising,* on the left-hand column in the *Marketing* section of your *Seller Hub,* is the **Promotions** link. eBay has a lot of ways for eBay sellers to promote their listings. By clicking on the blue **Create a promotion** button, you can choose from the following:

- **Order discounts** incentivize buyers to spend more money in your store by setting minimum discounts, such as B1G1 FREE offers and percentage/dollar-off discounts on quantity and order total minimums.
- **Shipping discounts** let buyers save on shipping when they buy more from you, either by meeting a minimum of spending a total items.
- **Volume pricing** incentivizes buyers to buy more quantities of your items by setting discounts on multi-quantity purchases such as "save 15% when you buy two or more items".
- **Coupons** allow you to create URLs that you can share via social media and email that give your customers percentage or dollar-off discounts.

- **Sale event + markdown** is accessible here or back over under the main *Marketing* page.

Markdown Sale: Back over on the left-hand side of the *Marketing* page is the **Markdown sale** link, which is also available under the *Promotions* tab. It's honestly easier to access under the *Promotions* tab from the drop-down menu. When you click on the blue **Create a promotion** blue tab and select **Sale event + markdown** from the drop-down menu, a new page will appear titled **Manage Promotions.**

eBay offers you three different **Create a sale event** options:

- **Take a percent off each item** (the drop-down menu offers you the option of anywhere from 5% to 80% off)
- **Take a dollar amount off of each item** (the drop-down menu offers you the option of anywhere from $5 to $1500 off)
- **Free shipping for all discounted items** (in addition to the percentage or dollar amount discount)

Let's say you want to run a 30% off sale. You would enter "30" as the percentage off discount and then click on the blue **Select items** button. You will then be taken to a new screen to **Select Items.** You can add up to 1,500 items to each sale. If you have more items to add, you simply create a second sale.

I typically run my sales on all the items in my store, so I simply check the box to select all of my listings. After you have chosen the items you want included in your sale, you then click on the blue **Confirm selections** button, which will take you to a screen showing all of the items selected for your sale. You have the option to **Remove** any listings you want OR to click on the **Add more items** button before clicking on the blue **Save and review** button.

After clicking the **Save and review** button, the final screen to set up your sale will appear, the **Review your sale event** page. Here you can enter **a Sale event name**, which only you will see. You could enter "30% off sale", for instance. You will be able to review your **Discount type and items** (in this case, 30% off 400 items; you have another chance here to edit these options).

Next is the **Date range**. You will need to select a start date and time AND an end date and time. I typically set my sale to start immediately and to end a week later. Finally, under the **Sale event banner**, you type in your **Sale event description** ("Save 30% Off Everything!" as an example) and **Select sale event image** (eBay will give you three of your listing thumbnails to choose from, or you can upload a different one).

The last section of this page is the **Preview sale event tile,** which shows you what customers will see on their end. If everything looks good, you simply click on the blue **Launch** button at the bottom of the page to start your sale. It may take a few minutes for your sale to go live, but soon whatever discount you opted for will be shown to customers. Once your sale is live, be sure to promote it via social media and on your website if you have one.

Buyer Groups: New for 2023 are Buyer Groups. According to eBay, "Our new buyer segmentation tool lets you create groups based on buyer type to help you stay connected and increase sales."

At the top of the page, EBay provides you with insights from **Your Buyers**, which is your year-over-year data of your total buyers, one-time buyers, repeat buyers and followers.

You can then create special offers based on groups of **Previous customers** and **Followers.** If you sell similar types of items, these features can be a great way for you to reach out to customers and followers who you know are already interested in your products. Simply click on **Get started** under each group, and eBay will walk you through creating coupon codes they will send out on your behalf. As you continue on your eBay journey, you will likely gain followers, so these targeted offers are a great way to get additional sales from those who have already purchased from you. As of this writing, I have nearly 1,900 followers!

Social: Back on the main *Marketing* page is the new **Social** section. Here you can link your social accounts to create custom posts and drive more traffic to your listings, categories, store, or profile. As of this writing, you can link a *Facebook Page* and/or an *Instagram Business Account.*

Advertising: Back over on the left-hand side of the **Marketing** page under **ADVERTISING**, click on **Dashboard** to access **Promoted Listings.**

Promoted Listings are a controversial offering from eBay, as sellers do not like to pay additional fees. However, I use *Promoted Listings* on all of my listings at all times. With so many other people selling on eBay, I have found that I need to pay for *Promoted Listings* to remain competitive.

eBay describes *Promoted Listings* as helping "your items stand out among billions of listings on eBay and be seen by millions of active buyers when they're browsing and searching for what you are selling, helping to increase the likelihood of a sale. You only pay when an item sells. *Promoted Listings* is available only to *Above Standard* and *Top-Rated Sellers* with recent sales activity."

eBay points to four key benefits of *Promoted Listings:*

1. **Boost Visibility:** Your items are more likely to sell when more people see them. *Promoted Listings* put your items in front of more buyers, boosting visibility by up to 36%.
2. **Pay Only For Sale:** You are not charged until a buyer clicks on your promoted listing and purchases the promoted item within 30 days.
3. **Guided Set-Up:** eBay's guidance tools help take the guesswork out and suggest items to promote and at what cost.
4. **Detailed Reporting:** Access detailed campaign metrics and sales reports to monitor performance and fine-tune your campaigns.

In the **Advertising Dashboard,** you will see the **Summary** date of any *Promoted Listings* you have already run, and you can set up a new campaign by clicking on the blue **Create new campaign** button near the top of the page.

After clicking on *Create new campaign,* a new screen will appear titled **Choose your campaign type.**

STANDARD offers a simple setup where you only pay when an item sells. *Standard* offers mean your items appear in ads across eBay's network, including on search and listing pages. You don't pay when someone clicks on your ad, only if that click leads to the item selling.

ADVANCED allows you to target top slots of search with additional controls. Unlike *Standard* ads, *Advanced* ads mean you pay every time someone clicks on one of your ads.

While *Advanced campaigns* target high-volume sellers, most eBay sellers who use *Promoted Listings* use the *Standard campaigns*. I only use the *Standard campaigns* myself.

Standard campaigns are available under three different types:

Simple: *Simple Promoted Listing Campaigns* are best for:

- Sellers who prefer a guided experience
- Visual listing and ad rate selection with recommendations
- Flexibility to select across different listing and ad rate strategies

Bulk: *Bulk Promoted Listing Campaigns* are best for:

- Sellers who prefer to promote in bulk with a .csv file or category selection
- Consistent inventory with low turnover rates
- Ad rate strategies that prioritize cost management

Automated: *Automated Promoted Listing Campaigns* are best for:

- Sellers who prefer a quick setup, daily ad rate updates, and automated listing promotion
- Dynamic inventory with high turnover rates
- Ad rate strategies that prioritize competitiveness

I will be completely honest with you and tell you that the only campaign type I ever use is the *Simple* campaign. It's quick and easy to set up, and I get results from it. In fact, half of my sales are typically the result of *Promoted Listings;* and the *Simple* campaign makes it easy for me to not only control my budget but also to get sales.

Setting up a *Promoted Listings Campaign* is easy. Click on the **Simple drop-down menu** and click on the blue **Create campaign** button. You will be taken to a new page titled **Create new campaign.**

The first section is **Name your campaign.** I rarely give my campaign's names, instead just going with whatever the default name eBay has filled in. I do, however, choose a **Start date** and **End date** under **Set your dates**. I start my campaigns immediately, but I end them on the last day of the month.

Why do I end my campaigns and not just let them run continuously? Why do I then have to set up a new campaign the following month?

I think letting campaigns end and starting new ones keeps my listings relevant to eBay's algorithm. It's like a reset, if you will, of my entire store every month that keeps my listings fresh on the site. Setting up a new campaign every month only takes a few minutes, and I feel it's worth the time.

The next section is **Choose your ad rate strategy.** According to eBay, "An ad rate is the percentage of your item's total sale amount (including item price, shipping, taxes, and any other applicable fees that you'll pay if your item sells within 30 days of a click on your ad."

The default setting here is **Dynamic ad rate,** which eBay always has set very high, typically around 25%. Here is where new sellers can lose a lot of money.

Whatever you do, do NOT select the Dynamic ad rate!

Instead, select Fixed ad rate!

You do not need to select a high ad rate. A rate of 2%, which is the minimum eBay allows sellers to choose, is more than enough to make your *Promoted Listings* effective. *Promoted Listings* work, but they are also another way eBay makes money from fees. They are a somewhat necessary evil for sellers. We know they work, and we have to pay for them; we just need to be careful and keep our costs low. I've used both high suggested rates and my own low rates, and I never saw a difference in sales.

After you have filled out the **Apply single ad rate** field under **Fixed ad rate,** you can choose which listings you want to promote. I always promote all of my active listings. You can do this by selecting **All** under **Categories**. However, you can select different ad rates for different items. The choice is yours.

Once you've entered your ad rate and selected your items, you simply click on the blue **Launch** button at the bottom of the page. Any new listings you create, after you start a campaign, will be automatically added to the promotion unless you manually remove the option within the listing.

After clicking on the *Launch* button, you will be taken back to the *Advertising* dashboard page you started at. At the bottom of this page, you will see your **Promoted Listings campaigns**, both active and ended. And just as with running a sale, you can pause, edit, or end your *Promoted Listings* at any time.

A website, social media pages, branding, sales, and promoted listings. There are so many options available to you as an eBay seller to market your listings. While it can all seem overwhelming, trust me promotion efforts become second nature after a while. The increase in sales will make all your extra time and effort worth it in the end!

CHAPTER TEN: MANAGING AN EBAY STORE

To open an **eBay Store** or not? That is the question I have been asked more times than I can count since I started giving out eBay advice in my books and on my YouTube channel!

The general rule of thumb is that if you consistently have at least 100 items listed on eBay, then an *eBay Store* makes sense financially. However, if you are a seller who sells things fast, that rule doesn't exactly apply. I believe that if you are consistently listing and selling on eBay, even if you aren't constantly maintaining 100 active listings, then a store subscription is a good idea due to the benefits it provides.

eBay Store owners get discounts on both listing and final value fees along with additional tools to manage their businesses. eBay currently offers five different store subscriptions:

Starter Store:

- For low-volume sellers who want an entry-level option that gives their business a storefront and a brand
- $4.95 a month when you commit to an annual subscription or $7.95 when you pay month-to-month
- 250 free fixed-price fixed price listings
- 250 free auction listings in the collectibles and fashion categories
- 30-cent listing fee above allocation
- *Final Value Fees* of 3-15% depending on the sale price and category
- Access to *Promotions Manager, Markdown Manager*, subscriber discounts, store home page, and a link to your eBay store in your listings

Basic Store:

- For sellers who are consistently listing on eBay but aren't at a full-time business level
- $21.95 a month when you commit to an annual subscription or $27.85 when you pay month-to-month
- 1,000 free fixed-price listings per month
- 250 free auction listings per month in the collectibles and fashion categories
- 25-cent fixed price listing fee above allocation
- 25-cent auction price listing fee above allocations
- *Final Value Fees* of 2.5-15% depending on the sale price and category
- Insertion fee credits for auction-style items that sell
- Access to *Promotions Manager*, *Markdown Manager*, subscriber discounts, store home page, and a link to your eBay store in your listings
- Access to *Terapeak Sourcing Insights*
- Coupon for $25 worth of FREE eBay-branded shipping supplies each quarter

Premium Store:

- For full-time sellers wanting lower listing fees and more business tools
- $59.95 a month for an annual subscription or $74.95 when you pay month-to-month
- 10,000 free fixed-price listings
- 500 free auction listings for collectibles and fashion
- 10-cent fixed-price listing fee above allocation
- 15-cent auction listing fee above allocation
- *Final Value Fees* of 2.5-15% depending on the sale price

and category
- Insertion fee credits for auction-style items that sell
- Access to *Promotions Manager*, *Markdown Manager*, subscriber discounts, store home page, and a link to your eBay store in your listings
- Access to *Terapeak Sourcing Insights*
- Coupon for $50 worth of FREE eBay-branded shipping supplies each quarter

Anchor Store:

- For high-volume sellers who want dedicated support
- $299.95 a month for an annual subscription or $349.95 when you pay month-to-month
- 25,000 free fixed-price listings per month
- 1,000 free auction listings per month
- 5-cent fixed-price listing fee above allocation
- 10-cent auction listing fee above allocation
- *Final Value Fees* of 2.5-15% depending on the sale price and category
- Insertion fee credits for auction-style items that sell
- Access to *Promotions Manager*, *Markdown Manager*, subscriber discounts, store home page, and a link to your eBay store in your listings
- Access to *Terapeak Sourcing Insights*
- Coupon for $150 worth of FREE eBay-branded shipping supplies each quarter
- Access to dedicated customer support

Enterprise:

- For the pros with large catalogs and high transaction volumes
- $2,999.95 a month

- 100,000 free fixed-price listings per month

- 2,500 free auction listings per month
- 5-cent fixed-price listing fee above allocation

- 10-cent auction listing fee above allocation
- Final Value Fees of 2.5-15% depending on the sale price and category
- Insertion fee credits for auction-style items that sell
- Access to Promotions Manager, Markdown Manager, subscriber discounts, store home page, and a link to your EBay store in your listings
- Access to Terapeak Sourcing Insights
- Coupon for $150 worth of FREE eBay-branded shipping supplies each quarter
- Access to dedicated customer support

All eBay Store subscribers receive:

- Access to *Terapeak Research*
- Access to *Promoted Listings*
- Access to *Promotions Manager*
- Customizable Storefront Homepage
- Customized Store Web Address
- Controllable "Featured Items"
- Store Categories

Note that if you choose to open a store and agree to the lower rate for a one-year commitment, you will pay the lower fee every month, not the entire cost for the year upfront. However, if you cancel or downgrade your store before the 12-month period ends, you will have to pay the difference between the yearly cost and the month-to-month cost for however long you have left in your agreement.

There are several things you can do to personalize your *eBay Store*. To access these customization tools, go to your eBay Store's front page (look for the **blue door icon** next to your username) and click on the blue **Manage My Store** button in the upper right-hand corner of the page.

There are a lot of features here to explore under the **STORE SETUP** on the left-hand side of the page, including:

Edit store: Here you can add a **store banner and** a **store profile picture**. You can edit your **store name** here, as well as **Stage your store** by selecting **Featured categories**. You can also **Feature your listings, Use a marketing banner**, and select the **category type** you want displayed in your store: *eBay categories* or your *Store categories*.

Under the **Tell your story** tab are fields are **About this store**, where you can write a short description about you and what you sell; **Store video** where you can upload a video clip about yourself and your business; and **Store Policies**, where you can customize things such as your shipping and returns rules.

Store categories: Back on the left-hand side of the page is the link for *Store categories*, which, in my opinion, is one of the best features of having an eBay Store. Not only can buyers narrow down their search when they are looking at your store, but it is helpful for you as a seller to keep track of your inventory.

The great thing about categories is you can add and delete them as you see fit. Perhaps you have a large stock of camera equipment to sell, so you create a "Camera" category. However, after you have sold all the cameras, you can delete the "Camera" category or simply leave it in your store set up as only categories with active listings show up. Inactive categories will still be visible to you in the *Manage Your Store* section, but they will only be seen by customers if or when you add items to them. You can create up to 300 unique categories in your store.

I like to arrange my categories alphabetically. While you can break down categories into subcategories, you are usually fine merely listing in the main category unless you have thousands of items listed. For example, if you have a category for figurines but have dozens of figurines of different brands, it could be advantageous to create sub-categories for each brand.

Once you have an eBay Store, you can select the store categories for your items whenever you go to list something. You can list each item in two of your store categories. Note that the store categories differ from the eBay categories, where you get one free and must pay for a second. With your store categories, both selections are free.

Store traffic: The next option on the left-hand side of the page is *Store traffic*. Here you can see the data including how many visits have been made to your store in the *Last 31 days*, *Last week*, *Last month*, *This quarter*, and *This year*.

Further down this page is a section titled **Optimize your store**. Here eBay provides direct links to help design your store, create coupons, segment buyer groups, build marketing campaigns, use eBay's social media widgets, and create a better shopping experience for your customers. There are a lot of options here, when you have some downtime, it's worth exploring these lings. However, remember that you want sourcing, listing, and shipping to remain your top priorities, not worrying about whether your eBay Store banner is perfect.

PROMOTE STORE: Back on the left-hand side of the page is another section titled *PROMOTE STORE*. Here you can access your **Store newsletter,** which allows you to create email campaigns and special offers for those you are following your store. Note that many of these features are also accessible under the *Marketing tab* in your *Seller Hub.*

Social: The *Social* link under *PROMOTE STORE* takes you to a page where you can link your Facebook, Instagram, and Pinterest business accounts to your store to share new listings with curated images, custom captions, and suggested hashtags. This process is more thorough than sharing listings directly within the active listing.

SUBSCRIPTIONS: The third and final section on the left-hand side of the *Manger My Store* page is *SUBSCRIPTIONS*. **Subscriber discounts** will take you to a page where you can access your **eBay Shipping Supplies** coupon (for *Starter* stores and up) along with **eBay Seller Capital**, which gives sellers loans to grow their businesses.

Manage subscriptions take you to a page where you can see your current store subscription details, including how much you are paying per month and when your subscription will end. You can change or cancel your store subscription here, although fees may apply.

Learning resources: The final tab on the left-hand side of the page is *Learning resources*. Here is where you can find links to store specific information and tutorials that have been created by eBay.

Store vs. No Store: As I mentioned earlier, one of the most common questions I get about selling on eBay is whether or not to open an *eBay Store*. If you are consistently listing and selling on eBay, then I firmly believe that a store makes sense. If you have not already subscribed to an eBay Store, you can always start with the lowest level and upgrade later. If you sign up for a store under the yearly rate, not the month-to-month rate, note that if you cancel or downgrade your store before your year is up you will have to pay the difference between the monthly and yearly rates.

New sellers often feel they must get their *eBay Stores* "ready" before opening them to the public. However, remember that an eBay Store is not like a brick-and-mortar store. Most customers will access your listings from eBay's search, not through your actual store. It will only be after you start promoting your store's URL address via social media that people will get to your storefront to see what you have for sale. Once you subscribe to an eBay Store, your listings will automatically be placed there. You cannot hide your store from users until you deem it "ready." Once your first listing is live on eBay, you are open for business, whether you have a store or not.

While I encourage you to have a great store design, you should prioritize getting your items listed. Once a listing is live, it will automatically be visible in your eBay Store. If you find that your sales are going well and that your listings are increasing, you can always upgrade your store subscription level; in fact, eBay will likely message you with special offers to upgrade your store if it is performing well.

Many sellers think having an *eBay Store* is all about the customer's experience. But the truth is that sellers gain a lot more from a store in terms of reduced fees and organization than buyers do from shopping in an *eBay Store* setting. Because most customers will find your listings in eBay's search, many will not click through your actual *eBay Store*. But even though most buyers will not venture into your "store," it does not mean you should not have one, as the savings on listing fees alone are typically worth the price of your subscription.

I have an *eBay Store* for my professional benefit as the reduced fees and organizational tools help me effectively run my shop. If customers happen to find it, that's just a bonus!

CHAPTER ELEVEN: EBAY ACCOUNTING MADE EASY

I get so many questions from eBay sellers who, like me, are not very confident with their math skills and are confused about how to track their eBay income and expenses. However, regardless of your mathematics abilities, it is essential to keep precise accounting records for your eBay business. Fortunately, it isn't hard at all once you establish a basic system for your recordkeeping.

In this chapter, I will explain exactly how to make the eBay accounting process as easy for you as it is for me. Trust me, if I can keep my eBay records using this system, so can you!

Hiring an accountant: Before we get to the actual accounting system, we need to cover some other important issues surrounding the finances of selling on eBay, including whether you should hire an accountant. Please note that these are my experiences; as with anything, be sure to do your own research on all aspects of your business, especially when it comes to accounting and taxes, as laws vary by state. When having doubts, it is always best to consult with a tax professional in your area.

When I started my business in 2005, I met with an accountant who set up the bookkeeping system I will share with you in this chapter. The simple system he set up for me years ago still works for me today. It has stayed the same whether I was selling gift baskets locally, wholesale items on eBay and Amazon, or secondhand items on eBay, Etsy, and Poshmark. I knew my accountant well from my previous office job and have always trusted his advice and knowledge.

However, while I keep my own books throughout the year, I hire my accountant to file my taxes. Tackling my own tax returns is not something I personally feel comfortable with. Because I have an easy system for my bookkeeping, I simply keep track of everything throughout the year and then turn it all over to my accountant at tax time. Since I have kept good records for the year, he can quickly and easily file my taxes for me, which drastically cuts down on the bill he sends me for his tax filing services.

It is essential to understand the difference between keeping your own accounting books and then hiring someone to file taxes versus hiring someone to do all your accounting. I keep my own books, but my accountant files my taxes. If my accountant kept my books for me and filed my taxes on top of it, I would be paying him a hefty monthly fee. I do know some small business owners who meet with their accountants quarterly to manage their books. It really depends on the person and the business itself as to how often someone should meet with their accountant over the course of a year.

If you are comfortable filing your own taxes, you will still be able to use the accounting system I show you later in this book. However, if you want to hire someone to do them for you, you will save a lot of time and money by having an accounting system in place. That way, when tax time comes around, you can simply hand over your records to a tax professional, and they will be able to file them for you quickly.

Again, the less time an accountant or tax preparer must spend sorting out your records, the cheaper their bill will be. While it may be tempting just to save up all your receipts and give them to someone a few days before April 15th, it is so much easier and cheaper to keep your own records and simply have someone file your returns for you.

There is no need for me to give my accountant a stack of receipts at tax time or for me to go over all my credits and debits line by line, as the system I use summarizes my gross sales and net expenses in one basic sheet of paper. I simply give my accountant my gross sales totals and my expense totals using the easy accounting system I have in place, and he handles the rest. At this point, I could probably just follow my accountant's template and file my own returns; but I prefer the security of having a CPA prepare and file my taxes for me.

Whether or not to hire an accountant is a personal choice. I must admit that I feel safer hiring someone to file my taxes for me. The IRS loves to audit small businesses, and I feel that having an accountant handling my returns offers an extra layer of protection for me. I even signed a form that gives my accountant permission to talk to the IRS on my behalf if any questions arise.

Another bonus of hiring an accountant to file your returns is that they are specifically trained to get you the most deductions possible. Most eBay businesses are run out of homes (mine is!), so there are many additional deductions available that are not for people who run brick-and-mortar stores. I can deduct the space I use in my home for my business, including property taxes and utilities. I also get deductions for using my car for business. My accountant keeps all this information in my file and just fills it in on my tax forms every year.

One final benefit for me of having an accountant has been that he can set me up to pay my income taxes every quarter rather than all at once at the end of the year. Using the previous year's returns, he coordinates with the IRS to figure out how much I will own. He then prepares tax forms for me to submit every three months. I simply cut a check and mail in the forms, both to my state as well as to the Federal government. Sometimes I still owe a bit more money in taxes at the end of the year, but that just means that I made more money. And with the changing tax laws, occasionally, I end up with a refund.

While it is nice to hope that you will always get a tax refund every year, paying quarterly definitely protects you during the years when you may have underpaid and then owe money. Paying my income tax quarterly prevents me from getting hit with a potentially massive tax bill from the IRS at the end of the year. If, at the end of the year, it turns out I have overpaid on my quarterly tax returns, I will get a refund. And since I am not skilled in IRS laws, I need my accountant to do this for me. When it comes to taxes, I would rather overpay than underpay, as the IRS will eventually come to collect what they are owed.

PRO TIP: Most self-employed individuals are generally required to file an annual return and pay estimated quarterly taxes. Whether or not you need to file quarterly depends on your net profit or net loss, which is something a CPA can easily do for you. Ignoring the possibility of paying quarterly income tax will mean you will own a large sum come tax time.

If you feel you need to hire an accountant or tax professional to prepare your taxes, be sure to ask around to your friends and family for their recommendations. There are many big accounting firms around that will charge you an arm and a leg to handle your returns. But many people run small offices or even work part-time from home and can do your taxes for a lot less.

Get recommendations from your friends and family, and then make a few calls. Ask what they charge for tax filing and ask if they do free initial consultations. Also, be sure to ask if they have experience filing taxes for home-based e-commerce businesses, specifically eBay, as they come with their own set of rules. If you use the accounting techniques that I will be sharing with you in this chapter, you will be able to tell potential CPAs that you keep your own books and are just looking for someone to submit your tax filings every year.

If the accountants you interview offer a free or low-cost initial consultation, take advantage of it. If you have started keeping your own records, take them with you to the meeting to see if they can work based on what you have or if they want to make changes to your system. Having a good accountant on your side is never wrong when running a business; plus, you can write their fees off as a business expense!

If you feel confident filing your own taxes, you can skip hiring an accountant. However, note that it is good to educate yourself on your state's specific tax laws. A little research can save you a lot of grief at tax time. Fortunately, you can use two FREE resources: **SCORE** and the **Small Business Administration**, both of which I discussed earlier in this book. Most large cities have these services available; a quick Google search will bring up the offices closest to you.

Both *SCORE* and the *SBA* can advise you about the potential need for you to hire an accountant, and they can also help you determine whether you want to set up your eBay business as a **sole proprietorship** or an **LLC.** As we've already discussed, the vast majority of eBay business owners are sole proprietors, which is defined as someone who owns an unincorporated business by themselves.

An LLC is a business that has legally been set up as an organization. Different tax laws apply to each. There are more tax benefits with an LLC, but an LLC is much more complicated to set up and complex to maintain. If you are going to form an LLC, you will definitely have to hire a CPA to assist you.

Again, a *SCORE* volunteer, an *SBA* employee, or an accountant can talk to you about whether a sole proprietorship or LLC is best for you. Still, unless you plan to hire employees, you will likely be operating as a sole proprietor. That means that you will be filing your business taxes under your given legal name.

As a sole proprietor myself, my legal name is technically my business name as far as the IRS is concerned. However, my name is followed by D.B.A., which means "Doing Business As" on bank statements and permits.

Note that a D.B.A. can also affect how you cash checks; most banks will only cash checks to accounts that match the checks' name, including the D.B.A. So, if you get checks made out to your D.B.A. name, a bank likely will not deposit them into an account that only has your name on it. This is something you will want to check with your bank about. If they feel you should have an account under your D.B.A., it should be easy to set up and may even link to your personal account. While your eBay transactions will be run online through eBay, if you need to file an insurance claim through the USPS, they will usually send you a check made out to your business name, which your bank may not cash unless it matches the name on your account.

Some banks may also require that you file a business license in your city with the D.B.A. name. If they do, do not panic, as the process is simple and relatively inexpensive to complete at your local courthouse. Again, your bank will be able to best advise you on this.

If you plan just to flip finds from garage sales, though, I would not worry about having a D.B.A. You can certainly create a business name for the fun of it, but legally just your name will likely suffice. However, suppose you plan to grow your business beyond just a part-time gig. In that case, you will want to consult a lawyer or your accountant to learn about the benefits of changing your business structure to an LLC. Even though my business has changed and grown over the years, neither my accountant nor I have felt it necessary to convert my business to an LLC yet.

Opening a business bank account: The whole point of selling on eBay is to MAKE MONEY! Therefore, it is a good idea to get a separate checking account dedicated solely to your business. Having a separate business account from your personal account makes keeping track of business income and expenses much easier.

As I discussed earlier, most banks will not cash checks that are made out to your business name into your personal account. So, a business account might be necessary if you plan to receive any payments using your D.B.A. name.

If you are not already a credit union member, look for one in your area, as they usually offer free account setup, free checking, and no ATM fees. You will want to get checks under your business account to buy things such as office supplies directly from your business account. I write very few checks but sometimes use them at estate sales when purchasing inventory.

Having a dedicated credit card for your business is also a good idea. I have a credit card that I keep on file with eBay as a backup funding source and use it when I buy something on the site. It's a card that I earn travel points on, and I pay it off every month to avoid paying fees.

In the rare instance that I must take a package to the Post Office for shipping (I do most of my shipping from home using *Carrier Pickup*), I use a credit card to pay for the postage. I buy shipping supplies locally from Staples and Sam's Club, and online from Amazon and eBay, all of which I charge to my business credit card. I also use credit cards when buying inventory at thrift stores, and a few of the estate sale companies in my area also accept them.

Charging business supplies, services, and inventory onto one credit card makes it easy for me to track my expenses. I chose a business credit card that offered rewards, too, so that I get something back for using it. However, be careful to pay off your credit card balance every month, or you will soon be using all your profits to pay for credit card fees. When I sold new gift items that I bought wholesale, I had to order them using a credit card; and the fees added up quickly.

Using one card is ideal as I can pull up the monthly statements online while doing my monthly bookkeeping. I can easily see what I spent, where I spent it, and what I spent it on, making it quick and easy to itemize my expenses.

My easy accounting system: Here we are at the heart of this chapter, which is how to keep your eBay accounting records. This system is so straightforward; trust me, if I can do it, anyone can. To say that math is not my strong suit is an understatement! But I can even do my eBay books this way.

How much money can you make selling on eBay? As much as you are willing to work for! As we've discussed, many people sell on eBay just for some extra money. Some do it as a part-time job. And others have expanded it into their full-time income. However, bringing in any amount of money requires accounting. As much as you may want to avoid bookkeeping, trust me when I say that when tax time rolls around, you will be so glad you started and stuck with a system at the beginning of the year. You cannot hide from Uncle Sam; the IRS will eventually catch up with you. And this accounting system is just too easy not to do!

When I started my business, I paid my accountant $300 for an hour-long meeting for him to set up my bookkeeping system. And it is this same easy system that I am about to lay out for you. Basically, it is just a check register, like the one you probably have in your checkbook. I keep track of my debits and credits and then hand off the totals to my accountant at the end of the year.

You can use a computer spreadsheet, a paper bookkeeping book, or just a plain notebook. Or you can use my **Reselling Planner & Accounting Ledger**, available on Amazon, which has this system all laid out.

Your business accounting breaks down into two categories: **DEBITS** and **CREDITS.**

Debits are your expenses (withdraws) on the check register.

Credits are the funds you earn (deposits) on the check register.

Just like you use your personal checkbook register to log the checks you write and deposit, you can track your eBay income and expenses the same way. Here's how most check ledgers are laid out:

- **Check #** (the number on your check)
- **Date** (the date of the transaction)
- **Transaction** (the transaction itself, such as "USPS" or "PayPal")
- **Debit** (the amount of money spent)
- **Credit** (the amount of money deposited into your business account)
- **Balance** (the total running balance after the most recent debit or credit)

That is all you need to track your day-to-day running numbers so that you always know how much money is in your account. At the end of the month, you will break your numbers down further to itemize your expenses.

Here is how I break down my numbers (I will use September as an example):

SEPTEMBER CREDITS: Credits are the deposits made into your bank account.

eBay Sales: Your gross sales numbers can be found by going to your **Seller Hub**, clicking on the **Performance** tab at the top of the page, and choosing **Sales** from the drop-down menu.

However, for accounting purposes, **you only need to account for your eBay payouts**. Gone are the days when sellers racked up a balance for fees and shipping. Now eBay automatically collects all listing and seller fees along with postage costs from your pending balance. To get this number, click on **Payments** in **Seller Hub**. Click on **Payouts** on the left-hand side of the screen. The default setting will show you your payouts from the past 90 days, but you can change it to the past 30 or 60 days. For the September example I am using, I would simply look at the payouts dated for September. I would add those up and enter the total under the *eBay Sales* section on my ledger.

Other Sales: If you sell on other platforms, such as Poshmark, WhatNot, Mercari, or Etsy, or if you sell locally via Facebook Marketplace or at an antique mall booth, you can add those sales numbers here on other lines. Most sites automatically deduct fees and postage from your balance before issuing you a payout, so you will only need to enter the amounts that were deposited into your bank account.

SEPTEMBER DEBITS/EXPENSES: Debits and expenses are the deductions made from your bank account.

eBay Fees: You can find a breakdown of your monthly eBay fees under the **Performance** tab in **Seller Hub**; simply select **Summary** from the drop-down menu to access this data. However, since eBay now automatically deducts your listing, final value, and advertising fees, you don't have to account for them on your accounting ledger.

The only eBay fees you do need to manually pay are if you have a store subscription. That cost will be charged to your backup funding source. In my case, it is charged to my business credit card. Therefore, I need to add that fee to my accounting ledger.

Even though you no longer need to account for most fees, it's still a good idea to check this section periodically to see how much you are paying eBay to run your business. There are several sections on this page, including a breakdown of your **Selling Costs**, details about where the **Traffic** to your listings is coming from, and your current **Seller Level.**

Cost of Goods: Cost of Goods, or COGs, refers to how much you spent on inventory during the month on items to resell. I track my sourcing costs via my credit card statement, checking account, and a notepad where I write down cash purchases. I usually charge thrift store purchases and will use my card at estate sales that take credit cards. One particular estate sale company accepts checks. And the rest of the time I pay in cash. I keep a small notebook in my car to jot down cash purchases.

Postage: This is for the money you spent out of pocket on postage, not the amount eBay automatically deducted from your balance when you printed a shipping label. Occasionally I take a package to the post office for postage or I buy stamps for my business. These are the costs I need to track.

You can look at your postage costs under the **Performance** tab in your **Seller Hub** under the **Selling Costs** section. There is a line item for **Shipping labels** that were purchased through eBay. If you have been offering "free" shipping where you pad the cost of postage into the price of the item, this number will be quite high and it may cause you to switch to having customers pay for postage. If you purchased your shipping labels through a site other than eBay, such as USPS.com or PirateShip.com, or if you take your packages to the Post Office for postage, you will need to account for those charges on your accounting ledger.

Advertising: *Promoted Listings* technically fall under *Advertising*, but eBay now automatically takes all *Promoted Listing* fees out of your account, so you do not have to track that amount. If you run Facebook, Instagram, or TikTok ads to promote your *eBay Store*, you will need to track those charges. And if you buy package enclosures, such as business cards, stickers, brochures, or magnets, you will add those costs here.

Office/Shipping Supplies: This is the total amount I spend on everything from labels and printer ink to poly mailers, to bubble wrap and shipping tape. Next to inventory, shipping supplies are typically the largest cost in a reselling business. I try to put all of the purchases on a credit card so I can easily track them.

Website/Phone/Internet Services: Make sure to track all of the technology services you pay for to run your eBay business. I add together my monthly internet fee and how much I pay for my phone. I also have a dedicated eBay store URL that I pay for through GoDaddy.

State Income Tax: I pay quarterly state income tax on all of my income so that I don't have to pay a large lump sum when I file my yearly tax returns. An accountant can prepare these for you; or if you do your taxes, the IRS will mail them to you directly.

Federal Income Tax: I pay quarterly federal income tax on all of my income so that I don't have to pay a large lump sum when I file my yearly tax returns. Just as an accountant can prepare these documents for you, the IRS will mail them to you directly if you file your tax returns.

Business Insurance: I carry insurance on my inventory and the part of the house I use for my business. Be sure to consult with your insurance agent to see if you need to add liability insurance to your home for people who may come to your home to deliver packages or pick up items you sold locally.

Bank/Credit Card Fees: Don't forget to track any fees you pay for your business bank account. If you are using a business card for purchases, you will also want to keep track of the fees you pay on the card.

Travel: You can claim any travel costs (gas, hotel) associated with your reselling business, such as trips out of town to source or if you attend any eBay events.

Meals: Track any food purchased in conjunction with running your reselling business (business meals, not the food you eat during your workday). This would include food you eat while traveling on business-related trips, such as sourcing out of town.

Monthly Health Insurance Premiums: If you pay out of pocket for health insurance, include that amount here. I get my insurance through the Affordable Care Marketplace at **healthcare.gov.**

Prescription Drug Copays: Tally up your monthly prescription drug copays here.

Doctor Copays/Deductibles/Dentist: Keep track of any out-of-pocket expenses you pay for health care, including at the dentist or optometrist.

Mileage: I use the app MileIQ to track my business mileage. It easily sorts personal trips from business trips and provides both monthly and yearly reports.

Office Space: I can also claim a portion of my home as office space; my accountant already has that figure in my files and inputs it into my returns every year.

Now, let's look at how I keep track of my transactions during the course of the month, using a purchase of office supplies as an example:

Let's say that I purchased copy paper for $10 at Staples on September 4th. On a checkbook-style ledger, I write "9/4" under "Date" and "Staples" under "Transaction." Since I spent money, I wrote "$10" under the "Debit" column. I then subtract $10 from the current "Balance" to give me my new business account balance.

See how this is done just as I would have if I had been using my household checkbook? You can also do this on a computer using an Excel spreadsheet. I just prefer to use paper and pen!

At the end of the month, I look through my "Debit" column. I add together all the expenses related to "Office/Shipping Supplies" and enter that number into my monthly expenses sheet.

At the end of the year, I add up all the total amounts under "Office/ Shipping Supplies" to get my total yearly expenses for that section. That final number, which goes onto my year-end sheet, is the only number I have to provide my accountant with.

I do the same for the other expense categories, too, and I give all the category totals to my accountant at the end of the year.

I then add up all of my eBay deposits for the year. Subtracting my total expenses (debits) from my total deposits (credits) gives me my NET profit for the year.

Figuring out your **NET** versus **GROSS** income is KEY to running any business.

GROSS income is the total amount of money, the "credits," you bring in BEFORE expenses are taken out.

NET income is the total amount of money you have left AFTER your expenses, the "debits," are taken out.

After you have accounted for all your expenses, or "debits," you will have your NET income, which is the actual PROFIT you made. **GROSS SALES minus EXPENSES equals NET PROFIT.**

In other words, **CREDITS minus DEBITS equals NET PROFIT.**

At the end of the year, I total my monthly debits and credits and combine them into yearly totals. I give my accountant my GROSS sales number, which is the total of all my credits. I then give him all my EXPENSES, which are all my debits. Subtracting my DEBITS from the CREDITS gives me my NET income for the year, and the NET income is what I pay taxes on.

Since I have other sources of income (books, YouTube, two Etsy shops, and affiliate marketing), I usually have several tax forms for my accountant to process. However, if your only business is eBay, then you will either have the 1099 tax form eBay provides you (if you sell over $600) or the numbers you have kept yourself for your accountant to work on (or for you to process if you are planning on filing taxes yourself).

As I noted on my accounting sheet, I also have other deductions that I give to my accountant, such as self-employed health insurance and prescription drug costs. I can also claim the areas of my house that I use for my business, including the utilities and property taxes.

Another thing I claim is the mileage from driving to the Post Office and going to estate sales and thrift stores. An easy way to do this is to keep a small notebook in your vehicle and write down your miles anytime you drive around on business. Or, as I said, you can use an app such as MileIQ.

My accountant has set up an income tax payment system for me, where I pay quarterly. He prepares four forms for me every quarter so that I mail a form and a check to the IRS every quarter. That way, I keep up with my income tax throughout the year and do not get hit with a hefty bill when I file my taxes. This is something he does as part of my yearly tax filing. If you file your taxes, you will get these forms directly from the IRS.

So, to recap: **My accounting system is basically a check register where I log my debits and credits.** I tally up the totals in each column at the end of the year and hand them off to my accountant, who then files my taxes.

There is no big box of receipts to keep track of. I do not have to spend hours in my accountant's office reviewing my records. It takes me about 30 minutes a month and around an hour at the end of the year to add up all my columns, and I then just give those numbers to my accountant. He factors in my deductions and files my tax returns for me.

EASY!!!

And to make it even easier for you, as I mentioned earlier, I also have reselling planners and accounting ledgers that I sell on Amazon. My

Reselling Planner & Accounting Ledger is available exclusively on Amazon. This 8.5x11-inch book is designed to help you keep track of your monthly and yearly sales and expenses as well as your weekly schedule. The bookkeeping pages offer space for not only eBay but also any other reselling platforms you may sell on.

Paying Yourself: Two questions I get asked a lot are, **"How much should I pay myself?"** and **"How much money should I reinvest in my business?"** After all your expenses are accounted for, and you know your net income, you will need to decide how much to keep for yourself and how much to put back into your business.

However, with eBay, your sales, and therefore, your cash flow, can vary wildly, which makes answering these two questions nearly impossible. All I can really do in this instance is to share with you how I handle this division of paying myself versus reinvesting in my business.

After filling out my accounting ledger at the end of the month, I see what my NET income for the month is. I pay all my personal bills (not my business expenses, as those were deducted for me to get my net income) from that total, and I am then left with a new amount.

If it has been an excellent sales month, I will have extra money to take out for myself while setting aside some for buying more items to resell. However, if sales have been slow, I may find that there is not much money left. So, I must choose: put that money back into my business for supplies and inventory or put it into my pocket for fun.

Let's say your NET income for January was $3000. Remember, NET means all your business expenses, including fees and inventory, have already been deducted. Out of that $3,000, you have $2,000 in personal bills that you need to pay, which leaves you with $1,000. After looking at prior months, you realize that you have spent around $500 a month to buy items to resell, so you decide to dedicate $500 to buy items in February, which leaves you with the remaining $500 for yourself.

Again, this is just an example. You always want to remember that you are selling on eBay to make money for yourself, not to funnel into your business continually. Keeping a ledger will help you track your cash flow and expenses to make an informed decision about how much money to take out for you and how much to leave in for your business. Don't get caught in the trap of reinvesting everything you make back into eBay; be sure to pay yourself or you will risk burning out and becoming disillusioned with reselling.

In business, you must spend money to make money. Selling on eBay means you will be spending money on inventory, supplies, and taxes. In fact, during months when you invest a lot into your business, you may find that you barely break even...or, worse, even lose money. With that, here is some advice on how to save money when you are selling on eBay.

> 1. Do not pay up for listing extras such as subtitles and second categories. Most of the "upgrades" eBay offers are not worth the money.

> 2. Repurpose shipping supplies when you can and ask friends, family, neighbors, and co-workers to give you their extra boxes and packing peanuts.

> 3. When you purchase shipping supplies, buy them in bulk to save money.

> 4. Plan your car trips to cut down on excessive gas usage.

5. Pay with cash as much as possible. If you do use a credit card, use only one. And try to pay off the balance every month to avoid interest charges.

6. Do not invest in fancy photography backdrops and expensive camera equipment. I use a white poster board from the dollar store for photos and use my iPhone to take my pictures.

7. Do not go sourcing until what you already have is listed. Shopping for inventory is the best part about reselling, but you cannot sell if your items are not listed. Your death pile is a money pile; do not bring any more items into your space until you list what you have.

8. Always look at the available shipping options for each order before purchasing postage to see if you can save a bit of money by choosing a different service or carrier.

9. Utilize USPS FREE Carrier Pickup to pick up your eBay packages to save a trip to the Post Office.

10. Don't invest in a fancy printer until you can pay for it in cash; I have run my business since 2005 without a DYMO or ROLLO thermal printer, and you can, too

Whether you are selling on eBay as a hobby or a full-time business, remember that your end goal is to make a profit. Too many resellers focus on shopping more than selling, tying up their money in unlisted inventory. But by implementing a simple accounting process such as the one detailed in this chapter, you can ensure that you are making money and not losing it!

CHAPTER TWELVE: TAKING YOUR EBAY BUSINESS TO THE NEXT LEVEL

When you own your own business, there is no difference between part-time versus full-time in terms of the hours you will work. Selling on eBay on even a part-time basis is an everyday commitment; you need to be available to answer customer questions and ship out orders promptly. If I am away from home for more than 24 hours, I put my *eBay Store* on vacation, now called *Time Away*.

But when I talk about a part-time versus full-time eBay business, I am really talking about income. I view a full-time eBay business as one that provides the same income level as an average 40-hour-a-week job, enough to completely support one person by covering all their living expenses. For some, however, a full-time income means making enough money to support an entire family.

Only you know the level of income you want or need, determining how many hours you put into reselling. The great thing about eBay is that if you want more money, you just need to source more items and create more listings. Consistently listing new items on eBay is the fundamental key to making money on the site. To grow an eBay business you want to list daily, if possible.

Most eBay sellers who view reselling as their business are part-time sellers. Many rely on a spouse's income for most of the household budget. They themselves may also work another part-time or even a full-time job in addition to eBay to earn enough money to support their family. Benefits such as health insurance are also a big reason many eBay sellers have other income sources.

I often joke that being a hobby seller on eBay is a part-time job, that being a part-time seller on eBay is a full-time job, and that being a full-time seller on eBay is the equivalent of working TWO full-time jobs! While social media paints a picture of reselling as simply filling carts at thrift stores, the truth is that selling online is WORK. Selling on eBay is a JOB. And no job is fun all the time.

Selling on eBay isn't necessarily hard, but it is time-consuming. Sourcing, photographing, listing, shipping, and customer service all take time to do properly. And they are physically taxing tasks. I typically end up a sweaty, exhausted mess after shopping at an estate sale as carrying items throughout the house, loading my car, and then unloading my purchases when I get home is a dirty job. And then comes the cleaning of everything before it's ready to be photographed and listed.

The reward of putting more time into eBay is larger profits. But the more you buy, the more you have to list. The more sales you have, the more shipping you have to do. And when your money is tied up in inventory, the pressure to make sales can be overwhelming.

While reselling on eBay can be very profitable, it can be hard to cover all household expenses and insurance costs by only selling online, especially as sales can go up and down depending on the time of year. I sell the most from October through March, but June through August is a painfully slow time, which is difficult because the summer is prime sourcing season with garage sales, church sales, and estate sales filling up the weekends.

However, don't let fear discourage you from your dream of starting a full-time home-based eBay business. With a ton of hard work and dedication, you can make a full-time living on eBay. However, I believe it is best to start slowly by viewing an eBay business first as a way to earn a little extra money, then expanding it to an actual part-time job while maintaining any other jobs you have. If you want to pursue it full-time after that, don't leap until you are bringing in the same amount of income as your regular job, if you have one.

If you follow the business advice in this chapter, you will already be prepared as your eBay business grows. Perhaps you are a stay-at-home mom or dad looking to supplement your spouse's full-time income. eBay can be an excellent job for you as it offers the flexibility of staying home with your children while running your own business. Plus, you retain the benefits from your spouse's job.

If you already have a job, I would advise keeping it and growing your eBay business slowly. I would never tell someone with a good-paying job and the benefits of quitting it to sell on eBay. However, maybe you have found yourself without steady employment. If you need a job now and see self-employment as your only option, there is no better home-based business, in my opinion, than eBay.

Whether you go part-time or full-time, earn a few thousand dollars a year, or an income in the six figures, make sure you treat eBay as a business. Even if you don't, Uncle Sam certainly will, as if you sell more than $600 on the site in a year, eBay will issue you a 1099 tax form and report your income to the IRS.

Speaking of taxes...oh, how they make people nervous. I get asked a lot about whether people should get a **Sales Tax Permit** and/or an **Employer Identification Number** for their eBay business. The answer is.... well, it depends.

Sales Tax Permit: If you plan to purchase items from wholesale companies, you will need a *Sales Tax Permit*. A *Sales Tax Permit* allows you to buy products at wholesale cost and not pay taxes on them. However, having a *Sales Tax Permit* means that you will need to collect and remit taxes on anything you sell to customers within your state.

Fortunately, eBay now handles the collection and remittance of sales tax on the sellers' behalf. When a customer buys an item from you if they live in a state that requires sales tax to be charged, the customer will pay the sales tax, but eBay will then automatically route that tax to the respective state.

However, if you have a *Sales Tax Permit*, you will still have to file sales tax quarterly with your state. Yes, even though eBay collects and remits the tax, you still need to fill out a form on every corner, even if you don't own anything. So, if you do not plan to use a *Sales Tax Permit* to purchase items at wholesale, you are better off not getting one.

Most liquidation companies do not require a *Sales Tax Permit* for you to buy from them. While wholesale companies act as a middleman between the manufacturer and retailer and usually require retailers to provide a *Sales Tax Permit*, liquidation companies buy from the retailers themselves, looking to offload returns, damages, and overstocks. So, if you plan to buy liquidation to resell, chances are you will not need a *Sales Tax Permit*.

Employer Identification Number (EIN): An *Employer Identification Number* or *EIN* is for business owners who plan to hire employees. However, some wholesale companies do require an *EIN* to place an order from them. An *EIN* is free and easy to apply for. Just as most liquidation companies do not require resellers to have a *Sales Tax Permit,* most do not require an *EIN*, either. Both *Sales Tax Permits* and *EINs* place a tax reporting burden on you that is avoidable if you do not have them or do not use them.

Business Insurance: If you plan to have an ample supply of inventory, you will want to carry business insurance to protect it in case of fire, theft, or other damage. You may also be liable for anyone who is injured coming to your home or business, including delivery people. If you plan to store thousands of dollars worth of merchandise in your home, you want to consider insuring it all.

If you plan to sell on eBay for others via consignment, you will need to get insurance to cover any damage to or loss of their items. You also want to protect yourself from consignment clients coming to your home and being injured. Call around to various insurance agencies and ask if they offer home-based business insurance coverage. If they do, ask for a free quote.

Health Insurance: If you have a spouse whose health insurance plan you can join, you are luckier than me. I have been purchasing my own health insurance since 2005, and I have paid upwards of $600 per month for my premiums, co-pays, and prescription drugs.

The **Affordable Care Act** now makes health insurance coverage more accessible and affordable for millions of Americans with the available tax credits. However, eligibility to buy insurance off the exchange is dependent on several factors, so make sure you find out if you qualify for ACA insurance before you quit your job to sell on eBay. Visit healthcare.gov for more information.

If you are looking for eBay to be your full-time income, you will want to examine the insurance costs involved as you will likely spend more on insurance than office supplies. And it is not just health insurance but also life insurance, injury insurance, sick time, vacation time, and retirement accounts. While you can purchase those benefits as an individual, they are very expensive. Again, you do not want to give up a good-paying job and benefits for an eBay career unless you are 100% sure it will provide for you and your family!

If you are serious about making eBay an actual business, it is helpful to talk to someone with business experience. If you want to work from home selling on eBay for a part-time or full-time income, two organizations can assist you: **SCORE** and the **Small Business Administration.**

SCORE stands for the Service Corp of Retired Executives. *SCORE* volunteers are former business owners who offer FREE, confidential counseling to anyone starting or expanding a business. They have 350 chapters in the United States, so you will likely be able to find an office near you.

Note that *SCORE* volunteers are retired and older; while they do have a lot of business experience, they may not know about eBay or online retailing. However, they can help you figure out any local or state laws regarding home-based businesses; and they will know some necessary information regarding taxes and permits. *SCORE* volunteers can also help you craft a business plan, which you will need if you plan to seek out a business loan from a local bank.

To learn more about *SCORE* and to find an office near you, visit **Score.org.**

The **Small Business Administration,** or **SBA**, offers confidential counseling and classes to anyone wanting to start a business, as well as services for those already running a company. *SBA* employees can provide you with information on what you need to operate a business in your area, including permits, licenses, and taxes.

Most offices have a small library of business books you can borrow, as well as computer labs. Classes are incredibly low-cost. They also offer incubator spaces for businesses needing a start-up location. As with *SCORE, SBA* staff can assist you in writing up a business plan, which at the very least, is a guide to helping you along with your business, and, at most, is crucial if you want to get funding.

To learn more about the *SBA* and to find an office near you, visit SBA.gov.

eBay's Seller Help: eBay itself is a fantastic resource for both new and experienced sellers. Visit ebay.com/help/selling to access articles and tutorials. At the bottom of the page is the **Need more help?** section where you will find a **Contact us** button, which will take you to the Customer Service page where there are several options for you to choose from:

- **Selling**
- **Buying**
- **Account**
- **Shipping & Tracking**
- **Returns & Refunds**
- **Fees & Billing**

Clicking on any of these sections will bring up several options that you will need to select to access the **Chat with our automated assistant** feature.

The eBay Community: When I first started selling on eBay, the eBay *Community* was a wealth of information for me. You will find the link to *Community* at the very bottom of all eBay pages. It resembles a social media platform with sections for announcements, articles, and message boards. Note that the message boards can be a bit intimidating for new sellers. I recommend you lurk on the boards for a bit before posting yourself to get a feel for the environment and decide if it's a place you want to be.

Facebook: If you have a Facebook account, you will find many groups dedicated to selling on eBay. The **eBay for Business** Facebook page also posts daily; it is the best place to go to get up-to-the-minute announcements directly from the company. And you can join the private **eBay for Business Podcast Group**, too.

PRO TIP: If you are having difficulty getting help through the eBay site directly, as a last resort, try messaging the *eBay for Business* Facebook page directly. You may have better luck getting a faster response and help for your problem.

Instagram: There is an active "reselling community" on Instagram that shares tips and tricks for selling on all online platforms, including eBay. Search the hashtags #reseller, #reselling, and #resellingcommunity to find like-minded online sellers. Whether you need specific questions answered or just want to find fellow resellers to connect with, you will find a great community on Instagram.

YouTube Videos: eBay has its own YouTube channel where they post videos of seminars from eBay events. There are also many reselling videos made by eBay sellers, including myself. Just as there is an active "reselling" community on Instagram, there is also one on YouTube. So many eBay sellers are sharing their tips and tricks for making money on their own YouTube channels. Whether you are looking for tutorials, hauls, or thrift-with-me videos, you will find them all within the reselling community on YouTube.

PRO TIP: The best way to grow your eBay business is to focus on sourcing sellable products, creating great listings, and committing to providing excellent customer service. Many successful eBay sellers don't have a social media presence. Make sure you've mastered all of eBay's tools and features before you spend the time to grow a social media presence. However, if you are craving community, social media can not only help you connect with other sellers but also drive more traffic to your listings!

CHAPTER THIRTEEN: PROVIDING EXCELLENT CUSTOMER SERVICE

There is a lot of misinformation and even fear about buying and selling on eBay, which spreads like wildfire on social media. Rumors about scams and people getting ripped off are rampant. However, eBay is overall a safe and secure place for both shoppers and sellers. In this chapter, I will hopefully clear up some common misconceptions about eBay along with giving you some practical advice about protecting yourself as a seller on the site.

eBay Support: eBay support is available by phone or through messaging, although eBay doesn't make contacting them easy. First, you can click on the **Help & Contact** link at the top of any eBay page to access their **Customer Service** section. Here sellers can click through several options:

- Returns & refunds for sellers
- Request to remove feedback
- Request to remove defects
- Review policy issues
- Request a selling limit increase
- Getting paid

You can click through any of those options to see if your question is answered in one of the posts. But you can also scroll to the very bottom of the page to find a **Contact us** section. A new page will open; click on any of the listed options to bring up a new window where you will finally find the link to **Chat with our automated assistant** or to **Ask an expert seller.**

PRO TIP: If you want to speak to a live eBay agent, first try typing AGENT into the chat box, which should bring up an option for you to ask that someone from eBay call you. You can also try calling 1-866-961-9253 to get through to an actual person.

Privacy/Safety: While the internet offers a level of anonymity when you are on eBay, there are some extra precautions you want to take. First and foremost is guarding your eBay account information. Change your passwords often, and make them a combination of letters, numbers, and characters so that they will be nearly impossible to hack.

The only legitimate messages from eBay will come to you via the eBay messaging system that you access when you are logged into your account. When you are logged in, you will see a **My eBay** link at the top of all pages. Click on that and select **Messages** from the drop-down menu. Unless you have opted for copies of all messages that Bay sends to you to also be emailed to you, the only messages from eBay will be found here.

eBay does not send sellers direct email messages off the site, only copies of messages that they sent to you through your account. If you get an email from eBay that is not also found in your *Messages* box, know that it is a scam. Scammers have been known to send emails to sellers disguised as messages from eBay saying that you need to click a link within the email to reset your password or log into your account. NEVER click on these email links, and do not give your eBay information to anyone claiming to be from the company either by phone or email.

Keeping your home address private is another concern for eBay sellers. I never worried too much about this until recently, when I finally got a P.O. Box so that I could make that my return mailing address for packages. And I mainly did this as I have a social media presence, not because of eBay customers directly.

Remember that your address will print out with your shipping label, so if you send out a lot of packages, you may want to make that address someplace other than home (such as your spouse's work or a P.O. Box). While this should not be a huge concern (after all, people have been using their home addresses for years), it may be something you want to consider if, like me, you have a public social media presence.

I have a designated email set up expressly for eBay, to which all copies of eBay communications go. Although some large sellers, typically those with warehouses or brick-and-mortar stores, set up a number specifically for eBay customers to call, I guard my phone number.

I also do not engage with customers outside of the eBay system. Several times over the years, buyers have gotten a hold of my phone number and called my house, leaving me messages asking me to return their calls. I do not return calls from anyone who calls my home, nor should you. I do the same with direct emails; I delete them without responding. If an eBay customer wants to communicate with me, they need to contact me directly through eBay's *Messages* system.

eBay Selling Practices Policy: It is important to remember that you need to adhere to eBay's rules to utilize their site. As I have said before, eBay is not YOUR business; it is a TOOL you use for your business. eBay has given us the following policies, which all sellers are expected to follow:

◈ Promptly resolve customer issues

◈ Ship items on time, within your specified handling time

◈ Manage inventory and keep items well-stocked

◈ Charge reasonable shipping and handling costs

◈ Specify shipping costs and handling time in the listing

◈ Follow through on your return policy

◈ Respond to buyers' questions promptly

◈ Be helpful, friendly, and professional throughout a transaction.

◈ Make sure the item is delivered to the buyer as described in the listing

eBay warns sellers that not meeting buyers' expectations can result in the following issues for sellers:

◈ Not meeting the late shipment rate requirements

◈ Exceeding minimum requirements for the defect rate

◈ A bad experience for you and the buyer

◈ Low-detailed seller ratings

◈ Negative or neutral feedback from a buyer

◈ A buyer requesting a return or reporting that an item was not received

◈ A buyer is asking us to step in and help with a transaction issue

And issues with buyers affect **eBay's Transaction Defect Rate Requirements,** which is the percentage of transactions that have one or both of the following defects:

◈ *eBay Money Back Guarantee* cases closed without seller resolution

◈ Seller-initiated transaction cancellation

To meet eBay's minimum standard selling requirements, sellers can only have up to 2% of transactions with one or more defects over the most recent evaluation period. To qualify as a **Top-Rated Seller**, which places your listings higher in search and gives you fee discounts, you can only have up to 0.5% of transactions with one or more defects over the most recent evaluation period. Only your transactions with US buyers count toward your seller performance rating.

According to eBay, *The defect rate won't affect your seller performance status until you have transactions with defects with at least five different buyers, or at least four different buyers, to impact Top-Rated status within your evaluation period. You can have a maximum of 0.3% of eBay Money Back Guarantee closed cases without seller resolution over the most recent evaluation period. That means the buyer reported they didn't receive an item, asked to return an item, or opened a case and you weren't able to resolve it, the buyer asked us to step in and help, and we found you responsible.*

They go on to explain, *Sellers with 400 or more transactions over the past three months are evaluated based on the past three months, and sellers with fewer than 400 transactions are evaluated based on the past twelve months. Buyers won't see your defect rate. Keep in mind that buyers still see your feedback rating and all four detailed seller ratings.*

Regarding shipping defects, EBay states that *sellers will be recognized for on-time shipping if tracking shows your item was either shipped within the stated handling time or delivered by the estimated delivery date. If there's no tracking available, we'll check with your buyer. If your buyer confirms the item was delivered on time—you'll be recognized for on-time shipping.*

eBay will only consider a shipment as late if:

◈ Tracking shows the item was delivered after the estimated delivery date **unless** there is an acceptance scan within your handling time or there is confirmation from the buyer of on-time delivery.

◈ The buyer confirms the item was delivered after the estimated delivery date **unless** there is an acceptance scan within your handling time or there is delivery confirmation by the estimated delivery date.

eBay's Money Back Guarantee: Buyers can have confidence when shopping on eBay due to the site's *Money Back Guarantee.* And while this policy can frustrate sellers who may feel that a buyer is taking advantage of them, the policy is in place to ensure that all customers feel safe when shopping on eBay so that they will return to the site again and again.

According to eBay, *When a buyer initially starts a return because the item didn't match the listing description or reports that they didn't receive an item, the transaction issue is called a "request." If the buyer and seller can't resolve the problem, and the buyer or seller asks us to step in and help with the transaction, the request then becomes a "case."*

These policies are not just public relations soundbites; they are what eBay uses to evaluate our seller performance standards, which allow us to continue selling on their site. However, eBay also offers many **Seller Protections,** including their **Abusive Buyer Policy**, which prohibits buyers from:

⬦ Demanding something that was not offered in the original listing

⬦ Making false claims about an order

⬦ Misusing returns

⬦ Misusing eBay's messaging system or bidding platform

⬦ Abusing the buyer protection program

eBay also recognizes that some situations are out of both the seller's and buyer's hands; fortunately, they offer protections for events outside of a seller's control, including:

If an item arrives late but tracking shows that you shipped it on time, eBay will automatically adjust your late shipment rate and remove feedback as long as the carrier scan shows you shipped within your handling time; or the carrier scan shows that the item arrived by the estimated delivery, even if you shipped it late.

If there is no tracking, the order will not be counted as late as long as the buyer does not indicate that it was late. This could happen if perhaps you mailed a small, flat item via *First Class Letter* mail that didn't get scanned in or stuck between other letters; or if your postal carrier did not scan the package. All eBay labels print with a barcode that carriers need to scan, but sometimes they are missed.

eBay is also particularly good about protecting sellers due to severe weather or other carrier disruptions by automatically adjusting the late shipment rate, removing canceled transaction defects, and removing feedback if you are in an area identified as experiencing delivery delays if the shipment receives a carrier scan within your handling time.

eBay updates us on their **Announcement Board** and the **eBay for Business Facebook** page whenever they identify a widespread carrier delay issue.

Messages: It is against eBay's policies for buyers and sellers to communicate off the eBay site regarding a transaction. All communication needs to be done through the eBay messaging system. Not only does this provide an easy way for you to keep track of all messages from both eBay and customers, but it also protects you as a seller as there will be an online record of all communications. So, if you are ever harassed or threatened by a customer, you can easily report it to eBay, and they will handle it.

At the top of all eBay pages is a link for **My ebay** with **Messages** as an option from the drop-down menu. You will find all messages that are sent to you and where you can send messages yourself. At the very bottom of all messages is an **Action** button. Click on it will access a drop-down menu with **Report message** and **Block this member** as options.

You can modify your messaging settings under the **Messages help** link on the left-hand side of your *Messages* page. You will be taken to a new page with a section titled **Managing your account**. Click on the **Messages** link to access these settings.

You need to keep communication with your buyers friendly and professional and not send messages to them needlessly. When a customer buys an item, eBay automatically sends them a notice that they have committed to purchasing the product and, if the item was won at auction, need to pay. Payment for *Fixed Price* sales is processed automatically.

There is no need for you to send customers messages demanding payment. I have seen so many new eBay sellers get into trouble doing this. If a buyer hasn't paid within 4 days, eBay will automatically cancel the sale and refund you all of your fees. If you choose to, you can also authorize eBay to automatically relist the item for you.

Accuracy: Ensure your listing titles, item specifics, and descriptions are all accurate. Any mistakes in these areas can lead to a customer filing an **Item Not As Described** (i.e., INAD) case against you. As I've mentioned, I try to "under promise and over deliver." My items are usually in better condition than described and I ship faster than promised, both of which lead to happy customers.

Non-Paying Buyers: From time to time, someone will bid on an item at auction and not pay. This is the nature of eBay, so expect non-paying bidders to pop up now and again. If I have an item up for auction and it ends with a winning bidder, I log onto eBay and send them an invoice for the order. If they do not pay by the following day, I send them a friendly note reminding them that their payment is due. But then I leave them alone as eBay requires buyers to pay within 4 business days before automatically closing the case and refunding the seller all fees.

Newbies: As a new seller, you may have to deal with people preying on your inexperience by sending messages to get you to sell them an item for less than you have listed. If you are open to accepting offers, you need to set up the *Best Offer* option in your listing; buyers should NOT contact you to request a discount or ask you to sell things off EBay. To stay safe, keep all your transactions ON EBay and report anyone trying to get you to deal with them offline.

Shipping: Another way to keep customers happy is to charge fair shipping prices. While it is okay to slightly pad flat rate shipping prices to cover handling fees, keep your postal charges as close to the actual price as possible to avoid customers giving you a low rating on your shipping, i.e., "dinging your stars."

I advocate using *Calculated Shipping* so that buyers pay the exact shipping cost based on the item's weight and the zip code it is going to. Ship your items the following business day (i.e., weekday). If you get a sale on a Saturday, go ahead and print the label out and prepare it for shipment on Monday. Ship your items in clean packing materials. Upgrade shipping from economy (slow) to expedited (fast) when possible to exceed your buyer's expectations.

Keeping a Schedule: To sell on eBay successfully takes a lot of WORK. Between sourcing items, listing them, answering customer questions, and preparing shipments, it is easy for eBay to take up every waking moment of your life. While attending to customers and shipping out items should always take priority, it is also essential to set realistic daily goals, so you do not get overwhelmed.

What has worked for me is to go out "picking" (i.e., shopping at estate sales and thrift stores, often referred to these days as "sourcing") only on certain days. I take photos on another day. I list on the days I am not sourcing or taking pictures. By only focusing on one area of business on a given day, I can commit to it fully and not get overwhelmed by trying to do it all in a single day. The only tasks I do every single day are answering customer questions and shipping out orders.

I also make sure to take some time off now and then. A day or two off from eBay ensures that you do not burn out on your business. Even a few hours away from the computer to do something fun like meeting a friend for lunch or going window shopping can help you return to eBay with renewed energy. After all, you likely started a home-based business so that you would have more freedom and time with your family, so do not forget to take time for yourself!

If a buyer ends up not paying and eBay automatically cancels the sale, I relist the item and block the buyer. I try not to harp on the lost sale. It happens. The best thing to do is move on and focus on the customers who have paid.

Under-Promise & Over-Deliver: As I've mentioned, one of the best pieces of advice I got when I started selling on EBay was to "under-promise and over-deliver." If you say you will ship items in two days, ship them in one. Print the label out as soon as possible after payment clears so that the buyer will get a notification that the item has shipped. If an item is in excellent condition, list it as "very good" so the buyer gets more than they expected. Use clean packing materials and wrap items well inside their boxes to protect them during shipping. Upgrade shipping when possible, so customers get their orders faster than expected.

Returns: No one who sells online likes returns. It is so exciting to sell an item and get paid, and it is a huge letdown when the customer contacts you wanting to return that item. Issuing refunds is no fun.

For years, I set my return policy so customers could return items they simply did not like at their own expense within 14 days. In 2019, eBay changed the time frame to a mandatory 30 days; and they also started pushing sellers to accept "free" returns, meaning sellers had to pay the return shipping.

At that point, I opted out of returns altogether as it just was not financially feasible for me to accept returns, especially since I usually offer "free shipping" on most of my items. Paying for the shipping to AND from a customer would leave me with no room for profit when factoring in all the other fees and business expenses related to selling on eBay.

However, if I have made a mistake when listing the item (I described the fabric wrong or took incorrect measurements), then the error is mine, and I will issue the buyer a full refund, including postage. Unless it is a high-priced item that I can easily resell, I usually just tell the customer they can keep the item to give to someone else or donate so that I do not have to pay the return postage. If I am going to have to throw the item away myself, there is no sense in paying for the buyer to ship it back to me.

For example, if I originally paid $1 for a shirt and listed it for $15.99 with free shipping, my actual profit is only about $8 after postage and fees, including my business expenses and taxes. I will not spend another $6 to have the customer return it to me so that I can relist it and only end up with a couple of dollars left in profit. Small sales like this usually are not worth the hassle of dealing with a return, and since it was my mistake, issuing a refund makes the buyer happy and lets me move on to my other sales.

Some clothing sellers accept returns if the buyer pays the shipping, and a small handful of sellers offer "free" returns on everything they sell. What you do is up to you, but if you are just starting out selling clothing specifically, you might find it beneficial to accept returns until you build up your feedback and get the hang of selling clothes. eBay's bulk editing feature can easily change your return policy anytime.

The best way to prevent returns or complaints is to do everything possible to accurately describe the items you are selling in the first place. Ensure you take lots of good photos, provide accurate measurements, and are honest about the item's condition. If a shirt has a tiny mark on it, disclose that in the listing AND show a picture of it. If a coat has a button missing, put that in the item condition field AND in the item description field AND take a close-up photo of it. Items with minor flaws can still sell, but to ensure the sale sticks and that the buyer does not return the item, you need to be upfront and honest in the original listing.

Buyers can get around a "no returns" policy by stating that an item was not as described (in eBay speak, this is called an **INAD**, i.e., **Item Not As Described**). Unfortunately, some buyers use this trick to return clothing they do not like. And eBay usually backs them up, meaning you have no choice but to accept the return and pay for the postage AND refund the buyer their total original price, including shipping. While this is highly frustrating, it happens to everyone at some point when they are selling on eBay. I deal with this by accepting the return and relisting the item, and I also block the buyer.

Remember that when dealing with any customer issue, you want to stick to communicating only through eBay's messaging system. If a buyer wants to make a return, they need to go through eBay's return process, not contact you directly to arrange the return. If a buyer does contact you directly wanting to return a piece of clothing, give them these directions:

- To start a return, find the item in the **Purchase History** link under **My eBay** at the top of any eBay page
- Select the reason for the return.
- Print a return shipping label and packing slip.
- Pack the item carefully.
- You can track the returned item's status in My eBay's *Purchase History* section.

By going through eBay's return process, both you and the buyer are protected. You can track the package and issue a refund upon the item's return to you as a seller. If you do not receive the item back and tracking proves this, eBay will close the case and protect you from the buyer retaliating with negative feedback.

However, if you get the item back in the condition you initially shipped, you need to log into eBay and close the return case. eBay will automatically issue the buyer a refund, taking the funds from your *Pending Balance* account. At that point, you can easily relist the item. Items that are returned and then relisted have a higher sell-thru rate as eBay's algorithm favors listings with a sales history, so sometimes returned items sell almost immediately after you relist them.

So, what is the best way to keep your account in good standing, even when dealing with unexpected emergencies or demanding customers? Here are my tips:

1. Ensure your listings are accurate with the correct measurements, conditions, and item specifics. Also, provide lots of clear photos showing the item from every angle so that customers know exactly what they are buying.

2. Do not steal other sellers' photos or use stock photos unless you have permission from the company.

3. Make sure you meet your handling time. My handling time is two business days, but I almost always ship the next business day. However, the extra day is a buffer in case something comes up.

4. Upgrade shipping when possible. Be sure to check all the shipping options available when you go to print your

postage. You may find that you can provide an expedited shipping service for the exact cost as the economy option.

5. Respond to customer questions promptly and professionally.

6. Package your items well to prevent breakage.

7. If you get a return request or a message from a buyer saying the item arrived damaged, take a deep breath, and direct them on how to use eBay's return system to file a claim. Do not get into a fight via messaging; eBay's system is set up to handle claims and returns.

8. If eBay sides in a buyer's favor, it is okay to be upset but do not let it ruin your day or your business. See if you could have done anything differently to affect the outcome and implement those lessons as you continue selling.

9. Do not use the eBay messaging system for anything other than talking to eBay customers about specific listings. Do not offer to sell something off the eBay site. Do not give buyers your phone number or email address. Do not reply to harassing messages; report those immediately to EBay and let them handle it.

10. Over-promise and over-deliver!

The following are some of the most common questions I have gotten over the years in regards to problems selling on EBay:

HELP! A customer wants me to end an auction early and sell an item to them for a set price! When you place an item up for auction, you may have someone message you that they will buy the item if you end the auction.

Do NOT do this! People like this are likely trying to lowball you because they think they can get the item for less than it will go for at auction. When I get messages like this, I reply that the auction is already in motion with watchers and will not end early. If you want to add a *Buy Now* or *Make Offer* to your auctions, you can; but if you didn't want to accept offers when you created the listing, stick with your decision and allow the auction to run its course.

HELP! A customer claims they have not received their package, yet tracking shows it was delivered! This comes up every so often, and it is usually a case where someone else in the home has taken in the package, or it was delivered to a neighbor. I ask the customer to double-check, reminding them that tracking shows their order was delivered.

Once they know you have tracking (which is why you should always ship through eBay as the shipping labels are printed with a tracking bar code and number), you will be amazed at how quickly buyers find their missing packages! Sadly, some people will try to get full refunds on their orders by saying they have not arrived. But as long as you have shipped your packages through eBay and have a valid tracking number, eBay will back the transaction up in your favor.

HELP! A customer says their item arrived broken! When a customer messages me that their item arrived broken, I calmly reply that I am so sorry and ask them to provide me with a photo of the damage. Do NOT just blindly give out refunds; it is important to ask for proof. eBay has added the ability to attach photos to its messaging system, making it easy for buyers to send you a picture.

There are scammers out there who break their own item, buy a replacement on eBay, and then try to pass off their original broken item like the one they just bought. While these scams are very rare, they do happen. If you are selling expensive items, consider marking them in a way that will be impossible to replicate to prevent customers from making a switch.

If you get a picture of an item that is broken, you will have to issue a refund. If you do not, the customer will file a claim with eBay, and eBay will automatically refund their money by taking it out of your pending balance. While this can be frustrating, it is just a part of selling online. And it will make you want to ensure that your orders are packaged to the best of your ability. If you are shipping the package through USPS *Ground Advantage* or *Priority Mail*, it is automatically insured for up to $100, so you can file a claim with the Post Office to recoup your loss.

HELP! I got an email from eBay saying I need to reset my account/my account has been suspended/I need to verify my identity and click on a link in the email! Remember that ALL eBay messages go through eBay's messaging system; you will NEVER get an email from eBay or sent directly to your email address without a copy of it also being in your eBay messages. Any email asking for your password or for you to click on a link to take a survey is a SCAM. Ignore it and delete it! Only respond to eBay messages WITHIN your eBay messaging system WITHIN your eBay account!

HELP! My item isn't selling! Does your item have any watchers? Has anyone asked you questions about it? Take a good look at your listing to see if you can improve it by writing a better title, including more photos, or adding to the description. Maybe your price was too high, or you had it at *Auction* when it would sell better at *Buy Now*. End the listing, click on **Sell Similar**, and then edit it. If it does not sell after another long period and is not getting any traffic or watchers, it may be better to pull it to donate or sell at your garage sale.

HELP! A customer is threatening to leave me negative feedback if I don't do something, and/or they are cursing at me! Feedback extortion is NOT allowed on EBay; neither is foul nor threatening language. Report messages like this immediately!

PRO TIP: In business, the customer is always right (even when you know they are wrong!), so it is essential to have a good set of customer policies in place so that both you and the buyer understand what is expected of one another. eBay, of course, has its own set of policies that you must adhere to, such as giving buyers 4 business days to pay for their items. You cannot demand someone pay you within an hour as that is not eBay's rule. When you sell on eBay, you must first follow eBay's rules.

Remember what we've already discussed: eBay is not YOUR business; it is a TOOL you use in your business. Use the tools they provide to make your eBay journey a success!

BONUS: RESELLING CLOTHING ON EBAY

Clothing is the largest category on eBay and the one where you will find the most full-time sellers. Whether it's clothes purchased at thrift stores or from liquidation companies, clothing is an in-demand product that almost any seller has access to. Therefore, I am adding this bonus section dedicated to selling clothing on eBay.

This section is for those who want to sell clothing on eBay, whether because your favorite resellers on social media do or because you have a genuine interest in it. Or it may be that you are already reselling but simply want to add in some clothes to diversify your inventory. Clothing is different from reselling hard goods, hence why it deserves a dedicated section in this book.

Why is clothing such a great item to sell on eBay? Not only are clothes highly sought after by buyers on eBay, but clothing is extremely easy and cheap for sellers to find for resale. Garage sales, yard sales, rummage sales, estate sales, charity sales, consignment stores, and thrift stores arc all bursting at the seams with clothes. No matter what the climate is where you live, you can always find clothing somewhere in your area to buy for resale on eBay!

Clothes to resell can be found in numerous places, including:

Thrift Stores: My favorite place to buy clothing to resell in my area is the thrift stores. Since I'm not a full-time clothing seller, I only pick up clothes at rock-bottom prices. Our Goodwill stores have a different color sale tag every day that gets shoppers half off. This is their way of making sure inventory moves quickly.

You likely have Goodwill locations in your area, but there are many other secondhand stores across the country. From large chains such as Savers and Value Village to locally run Salvation Army stores and other charity shops, search out all the thrift shops in your city to find which ones are worth sourcing clothing at.

While all thrift stores are managed differently, most have discount days or other sale promotions. However, not all advertise their sales. You must be proactive and ask the clerks about sale days or discount cards. Many stores also have social media accounts, so find the locations near you on Facebook and Instagram to keep up with their sales announcements. And be sure to check their websites for sale calendars and email lists you can sign up for so that you do not miss any special offers.

You want to ensure you are paying as little as possible for clothing as it is a crowded eBay market on eBay. The regular everyday prices at my Goodwill are too high for me to make a profit on, so I can only shop during the sales. Plus the brands in my area are typical mall brands that don't bring as much money as higher-end pieces. You may be one of the lucky people whose thrift stores are bursting with high-end goods at low prices, but most resellers have to hunt. However, most clothing resellers LOVE clothes, so, for them, thrifting is fun.

As with any item you are buying to resell, you want to buy low and sell high (i.e., buy it CHEAP and sell it for a big PROFIT!). Size, style, brand, and condition all factor into what you can sell an item for on eBay. If you are just starting, try to pay as little as possible as you learn what sells, how to list clothing, and how to properly ship it.

Goodwill Outlets: Goodwill has pay-by-the-pound outlet stores in some markets, also referred to as "The Bins." The outlet stores sell merchandise that did not sell in the regular Goodwill locations. Sometimes, if an area has an abundance of donations, items skip the regular stores altogether and go straight to the outlets.

Most *Goodwill Outlet* stores use big plastic blue bins on rollers to bring merchandise out onto the sales floor, hence the nickname "The Bins." Shoppers must dig through these giant bins to find what they want to buy; at checkout, they roll their shopping carts onto a big scale to see how much they have purchased in weight (minus the shopping cart as the stores calibrate their scales to account for the heavy metal carts).

Every *Goodwill Outlet* location is run differently. Some charge the same per-pound rate for all items, while others separate clothing from hard goods. Some locations only sell clothing, and others sell a mix of both clothes and hard goods such as books, dishes, toys, and décor. Some outlets are very clean and orderly; some are a dusty, dirty mess. Some have very strict rules about when you can and can't touch the merchandise as it is being rolled out. And some require that you wear gloves.

Condition is a huge issue when sourcing clothing at *Goodwill Outlets*. Again, most of the pieces were for sale first in a regular Goodwill store but did not sell there, hence why they were sent to "The Bins." There may be a reason that an item did not sell at the regular store, such as it perhaps having a stain or tear. But, as I mentioned, sometimes unsorted donations go straight to the outlets, meaning you'll have a better chance of finding hidden treasures.

Garage Sales: In addition to thrift stores and "The Bins," you can also find clothing at garage sales, yard sales, tag sales, and rummage sales, which are all the same thing but seem to be called something different depending on the area of the country you live in. As a reseller, I used to cringe when I would drive up to a garage sale and see racks of clothing. However, now I know that garages full of clothing can be gold mines.

In my city, garage sales are advertised in the local newspaper and on Facebook. Several Facebook groups are dedicated to posting local garage sales online, and some cities even post their sales on mobile apps. And some people skip the ads altogether and just put signs up when they are having a sale.

Garage "sail-ing" usually requires a lot of driving from house to house looking for treasures, but garage sales can pay off big time for those who love hunting deals. A bit of planning the night before you go out is essential; I create a map of the advertised sales and always find unadvertised ones as I drive around my area.

When hitting up garage sales, be sure to have a lot of cash on hand, mostly $1 and $5 bills. If you buy clothing, try bundling several pieces together and asking for a deal. While getting to sales early means you get the best selection, showing up toward the end of the sale might pay off if the homeowners are desperate to unload their unsold items. If you go to a sale and the prices are too high on their opening day, try going back during their last hour to see if they are willing to sell to you at a discount.

Charity Sales: Charity sales are held everywhere, from churches and schools to community centers and senior homes. Since multiple people usually donate goods to these sales, they attract huge crowds. Most charity sales I have been to sell clothing for $1 apiece or by-the-bag for $5.

Since charity sales tend to attract many shoppers, I try to ensure I am in line early to score the best deals. However, attending on the last day of these sales can also be advantageous as many organizations are desperate to sell all remaining items and may offer discounts, including fill-a-bag deals. Most charity sales are cash only, so be sure you are ready with $1 and $5 bills.

Estate Sales: Estate sales are usually held by professional liquidation companies and are in the homes of someone who is moving or has passed away. While most people go to estate sales searching for antiques and collectibles, many estate sales also have clothing. If it is the estate of an older person, you may luck out and find vintage clothes. I love finding vintage jackets and hats at estate sales.

Research all the estate sale companies in your area and start attending their sales so that you learn how they price their items. Most also have Facebook pages where they post photos of their sales. Also, find out what payments they accept; in my area, some only accept cash and checks, while others only accept cash and credit cards. Some companies may want you to bring your own bags and provide your own manpower, while others insist on bagging your items for you and carrying them to your car.

Be friendly and get to know the staff. Remember that estate sale companies are working for the homeowners while also paying their own business expenses. They are often unwilling to negotiate prices, especially on the first day. However, most companies offer the remaining items at half-off on the last day or in the final hours. Usually, the more you buy, the more they are willing to negotiate with you.

Flea Markets: Flea markets are typically outdoor events where numerous sellers set up tables and racks to sell their goods. Flea markets are typically thought of as the place to find collectibles and antiques but don't discount them for sourcing clothing, especially vintage and retro pieces. Be sure to have plenty of cash with you and also bring bags to carry your purchases in. If the flea market is outdoors, be sure you are conscious of the weather and wear a hat and sunscreen if necessary. Also, wear comfortable shoes and bring water and snacks.

Consignment Stores: Whether it is a big chain store or a small local operation, consignment stores are typically full of clothing. While prices can be high on the newest items put out on the sales floor, the longer an item sits, the more it gets discounted. Plus, most stores have frequent sales. Visit the consignment stores in your area to learn about their pricing and sale calendars and see what sorts of merchandise they sell. Also, see if they have social media pages, specifically on Facebook, that you can follow for updates.

Plato's Closet and Buffalo Exchange are two national consignment stores that focus on trendy clothing for younger people. Both stores buy items outright from patrons who bring in their unwanted clothing. Our Plato's Closet has frequent sales, discounting pieces as low as 90%. Some stores offer dollar days and even fill-a-bag sales.

In Iowa, we have a chain of consignment stores called Stuff Etc. Not only do I shop at Stuff, but I also consign there. Stuff Etc. stores are massive and carry every category of item that regular thrift stores do. The difference is that the items are more carefully curated. Stuff only accepts clean, in-season items, so the selection is often better than Goodwill.

However, with that curation comes higher prices. I can rarely buy anything at full price at Stuff Etc. to resell, but I find quite a lot when the items go on clearance. Stuff Etc. reduces the price of an item by 50% once it's been in the store for 60 days and down to 80% when it's been in the store for 90 days. After that, they sometimes pile the clothing into shopping carts for 90% off. It's like *Goodwill Outlet* shopping without having to dig as much as the items are of better quality.

If you live in or near Iowa, visit *shopstuffetc.com* to see where the closest Stuff Etc. store is to you. For other consignment store locations, search on Facebook to see if there are any near you. Independently owned consignment stores typically don't have a marketing budget, meaning they rely on social media to advertise.

Facebook Marketplace: "For Sale" ads used to be placed in local newspapers, but many people sell their items on *Facebook Marketplace* these days. I often see people selling lots of clothing (usually in a specific size as they are cleaning out their closets) for next to nothing. While you will likely end up with some pieces that you cannot resell due to style or condition, it is a quick and easy way to get a large amount of inventory, which is especially nice if you are just starting to resell clothing.

Facebook is also a great place to advertise that you are looking to purchase clothing in bulk. Be sure to specify the brands, styles, and/or sizes you are looking for and what you are willing to pay. Also, be clear that you only purchase from smoke-free homes. When meeting people from Facebook to buy items, stay safe, and choose a public place during the daytime. If possible, take someone with you, just to be safe.

Friends & Family: Let your friends and family know that you are looking to purchase any clothing they want to part with. Posting this to your personal Facebook page is a great way to spread the word. Be ready with a list of the brands, sizes, and styles you are looking for, along with how much you are willing to pay for each piece. Have this information firmly established, so you do not get guilt-tripped into buying items you do not want to resell, such as worn-out kids' clothing or extra small-sized tops from Walmart.

Liquidation & Wholesale: In *Chapter Four*, I covered several companies where you can buy both secondhand and new goods in bulk, including clothing. Please refer back to that chapter for all of the details, but I will provide the list of the companies that specifically deal in clothing again here:

- **B&G Trading**
- **Bstock.Com**
- **Bulq.com**
- **Continental Wholesale**
- **Fox Liquidation**
- **Goodwill Bluebox**
- **Liquidation.com**
- **Merchandize Liquidators**
- **Quicklotz.com**
- **ViaTrading**
- **Wholesale Ninjas**

Consignment: As I discussed in *Chapter Four* of this book, another popular eBay business model is to sell items on consignment for other people. Please refer back to that chapter for more details about selling items for other people, but just know that it can be an especially profitable business model for clothing, especially.

So, we have established that clothing is available no matter where you live, and you now know it can be had for cheap. However, just because clothing is easy and inexpensive to source does not mean you should buy it all up to resell on eBay. Style, size, condition, and brand name all factor into how much an item will sell for or if it will even sell at all.

CLOTHING CATEGORIES: Clothing covers a wide variety of categories on eBay, from accessories and shoes to outerwear and underwear. Here are just some of the categories of clothing that you can sell on EBay:

Belts: Resellers often overlook the belt category, but there is a market for belts on eBay. Look for higher-end brand names and larger sizes; genuine leather pieces sell best as do exotic reptile skins.

Blazers: Both women's and men's blazers (also called suit jackets) are expensive to purchase new, which is why many shoppers turn to eBay to find them secondhand at a great price. When sourcing blazers, be sure to check that all the buttons are intact, including those on the cuffs. Also, make sure the piece hasn't been altered as that will change the size versus what is on the label.

Bras: Bras in large sizes and from popular brands, such as Victoria's Secret, sell very well on eBay. I used to cringe when I saw a table full of bras at a garage sale, but now I kick myself for passing them by. The larger the size, the better. Vintage bras can also sell well, especially if they are still in their original package.

Coats & Jackets: I love to pick up coats and jackets in the off-season when no one else is looking at them. I focus on better brand names and larger sizes, and I double-check all buttons, zippers, and linings to ensure there are no missing pieces or flaws. I also look to see if the coat initially had a detachable hood; I pass up many coats that end up missing their hoods. The same goes for missing belts on trench coats.

Corduroy Jackets: Be careful to differentiate between denim and corduroy jackets in your listings; I once described a corduroy jacket as denim and had to accept a return on it. While both corduroy and denim are usually 100% cotton and have the same structure, corduroy, which is thick and textured, has a much different feel than denim.

Denim Jackets: Blue jean denim jackets have always been my best-selling clothing item. They are the one item where the brand does not matter as much as any good-looking jacket seems to sell well. Denim jackets in colors other than blue (such as black, red, white, or pink) are incredibly hot on eBay, as are coats in larger sizes. Note the fabric makeup when listing jean jackets as some have stretch via spandex, which is a feature many customers want. While denim holds up very well, make sure all buttons are intact.

Dresses: New dresses are expensive and are an item that many people only wear once, which is why so many shoppers turn to eBay to find their special occasion dresses at a discount. However, do not just focus on sourcing formal dresses as casual summer dresses and career wear dresses sell just as well, and sometimes even better. Do some research to see what is on trend and look for those pieces. For example, if maxi dresses are currently the hot style, look for those first over mini dresses.

Handbags: You will likely find purses, totes, and wallets displayed near the clothing at most thrift stores. Look for brand-name bags with little to no wear (including on the inside) to flip on eBay. Check to ensure the zippers work and that all details, such as studs and jewels, are intact.

Many bags were initially sold with detachable cross-body straps; if you pick up a purse that is missing this extra strap, it can still sell; make sure you disclose that the strap is missing. Also, look over the bag's interior lining; this is where I often find the most issues as the linings are often dirty and stained.

Note that there are many counterfeit designer handbags out there. Even purses marked as Coach or Kate Spade can be fakes. If you are found to have listed a fake bag on eBay, they will pull the listing. Before you list a bag online, do some research to ensure it is authentic.

Jeans: Blue jeans are one of the largest clothing categories on eBay, and fortunately for resellers, they are in abundance at thrift stores and garage sales. Check the crotches for rips, and make sure the inside labels are intact. Denim jeans are usually easy to list as many have the style and size (waist and inseam) on the label. As with most items, larger sizes tend to sell best, although high-end denim usually sells despite the size. Make sure the jeans haven't been altered; regardless of what the inseam label says, do your measuring to ensure they weren't shortened.

Men's Hats: Vintage fedora and cowboy hats have always been quick and easy sales for me on eBay, especially when they are leather or suede. Vintage snapback baseball and trucker hats are also good pieces to pick up. Vintage hats with patches sewn onto them are particularly in demand.

Men's Flannel Shirts: Cotton men's flannel shirts are highly sought after on eBay. The softer and thicker the material, the better it sells. Though the best-sellers are vintage, any shirt with pearl snaps will typically sell the fastest regardless of age. Woolrich is a very popular brand of flannel.

Nylons: I have had great success selling new-in-the-package women's nylons, which I can usually find at Goodwill in an out-of-the-way bin. I also find hosiery at estate sales. Usually, I can find several packages of the same size at thrift stores and estate sales. Unless they are vintage (vintage nylons can bring hundreds of dollars per pair!), I sell nylons in lots by size.

Overalls: Blue jean denim overalls are hard to find new in the stores, which is why they are popular with customers on eBay. Maternity overalls are an incredibly hot seller. I have found that the brand does not matter regarding overalls. I pick up full-length and short styles and overall dresses and skirts.

Puffer Coats & Vests: Outerwear in the "puffer" style (quilted and puffy) is always a good seller on eBay for men, women, and children. However, note the size and weight before picking up puffer jackets, as the larger ones will not fit into a Flat Rate Priority Mail padded mailer, which is a popular envelope among clothing resellers. They are still okay to buy to resell; just note that the shipping cost will be higher as they will have to ship in a larger poly bag or box.

Shoes & Boots: The secondhand shoe market on eBay is enormous. Good, clean shoes from better-known brands can bring in good money. Familiarize yourself with the season's trends to know what to look for when sourcing. As with clothing, larger sizes of shoes tend to sell the fastest. High-end boots in leather and other animal skins are also good sellers.

Sweaters: Well-made sweaters, especially cashmere ones, are in demand during the fall and winter on eBay. While I do not live in an area where designer brands are sold, I can still find sweaters from Land's End, Eileen Fisher, and L.L. Bean that sell well online. Beware of cheap itchy acrylic sweaters as they do not sell well.

Vests: My Goodwill stores (there are three locations close to where I live) all have designated racks for vests. I always look through them, searching for designer brands and outerwear (as often puffer vests are placed in with the vests rather than the coats). Vests with novelty patterns and prints are usually good sellers as are those made of leather or denim.

Vintage Tee Shirts: Tee shirts from the 1990s and before can be highly collectible. I look for concert and sports tees in good condition, although sought-after designs can sell regardless of condition. "Single stitch" is the most desirable. Modern tees have a distinct double line of stitching around the arms, collars, and hem.

One line of stitching indicates it is a "single stitch," and therefore vintage.

Women's Shirts: After denim jackets, my favorite items to pick up at thrift stores and garage sales to resell are women's shirts and tops. They are often lightweight, making them easy to list and ship. As with all clothing, I focus on better brand names and larger sizes when sourcing shirts.

As a reseller who only sells a bit of clothing, I deal primarily with men's and women's tops and outerwear. Since those are the categories of clothing I am most familiar with, those are the pieces I am naturally drawn to when I am out at garage sales and thrift stores. If you only want to sell clothing, you can still narrow down your focus. I know resellers who only sell shoes while others only sell dresses. Choose a niche that works best for you.

For example, if you have kids, you may have a knack for children's clothing. If you love shoes, footwear may be just the item you hunt for. While I have shared the items that work best for my business model, please do not let that stop you from sourcing the styles you are most interested in. You will be much more successful in reselling items you like versus picking up items you hate.

SIZES: When selling clothing on eBay, size matters, especially when dealing with more common brands. High-end designer clothing will sell in any size (and let's face it, most of the prominent brand-name designers only sell smaller sizes, anyway). However, mall store brands that are readily available everywhere tend to sell best on eBay when they are in larger sizes.

In general, I stick to the "Small/Medium/Large" sizing, i.e., NOT specific fitted sizes such as "Size 4" or "Size 10." I find that someone is much more likely to buy a size "Large" shirt than a "Size 12" shirt. Most clothing sizes run differently according to the designer, too, so sticking to the "S/M/L" range is easier on me as a seller and for my buyers. I will be talking more about providing clothing measurements in your eBay listings coming up later in this chapter.

I always look for larger clothing sizes for women, specifically extra-large and up. Women's plus sizes are typically marked as "0X, 1X, 2X, 3X, etc."; or with a "W," such as "22W" or "28W." Clothes labeled "XXL," and "XXXL" are usually considered to still fall under "regular sizing"; however, they are some of my best-selling sizes. Let's be honest: most women would prefer to buy a "regular size XXL" than a "plus size 1X" (even though in many brands, they are the same size).

Larger sizes are always the first to sell out new in the stores, so they are usually easy to resell on eBay as they are in demand. If you've ever looked at the clothing clearance in a store, you know that there is usually an abundance of XS but very few XL. Some people are also very self-conscious of their size and are embarrassed to shop in a brick-and-mortar store, so they turn to eBay to shop in private.

While I steer away from "Petite" women's clothing, I always pick up "Tall" sizes. Very few brands make "Tall" sized women's clothing, so statuesque ladies must go on eBay to find styles that will fit them. "Petite" sizes do sell; they just tend to sell more slowly for me, so I focus on items I can move faster.

Men's large sizes are often the same as women's (i.e., "2XL, 3XL, 4XL"), although, with men's buttoned shirts, you get into neck and sleeve markings. I love finding big and tall men's clothing, which is usually marked with a "T" (i.e., "XLT, 2LXT, XXXT"). Just as "Tall" sizing is a niche category in women's clothing, it is also a specialty size in men's and is hard to find in the stores, meaning men must shop online for it. I will pick up a dress shirt from a lower-end brand if I find it in a "Tall."

However, as I have said, a high-end designer brand will usually sell despite the size. That is why it is important to look at the labels when sourcing clothing. A Gucci shirt will sell even if it is a size "XXS" just because it is Gucci. Likewise, an Old Navy jacket in a "XXL" will sell despite Old Navy being a common mall brand. I will pick up a Walmart brand if it is a size "4X" but won't even look twice at it if it's an "XL" or smaller.

CONDITION: Unless you are selling a hard-to-find, vintage, and/ or extremely high-end designer brand of clothing, the piece's condition is critical when it comes to selling it on eBay. It can be hard to give a piece of clothing a rigorous inspection in the middle of a crowded thrift store, but here are some things I make sure to look over before heading to check out:

Buttons: I look to ensure all buttons, including those on cuffs and pockets, are intact. I pass on items that need new buttons as I do not have the time to find replacements. Note that if you find a high-end designer piece that is missing buttons, you can still buy the item and remove the remaining buttons to sell on their own if they are stamped with the designer's name.

Labels: A mistake I have made several times is buying an article of clothing that was missing a size label. I sometimes get so excited by spotting a brand name that I miss the fact that the original owner of the piece cut out the label with its size. While you can provide measurements for a piece of clothing with its label cut out, most buyers want the labels intact. Remember that not all size labels are on the inside collar; some are on the garment's inside body or a label hidden in the pockets.

Pilling: Those little balls that form on your cotton shirts after they have been washed multiple times? It is called pilling, and it instantly screams that an item is in too worn of condition for resale. You can use a sweater shaver on these garments if the pilling is contained in one small area, especially if it's a valuable piece, but if the entire piece is covered in pilling, pass on it.

Pockets: Be sure to look at both the outside and inside pockets of garments (many trench coats, for example, have pockets in the lining) for rips. A bonus to checking pockets is that you might find some forgotten cash inside. Although, you also might find used tissues or unwrapped candies. Yuck!

Seams: I always give the seams a quick look to make sure there are no tears or rips. If you (or someone else in your house) can sew, minor tears along the seam can be repaired relatively easily. However, unless it is a high-end item, I do not want to waste my time doing any clothing repairs.

Stains: I always put back any item of clothing that has stains on it. While some stains can be treated and washed out, I do not have the time to deal with repairs. I wash almost all clothing before listing it on eBay; if a stain doesn't come out in the regular wash, it's likely set and the piece isn't salvageable if the stain is in a noticeable place.

Zippers: I ensure zippers are intact and functioning, i.e., not sticking. While there are zipper lubricants you can try on stuck zippers, I typically find that malfunctioning zippers are not worth dealing with unless they are vintage or designer pieces. Vintage zippers can be notoriously stiff. If you have a valuable designer piece, it can be worth the money to have the zippers repaired or even replaced.

WASHING & DRYING: Should you wash clothes before listing them on eBay? Some clothing sellers wash all items except those that are new with tags. Other sellers only steam clothing. And others list them as is.

Unless the item is dry clean only, I machine wash and tumble dry all clothing I sell on eBay. Many other eBay sellers do NOT wash the clothes they list, but I do for a couple of reasons:

First, since I source most clothing from thrift stores, namely Goodwill, the pieces almost always have an odor. None of the thrift stores in my area wash the clothes they sell, so many still have the original owners' scent on them. Plus, they pick up the odors from all the other items they are bunched in with. There is a "thrift store" smell that you become familiar with if you shop at secondhand stores!

Second, I have had garments that reeked of perfume while others stunk of body odor. Throwing them into the wash is just an easy decision for me. Also, remember that just because you do not detect an odor does not mean your buyer won't. I once sold a suede jacket that I had not washed because it was dry clean only and because it looked and smelled (to me) fine. However, the woman who bought it left me neutral feedback, complaining that it smelled strongly of perfume and that she had to have it professionally dry-cleaned to get the smell out. Had I just disclosed in the listing that the item was unwashed, I could have saved myself the neutral feedback mark.

And third, some thrift stores, especially the Goodwill Outlets, spray the clothing they receive through donations to kill potential bed bugs. This chemical solution causes me to have an allergic reaction when I touch the garment, so washing clothing from "The Bins" is especially crucial for me. Most resellers who source at Goodwill Outlets wash the clothing before listing it unless it is new with tags.

If you wash a piece of clothing that still has the original tags attached, it will no longer be new with tags, and therefore the value will be decreased. I do not find too many new with tags clothing items at the thrift stores, but when I do, I put them aside and list them as I found them. However, many full-time clothing resellers use handheld steamers to freshen up new-with-tags clothing as it's a quick and easy way to remove wrinkles and give the piece a fresh look for photos.

If you are sourcing new with tag clothing via liquidation, you do not have to worry about washing those pieces. However, depending on how they were shipped to you, you may need to steam them to get out wrinkles.

I use fragrance-free laundry detergent and non-scented dryer sheets for the clothes I list on eBay. While I want to clean the items, I do not want to add any scent to them. Some buyers are sensitive to any smells; I have had buyers specifically request that I NOT use scented dryer sheets on items or put dryer sheets into packages (some sellers try to get away with not washing clothing by tucking a dryer sheet in them). I would also recommend NOT spraying clothing with Febreze or any other fabric spray, as people can be sensitive to their fragrances. Even unscented products can adversely affect some customers.

For items that, for whatever reason, cannot be washed but have an odor, you can try leaving them outside to air out. Or you can place the item in the freezer, as the cold temperature typically kills the scent. I have used the freezer technique for vintage men's hats with a musty smell. Other resellers put shoes in the freezer to kill odors.

However, if you are still unable to remove a scent from an article of clothing, you can list it as-is and be very clear in the listing that the item has a noticeable odor. This is fine with vintage items, but not so much for newer pieces. After all, if someone is buying a pair of jeans that were released in the past year, they can find them from someone who has a pair that doesn't smell. That's different from vintage clothing, which is harder to find.

Freshly washed clothing is also just more pleasant for me to handle. Since I need to touch the clothes to photograph, measure, list, and then prepare for shipment, making sure they are clean makes the whole selling process much more enjoyable. After all, I do not want a pile of dirty, stinky clothes on my desk or on my skin!

Ironing: Since I sell a lot of shirts on eBay, ironing is sometimes necessary. I picked up an ironing board at Goodwill for $4, and I use an iron I have owned for years. While clothing will get wrinkled when folded up to be shipped out, ironing out wrinkles makes garments look much better in the pictures. Ask yourself if you would buy a shirt if the picture showed it full of wrinkles before dismissing the idea of ironing clothing.

It is not just shirts I iron, however. Jacket collars are notoriously hard to get to lie down flat, but a quick press of the iron usually takes care of it. I also run into hems that have turned up, as well as cuffs, but ironing makes the fabric lie flat.

Steaming: In addition to an iron and ironing board, I also have a handheld steamer that I use when an item only has a few wrinkles. Note that many full-time clothing resellers invest in large industrial steamers that will do the work of an iron, do. The great thing about a commercial-grade garment steamer is that it removes the wrinkles and sanitizes the item, meaning it does not need to be washed. A quality steamer is an investment, so I recommend waiting until you gain experience in reselling clothing before deciding if you want to splurge on one for your business.

RELIABLE BRANDS TO PICK UP: There are tens of thousands of clothing labels out there; some are hot sellers, but many you cannot give away. High-end designer clothing in good condition will, of course, always sell. But if you are like me and do not live in an area where expensive clothing is worn or even sold, you can still find sellable clothing.

I live in Iowa, and the clothing brands I find secondhand are from your typical mall stores. Yet, I have successfully added clothes to my inventory by looking for unique pieces in excellent condition. I would guess that you will find the brands listed below as well, which means you will be on your way to making money by reselling them on eBay!

Another benefit of being restricted to run-of-the-mill brands is that I do not have to worry about counterfeit clothing. I highly doubt anyone is making knock-off Old Navy coats the way they produce fake Gucci purses!

Here are just some of the brand names that I have personally sourced here in Iowa and have sold on eBay:

- **American Eagle** (denim jeans and women's tops)
- **Anne Klein** (women's suits, dresses, sweaters, and shoes)
- **Ann Taylor and Ann Taylor LOFT** (career wear, coats, and dresses)
- **Banana Republic** (leather jackets and dresses)
- **Cabela's** (hunting and fishing jackets and shirts)
- **CABI** (look for pieces with the most current logo on the label)
- **Carhartt** (thick, heavy men's work clothes and boots)
- **Calvin Klein** (women's dresses)
- **Chico's** (sizes 3, 3.5, 4, and 4.5, which are their versions of large and up)

- **CJ Banks** (the plus size sister brand of Christopher & Banks)
- **Columbia** (jackets and coats for men, women, and kids)
- **Disney** (look for officially branded Disney Parks clothing as well as Princess dresses)
- **Duluth Trading Company** (leather bags and jackets)
- **Eddie Bauer** (larger sizes and outdoor wear)
- **Eileen Fisher** (women's dresses, pants, and tops)
- **Express** (sizes large and extra large)
- **Gap** (denim jackets and blue jeans)
- **Harley Davidson** (shirts and jackets)
- **J. Crew** (shirts, shoes, and jackets)
- **J. Jill** (jackets, dresses, and cashmere sweaters)
- **Land's End** (cashmere sweaters)
- **Lane Bryant** (plus size clothing)
- **Levi's** (denim jackets and vintage jeans)
- **Life Is Good** (graphic tee shirts in larger sizes)
- **L.L. Bean** (boots, bags, and jackets)
- **Lucky Brand** (leather shoes, boots, jackets, and bags)
- **Nike** (graphic tee shirts in large sizes and sneakers)
- **Patagonia** (jackets, coats, and men's shirts)
- **Talbots** (women's career wear)
- **Tommy Bahama** (casual men's summer clothes)
- **Tommy Hilfiger** (women's pieces do better than men's on eBay)
- **Torrid** (plus size women's clothing)
- **Victoria's Secret & PINK** (larger size bras and clothing with a large PINK logo)

Again, please remember that these are the brands I have personally been able to find in my area and have successfully sold on eBay. You may be in an area that sells higher-end designer pieces, meaning you will have a better chance of finding more expensive clothing at your thrift stores.

Also, as I discussed earlier, size, style, and condition are crucial factors when sourcing clothing to resell. You likely will not have much luck selling a size small white tee shirt from Express that shows wear, but you will likely be able to sell a size large sparkly dress from Express that is in excellent condition.

Better Name Clothing Brands That Sell for More Money: If you live in a more affluent area, you will likely find higher-end clothing brands at thrift stores and the Goodwill Outlet. Brands that sell between $50 and $200 include:

- **Akris** (women's dresses and bags)
- **Alice + Olivia** (dresses)
- **Athleta** (women's workout wear)
- **Celine** (purses)
- **Chloe** (purses)
- **Citizens of Humanity** (blue jeans)
- **Free People** (women's clothing)
- **Johnny Was** (dresses)
- **Lily Pulitzer** (dresses)
- **Lululemon** (men's and women's workout wear)
- **Magnolia** (dresses)
- **Marc Jacobs** (purses)
- **Miu Miu** (shoes, purses, and dresses)
- **Mother** (women's jeans)
- **Roberto Cavalli** (purses and dresses)
- **7 For All Mankind** (blue jeans)
- **St. John** (women's blazers)
- **Tory Burch** (shoes and dresses)
- **Veronica Beard** (women's blazers)

STORING & ORGANIZING CLOTHING INVENTORY:
When you sell on eBay, you tend to accumulate a lot of stuff, but inventory usually takes up the most space. This is true whether you sell books, collectibles, or clothing. The one downside of clothing is that while one piece is relatively lightweight, a bunch of it together is heavy. I had broken several clothing racks over the years when I overloaded them with clothes.

I finally invested in industrial clothing racks that I found on Amazon. You can find sturdy ones (I recommend a rack that holds at least 250 pounds) for around $60 online. Make sure to get a rack with rollers to move it around easily. I have six of these industrial racks for hanging clothing.

However, if you do not want to invest in clothing, there are other ways to store clothes. Many full-time clothing resellers store their inventory in plastic bins. Once they have listed the item on eBay, they fold it and seal it in a clear poly bag. They then label the bag with the contents (some just write this on a piece of tape while others print out an inventory label) and store it in the bin. The bins themselves are labeled, making the item easy to find once it sells.

How To List Clothing on EBay: Too many people focus only on obtaining items to sell online and neglect the other essential parts of selling on eBay, especially getting the item listed for sale. A good listing makes all the difference in how fast your item will sell and how much and how happy the customer will be once they receive their order.

Clothing is tricky for several reasons. Some pieces may look like they are for a man but are sized for a woman. There are hundreds of categories and sub-categories to list clothing in. A "Small" in one brand may be a "Medium" in another. Some people take measurements one way, while you may take them differently.

It is very easy to make a mistake when listing a piece of clothing, resulting in an unhappy customer, a return, and possibly negative feedback. However, taking the time to list clothes properly will help cut down on any issues.

Men's vs. Women's Clothing: The first thing you need to do before you list an item of clothing on eBay is to determine whether it is for a man or a woman. I know you are probably thinking (or saying), "DUH! Of course, you will know if an item is for a man or a woman!" However, unless an item is marked on the label as being sized by gender, it can sometimes be hard to tell who the garment was made for, especially when dealing with shirts and coats.

Fortunately, it is usually easy to determine whether a piece is for a male or a female, and that is by looking at how the item is buttoned or zippered. The buttons are on the right-hand side for men's buttoned shirts, and the buttonholes are on the left. It is the opposite for women's buttoned shirts: the buttons are on the left-hand side, and the buttonholes are on the right.

For coats and jackets, the zipper pull tab is usually on the right-hand side for men and the left-hand side for women. When listing a zippered jacket on eBay, I often must double-check my own jackets to see which side the zipper is on!

If the buttons and/or zippers still are not clearing the issue of gender up for you, look at the piece's silhouette. Women's shirts and jackets tend to be tapered a bit at the waist. Also, check the measurements. A man's "medium" will measure larger than a woman's.

Of course, in today's world, there are those items that are unisex. While many unisex pieces are marked as such, not all are. I have had clothes that looked like they were for women but were sized for men. In these instances, I list the item as "unisex" and clarify in the listing that the customer needs to thoroughly review the measurements I have provided before buying the piece.

Clothing Categories: The first thing you need to decide when creating your eBay listing for an article of clothing is what category to put it in. Clothing accounts for a considerable portion of the listings on eBay's website, and there are many choices on how to categorize your item. Is the jacket you have a windbreaker or a parka? Are you listing the men's shirt as a dress or a casual one?

I always do a completed listing search of all items I list on eBay, whether it is a vintage collectible or an article of clothing. This enables me to see the going price (more about pricing clothing coming up), and I can also see what category other sellers are putting the same item in. You can get 90 days' worth of sold results in eBay's regular search or get 2 years' worth of data using **Terapeak**, which is located under the **Research** tab in your **Seller Hub**.

While the first category you list an item in is free, you can list that same item in a second category for an additional fee. However, I strongly advise saving yourself the fees and only listing your items in one category each. If you have a keyword-loaded title and have filled out the correct item specifics, customers should find your items no matter what category you have them listed under.

Writing A Great Title: A good, keyword-loaded title is essential for selling anything on eBay, including clothing. When listing an item of clothing, I include the brand, color, size, pattern, and anything else I can cram into the available title space. Remember that with an eBay title, you do not need to write a proper sentence but rather fill up space with keywords that will bring in the most traffic.

It is not enough to type in "Green Ralph Lauren Shirt." A better title would be "Mens Green RALPH LAUREN Polo Shirt EXTRA

LARGE Pony Cotton EUC." Notice how I only capitalized a few words; you do not want to type anything in all capitals as it comes across as yelling. I also added "EUC," which means "Excellent Used Condition."

Misspellings are common in eBay titles, so it is essential to double-check that you have correctly spelled the clothing item's brand name. You do not want to miss a sale because you left an "I" out of Tommy Hilfiger.

Another tip for writing any eBay title, including one for clothing, is to put both spellings of a word in. I often include both "grey" and "gray" in the title because people spell that color differently.

Do not clutter up your title with pointless words such as "LOOK!" Also, avoid punctuation marks as they not only take up valuable space but can also mess up search results. I always type "Mens" not "Men's" in my titles, for instance.

Accurately Describing Condition: After the title comes the condition field. eBay allows you to choose one of four condition choices for clothing:

- **New with Tags**
- **New without Tags**
- **New with Defects**
- **Pre-Owned**

Because I buy most of the clothing, I resell at estate sales and Goodwill, almost all of what I sell on eBay is *Pre-Owned*. I only list an item as *New with Tags* if it, in fact, still has the original price tags attached.

I rarely use the *New without Tags* or *New with Defects* options. The only time I list an item as *New without Tags* is if it came from my own closet, and I can guarantee it was never washed or worn (washing an article of clothing automatically makes it a secondhand piece), or if it came in a liquidation lot. Otherwise, I classify clothing without tags as *Pre-Owned* to ensure I am not misleading customers.

Technically, an item is *Pre-owned* once the original buyer purchased it, regardless of whether the piece was ever worn or even washed. So even if you buy an item at a thrift store that still has the original tags attached, it is still, to some people, considered to be *Pre-Owned*, although very few resellers will classify it as such.

Since I rarely find *New with Tags* clothing at thrift stores to resell on eBay, this is not usually an issue for me. However, even when I find clothing with the original tags still attached, I sometimes still list them as *Pre-Owned* if the tags are torn or damaged in any way. Customers expect *New with Tags* items to look like they just came off the original store rack.

Under the condition field is a section where you can **Highlight any defects, missing parts, scratches, or wear and tear.** It is important to be very thorough here and disclose all issues, no matter how small they may be. Filling out this section offers you, as the seller, a level of protection from a buyer coming back after the sale to claim you did not correctly describe the item. I include any flaws in this area and put the same information into the actual item description, too.

Photos: I have sold clothing on eBay for years and only occasionally use a mannequin, only using one for items that look significantly better on one. Otherwise, I just hang my items against a flat surface for photos. If you plan to make clothing the main part of your inventory or even a large part of it, then investing in a mannequin to take photos of clothing is a good idea. There are many listings available on eBay where you can find a good mannequin for around $50.

However, if you are only planning to sell clothes occasionally, or if you do not have a lot of extra room to set up a mannequin, don't worry, as there are ways to photograph clothing without one. For years, I took clothing photos hanging from a hook on the back of my bedroom door. I have since "upgraded" to hanging them on a hook on a white wall to give the items a clean background.

While clothing usually does look best on a mannequin, I prefer the ease of hanging clothes against a white wall. Some resellers invest in professional photo backdrops and expensive lighting, but I get by with my white wall next to a large window, which gives me a lot of natural light. Whether you use electric lights or the sunlight, you want to ensure the item's actual color comes through in the pictures and small details, such as the fabric's texture and the details on the buttons.

eBay allows you to add up to 24 photos to each listing, and I advise taking advantage of that number by providing as many pictures as possible. Take photos from the front, back, and sides of each item you list. Zoom in on any unique details. Take pictures of the labels, the size label on the collar, and the fabric label, usually found along the tops and jackets inside.

If there are any flaws on the item, even very tiny ones, take photos of them. Clothing with flaws can still sell if you are upfront and honest about its issues. Give your customers the feeling that they are holding the item in person, turning it over in their hands as they would if they were shopping in a brick-and-mortar store.

If you are unsure how to take pictures of clothing best, look around at other eBay listings to compare how different sellers present their items. While you do not want to copy someone else's photo style outright, you want to note which listings appeal to you as a shopper. Do you prefer clothing on mannequins? Do you like how clothes look hung up? What DON'T you like about some of the pictures you see? Use these impressions to guide you in your own photographing of clothing.

One thing that you may see other sellers doing is putting props in their pictures, such as flowers or even accessories. While this may be visually appealing, it can distract from the item you are trying to sell, and if you add jewelry and shoes in a picture of a sweater, buyers may assume they are BUYING everything in the photo. Online shoppers are notorious for purchasing simply based on the pictures and failing to read the actual listing. Avoid any confusion and possible customer backlash by ONLY showing the item for sale in your pictures.

Item Specifics: Depending on which category you are listing in on eBay, various clothing-specific fields will be available for you to select. For example, the fields within a listing of men's shoes will differ from that for a pair of children's pajamas. Providing as many details as possible on each piece of clothing will help sell it faster and will also cut down on customer questions or complaints.

Usually, these fields are for **Brand, Style, Size Type and Size, Color, Pattern, Material,** and **Country of Origin**. If you are unsure about the style, look at the completed listings to see what other sellers have categorized it as. Brand, size, material, and country of origin should all be described on the garment label.

You will also see fields for the collar and cuff type for certain items, such as men's dress shirts. Listings for pants will include size fields for the rise and inseam. While you will still want to type all these details into your description, you still want to fill out this section, as it is what buyers use to narrow down the search results.

In late 2019, eBay implemented a massive overhaul of its item-specific fields, most of them in the clothing categories. Now there are two distinct sections under **Item Specifics: Required** and **Suggested.** You MUST fill out all the *Required* fields, and you SHOULD fill out as many of the *Suggested* as possible. All fields will help buyers find your item among the millions of other eBay listings.

When filling out the item-specific fields, try to choose the options provided in the drop-down menus over typing in your information. The choices already in eBay's system are the ones that appear to buyers when they are searching the site. Entering your own specifics will result in your item being excluded from that section's particular search. When in doubt, leaving an item-specific field blank is better than writing in your own terms.

Writing A Great Description: After you have chosen a category, write a title, uploaded your photos, and selected the item specifics, it is time to write the description for the piece of clothing you are selling. While it is tempting just to list the facts, such as only the brand and size, taking a few extra moments to write a great description will help sell your item faster and cut down on customer questions or problems.

Because the clothing market on eBay is so crowded, it is important to make YOUR listing stand out from the rest. I always start by stating what the item is in bold fonts, such as "Mens Red Gap Puffer Vest." Under that, I try to really "sell" the item by writing something like, "This stylish red vest will keep you warm all winter long!" As you can see, I do not write an entire advertisement for the piece, but I do add a little extra to the listing to catch potential buyers' eyes.

After my title and "sales pitch," I then follow up with all the information I can give the buyer, including fabric (look on the label and copy down what is there), washing instructions, any zippers or buttons, pockets, and of course the size and measurements (more on taking measurements coming up). Whatever details you chose in the item specifics section should be repeated in your description. If I have washed the item, I always include "Comes to you freshly washed!" Finally, I provide the condition of the piece.

Providing an accurate statement of the condition of anything, especially a piece of clothing, is tricky. What may look to be brand new to you could appear worn to a customer. As with all items I sell on eBay, I tend to understate the condition. If a piece is in excellent condition, I describe it as great. Instead of saying an item is in very good condition, I will state that it is merely in good condition.

If an item still has the original price tag on it, I do state that it is brand new with tags. If the original hang tags are cut off, it immediately makes the piece pre-owned. Washed but never worn also means pre-owned. If I purchased the item at an estate sale and knew the owner did not smoke, I would state, "From a clean, smoke-free home!"

Clothing Measurements: If you want to sell clothing successfully on eBay, you must take measurements. A size "large" in one brand may fit like a "small" in another. If you only list what the label says, you will be inundated with questions asking you what the measurements are, so you might as well take them to start with.

While it may sound tedious, taking measurements is relatively easy to do. There are many ways to take measurements, though; here is how I take them:

I provide three measurements for shirts and coats: Across the Chest, Sleeve, and Body Length. As I mentioned earlier, I put an explanation of how I take these measurements in my listings.

To get **Across the Chest measurement**, I lay the item out on a flat surface, place the tape measure under the armpit on one side, and then stretch the tape measure out to the other armpit. I provide that number in my listings, although doubling the number is also an option as those give the buyer the chest size.

For the **Sleeve measurement**, I place the tape measure at the seam near the shoulder and stretch it down to the cuff. Another option is to measure from the top of the sleeve near the collar and down to the cuff.

For the **Length measurement**, I place the tape measure at the top of the piece at the seam next to the collar (but not including the collar) and bring it down to the longest part of the garment's hem.

It is also important to note if an item, say a women's shirt, is cinched in the waist. If it is, providing the waist measurement is helpful. Some customers will also ask for the shoulder size, meaning the width from one shoulder to the next. You will want to provide the hip measurements for garments that fall below the hip, such as trench coats. I take the waist, shoulder, and hip measurements just as I do across the chest by laying the item flat and measuring the width.

For pants, shorts, or skirts, I provide measurements for the **waist, hips** (measuring across the widest part), **inseam** (length from crotch to hem or cuff), **front rise** (length from waistline to crotch), **rear rise** (length from waistline to crotch in the back), and the **length from the waistline to the hem.**

Fortunately, many pants include the waist and inseam measurements on the label, but some buyers still want the actual measurements. For pants with the label measurements, you can always try listing them without additional measurements if you are open to providing exact measurements for those who ask.

I try to be proactive when listing and providing as much information as possible the first time. Otherwise, someone will inevitably ask for a measurement, meaning I will have to go into my inventory room to pull the item to measure it. However, some sellers will tell the customer that the only measurements they can provide are the ones they have already included in the listing, even if that is only what is on the garment label.

I measure across the chest, across the waist, and the length from the waist to the hem for dresses. If there is no waist seam, I measure the length from the collar seam back to the dress hem.

I sometimes sell accessories such as hats, neckties, purses, and shoes, in addition to clothing. For neckties, I measure the width at the widest point. For hats, I look for a label inside indicating the size. If there is not one, I measure the inside diameter. Customers shopping for purses want to know the width, height, depth, and handle drop, which is the distance from the top of the handle or strap to the top of the bag. Finally, when selling shoes, I include the size on the label as well as heel height and width.

Again, while taking all these measurements may seem like overkill, providing them will help you sell the item faster and cut down on customer questions. You are also protecting yourself from a buyer coming back and claiming an item was not the size you stated in the listing.

Shipping Clothing: A significant factor in pricing clothing is whether to offer "free" shipping. I put "free" in parenthesis because nothing is ever truly free; to offer "free" shipping, I must add the postage cost to the item's price. Therefore, I must know the shipping cost before I list an item on eBay.

As I have mentioned several times, clothing is the largest category on eBay, and the competition is fierce. I am an *eBay Power Seller* and a *Top-Rated Seller*, so my listings are supposed to be the first in searches. However, with so many other people selling clothing, it is easy for even a seller like me to find their clothing listings buried amongst all the others.

Offering "free" shipping is one way to bring your clothing listings to the top of the eBay search results. Most of the clothing I sell can ship in a poly bag via *Ground Advantage* or in a *USPS Priority Flat Rate Bubble Mailer*. For those items, I will usually offer "free" shipping. However, I do charge the customer shipping for bulky, heavy pieces.

I always give my customers two shipping choices on clothing, the first being the economy choice of *Ground Advantage* and the second option being the expedited choice of *Priority Mail*. If I'm offering "free" shipping, I would make the economy option "free" with customers who choose *Priority* having to pay. I also ship through eBay's *International Shipping* program, and all international customers pay for shipping.

Most clothing you sell on eBay will ship via either Ground Advantage or Priority Mail. Gone are *First Class Package*, which was for packages under one pound, and *Parcel Select*, which was for packages over one pound. Both of those services have been combined into the new which is a faster service that is still less than Priority.

While you can break down *Ground Advantage* into ounce ranges (1-4 ounces, 5-8 ounces, 9-12 ounces, and 13-15 ounces), when you are just starting, it's fine to list all items under a pound at the 15-ounce rate. You would then list items weighing between 1-2 pounds at 2 pounds; 2-3 pounds at 3 pounds, 3-4 pounds at 4 pounds, etc. As we discussed in the shipping section of this book, you simply round up to the next pound when shipping items over a pound.

I ship most clothing in plain poly mailer bags that I order online from Amazon or eBay. Or, if the piece weighs over a pound, I will likely use a *Priority Mail Flat Rate Bubble Mailer*. Most tee and men's dress shirts are light enough to ship via *Ground Advantage* at the 15-ounce rate, which costs around $6. If I am offering "free" shipping, I will add up to $6 to the price to cover postage. For example, if I have a shirt that I think is worth $25, I may price it at $31 with "free shipping to cover the postage cost. Even though the shirt is priced slightly higher because it has "free" shipping, it will show up higher in the eBay search results. Since some customers specifically search eBay for "free" shipping items, offering the "free" shipping option is sometimes the only way customers will find your item.

And here is a tip that will save you when you create your next clothing listing: Instead of starting from scratch every time you need to create a new listing, open a listing that is currently live and click on the **Sell Similar** option. Then you can just change all the item specifics, including the shipping options and weight. This makes your listing time fly by as you do not have to go in and set up the *Calculated Shipping* option every time you list a new item!

It is crucial that whatever you sell on eBay, especially clothing is CLEAN and from SMOKE-FREE HOMES. If you are a smoker, keep your inventory and packing supplies in an area away from the smoke. If your buyer detects even the slightest scent of cigarettes, they WILL complain.

Even though clothing isn't breakable, we still take the time to package it carefully for shipment. I wrap garments in packing paper before sliding them into their envelopes or boxes. If there is space between the wrapped piece of clothing and the box, we will add a bit more packing paper to prevent the item from bouncing around during transit.

One tip to get clothing into the *Priority Mail Flat Rate Bubble Mailer* is to put it into a small plain polybag, which then slides easily into the bubble mailer. This is especially helpful in shrinking down puffy coats and thick shirts to fit into the envelope. The bubbles inside the envelope can "stick" to the fabric, making it difficult to slide inside. Putting clothes into a smooth bag will help them slide in more easily.

Be sure to use plenty of packing tape, especially if you have a stuffed-to-the-brim bubble mailer. The last thing you want is the envelope busting open during shipment. Also, be careful of stuffing clothing too tightly into a poly bag as the customer could inadvertently cut it when trying to open the package.

There is a reason you see so many resellers posting on social media about selling clothing. It is easy to find, relatively cheap to buy, easy to list and store, and easy to ship. Even if you do not want to make reselling clothing your full-time business, it is still worth taking the time to learn about how to flip clothes for profit on eBay. By simply adding a bit of clothing to my eBay business, I was able to grow my sales by 30%!

CONCLUSION

Whether you picked up this book because you wanted to start selling on eBay or because you wanted to take your eBay business to the next level, I hope you found the information helpful!

I have been selling on eBay since 2005, and I have had to pivot my business model more times than I can count. eBay and the online selling landscape are constantly changing and evolving, hence why I publish new editions of this book every year. But regardless of how retail has changed over the years, one thing remains the same: eBay is still in the top three of online shopping sites. Whatever you have to sell, you will have the best chance of selling it on eBay.

From sourcing and photographing to listing and shipping, selling on eBay takes work. But the rewards can be well worth the time and effort you put into it. Whether you are just looking to earn a bit of extra spending money or want to start your own full-time home-based business, eBay offers sellers of every size the opportunity to earn an income.

The only thing standing in the way of you making money on eBay is YOU! The more you list, the more you will sell. So, get to listing and watch the money roll in!

Are you interested in more reselling content or other ways you can make money online? Be sure to visit my **Amazon Author Page at https://amzn.to/3wBF0WF** for all of my business books and planners, including:

- **Beginner's Guide To Starting a YouTube Channel**
- **Beginner's Guide To Amazon KDP**
- **Beginner's Guide To Selling On Etsy**

- **Beginner's Guide To Selling Antiques On Etsy**
- **Beginner's Guide To Selling Crafts On Etsy**
- **Beginner's Guide To Starting An Etsy Sticker Shop**
- **Beginner's Guide To Selling Digital Products On Etsy**
- **Beginner's Guide To Starting An Etsy Print-On-Demand Shop**
- **Beginner's Guide To Selling On WhatNot**
- **101 Items To Sell On EBay**
- **101 MORE Items To Sell On EBay**
- **Reselling Planner & Accounting Ledger**

ABOUT THE AUTHOR

Ann Eckhart is a writer, entrepreneur, and online content creator based in Iowa. She has numerous books available about how to make money online from home. For all of her books, visit her Amazon Author Page at: https://amzn.to/3wBF0WF

You can also follow Ann Eckhart on these social media sites:

FACEBOOK: https://www.facebook.com/anneckhart/

TWITTER: https://twitter.com/ann_eckhart

INSTAGRAM: https://instagram.com/ann_marie_eckhart

YOUTUBE: https://tinyurl.com/yxvqtwc7

COPYRIGHT 2023 Ann Eckhart

No part of this book may be reprinted or reproduced without the express written permission from the author.

Cover Design by Ann Eckhart

Don't miss out!

Visit the website below and you can sign up to receive emails whenever Ann Eckhart publishes a new book. There's no charge and no obligation.

https://books2read.com/r/B-A-UQFB-MOBTC

BOOKS 2 READ

Connecting independent readers to independent writers.

Also by Ann Eckhart

101 Items To Sell On Ebay
101 Items To Sell On Ebay
101 More Items To Sell On Ebay

2022 Home Based Business Books
Beginner's Guide To Amazon KDP 2022 Edition: How To Create
& Sell Books Using Kindle Direct Publishing
Beginner's Guide To Selling On Ebay 2022 Edition: How To Start
& Grow a Successful Online Reselling Business from Home
Beginner's Guide To YouTube 2022 Edition: How To Start & Grow
a Successful & Profitable YouTube Channel

2023 Home Based Business Books
Beginner's Guide To Selling On Ebay: 2023 Edition

Standalone
2020 Ebay Sourcing Guide
Ebay Seller Secrets

How to Start a YouTube Channel for Fun & Profit
Beginner's Guide To Amazon KDP: 2023 Edition
Beginner's Guide To Starting An Etsy Print-On-Demand Shop
Beginner's Guide To Starting An Etsy Sticker Shop
Beginner's Guide To WhatNot: How To Buy & Sell On The Live
Auction Reselling App
Reseller Liquidation Database: The Top 35 Liquidation &
Wholesale Companies for Online Sellers
2000+ Printable Products To Sell On Etsy
Beginner's Guide To Selling Digital Products On Etsy
Beginner's Guide To Amazon KDP 2024 Edition
Beginner's Guide To Selling Antiques On Etsy
Beginner's Guide To Selling Crafts On Etsy
Beginner's Guide To Selling On eBay 2024 Edition
Beginner's Guide To Starting a YouTube Channel 2024-2025
Edition

Watch for more at www.SeeAnnSave.com.

www.ingramcontent.com/pod-product-compliance
Lightning Source LLC
Chambersburg PA
CBHW061427150726
47987CB00001B/127